KT-572-518

47 RONIN

Writer
MIKE RICHARDSON

Artist
STAN SAKAI

Editorial Consultant
KAZUO KOIKE

Color by
LOVERN KINDZIERSKI

Lettering by
TOM ORZECHOWSKI and **LOIS BUHALIS**

DARK HORSE BOOKS®

Publisher ✦ MIKE RICHARDSON

Editor ✦ DIANA SCHUTZ

Associate Editor ✦ BRENDAN WRIGHT

Assistant Editor ✦ AARON WALKER

Design & Digital Production ✦ CARY GRAZZINI

Japanese Consultant ✦ MICHAEL GOMBOS

———————

47 RONIN

© 2012, 2013, 2014 Dark Horse Comics, Inc. All rights reserved.
Dark Horse Comics® and the Dark Horse logo are trademarks of Dark Horse Comics, Inc.
All rights reserved. No portion of this publication may be reproduced or transmitted, in any
form or by any means, without the express written permission of the publisher. Though based
on historical fact, names, characters, places, and incidents featured in this publication
either are the product of the author's imagination or are used fictitiously.

This book collects issues one through five of *47 Ronin*,
originally published November 2012 through July 2013 by Dark Horse Comics.

Published by Dark Horse Books
A division of Dark Horse Comics, Inc.
10956 SE Main Street
Milwaukie, Oregon 97222

DarkHorse.com

First edition: February 2014
ISBN 978-1-59582-954-2

1 3 5 7 9 10 8 6 4 2
Printed in China

President and Publisher Mike Richardson ✦ Executive Vice President Neil Hankerson
Chief Financial Officer Tom Weddle ✦ Vice President of Publishing Randy Stradley
Vice President of Book Trade Sales Michael Martens ✦ Vice President of Business Affairs Anita Nelson
Editor in Chief Scott Allie ✦ Vice President of Marketing Matt Parkinson
Vice President of Product Development David Scroggy ✦ Vice President of Information Technology Dale LaFountain
Senior Director of Print, Design, and Production Darlene Vogel ✦ General Counsel Ken Lizzi
Editorial Director Davey Estrada ✦ Senior Books Editor Chris Warner ✦ Executive Editor Diana Schutz
Director of Print and Development Cary Grazzini ✦ Art Director Lia Ribacchi ✦ Director of Scheduling Cara Niece
Director of International Licensing Tim Wiesch ✦ Director of Digital Publishing Mark Bernardi

四十七浪人
47 RONIN
The Tale of the Loyal Retainers

"To know this story is to know Japan."

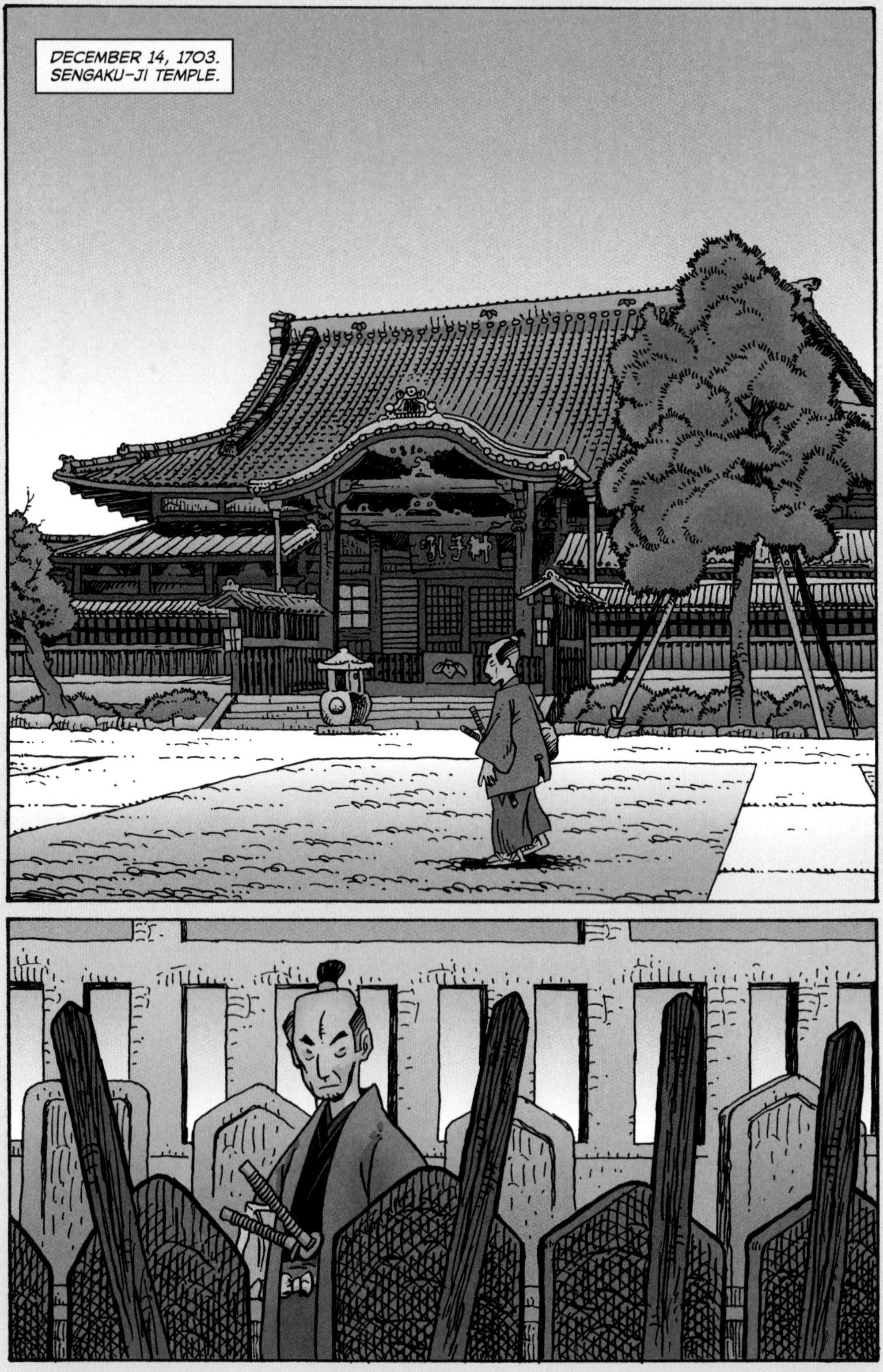
DECEMBER 14, 1703.
SENGAKU-JI TEMPLE.

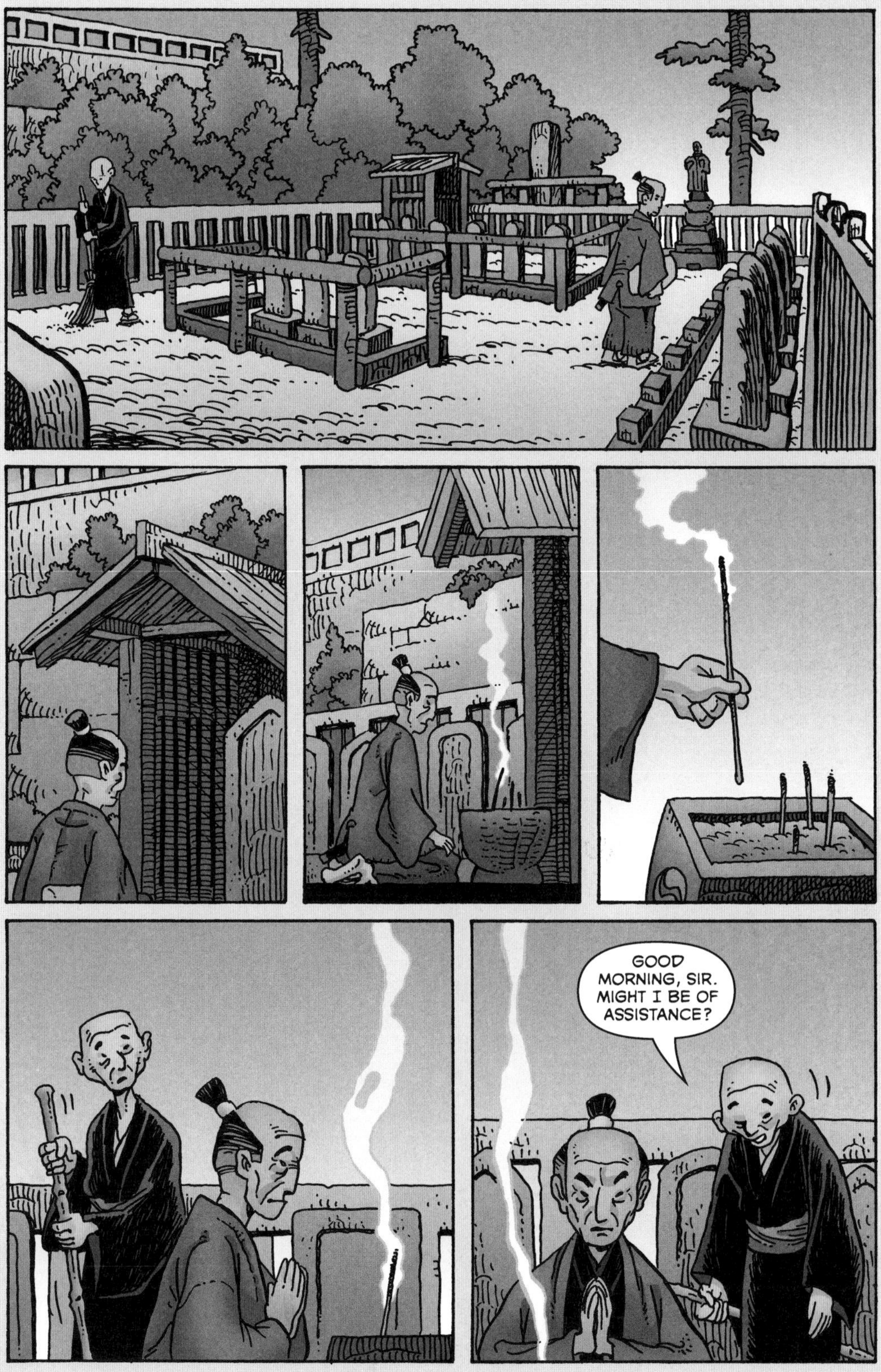
GOOD MORNING, SIR. MIGHT I BE OF ASSISTANCE?

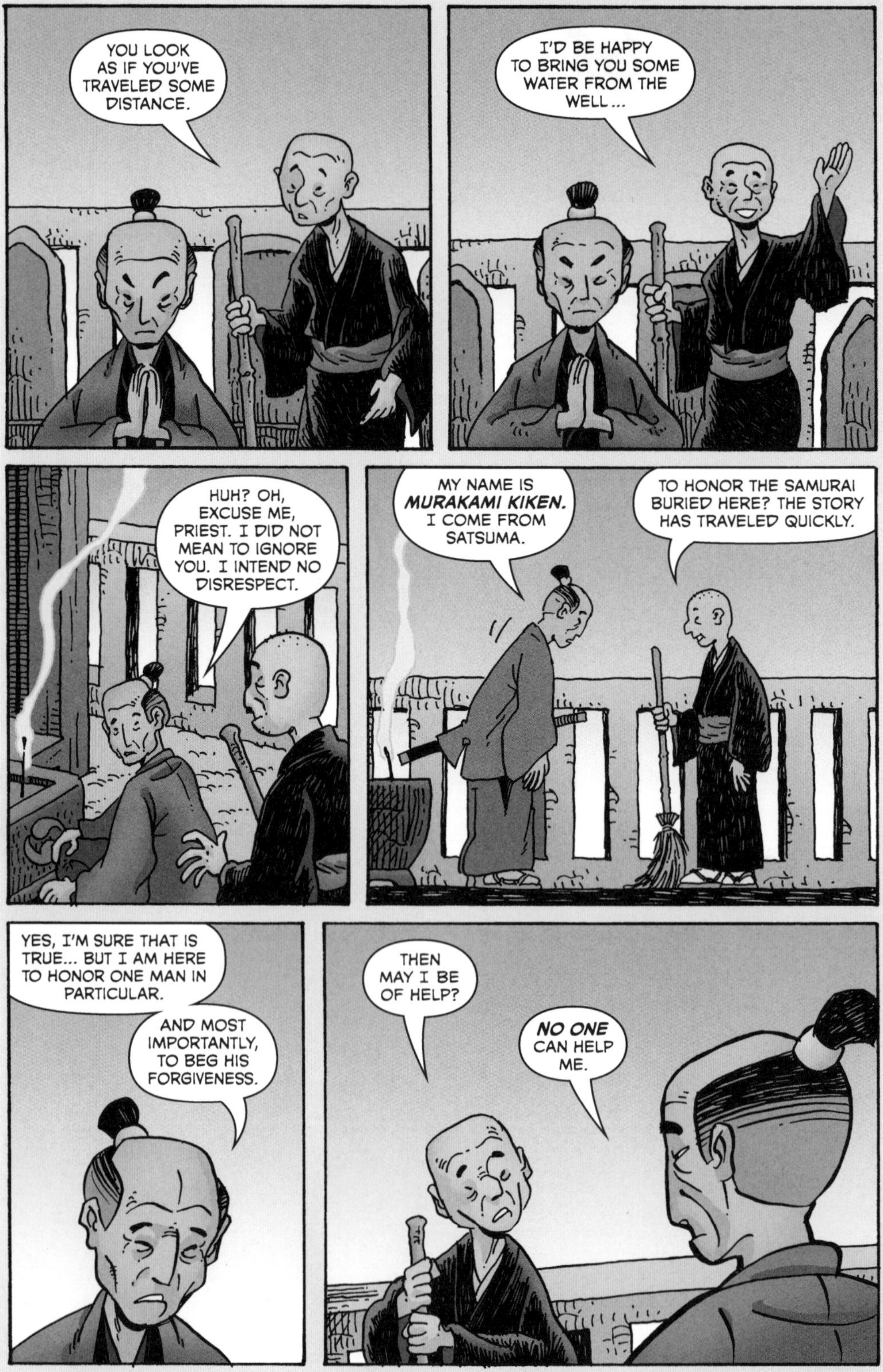

YOU LOOK AS IF YOU'VE TRAVELED SOME DISTANCE.
I'D BE HAPPY TO BRING YOU SOME WATER FROM THE WELL ...
HUH? OH, EXCUSE ME, PRIEST. I DID NOT MEAN TO IGNORE YOU. I INTEND NO DISRESPECT.
MY NAME IS MURAKAMI KIKEN. I COME FROM SATSUMA.
TO HONOR THE SAMURAI BURIED HERE? THE STORY HAS TRAVELED QUICKLY.
YES, I'M SURE THAT IS TRUE... BUT I AM HERE TO HONOR ONE MAN IN PARTICULAR.
AND MOST IMPORTANTLY, TO BEG HIS FORGIVENESS.
THEN MAY I BE OF HELP?
NO ONE CAN HELP ME.

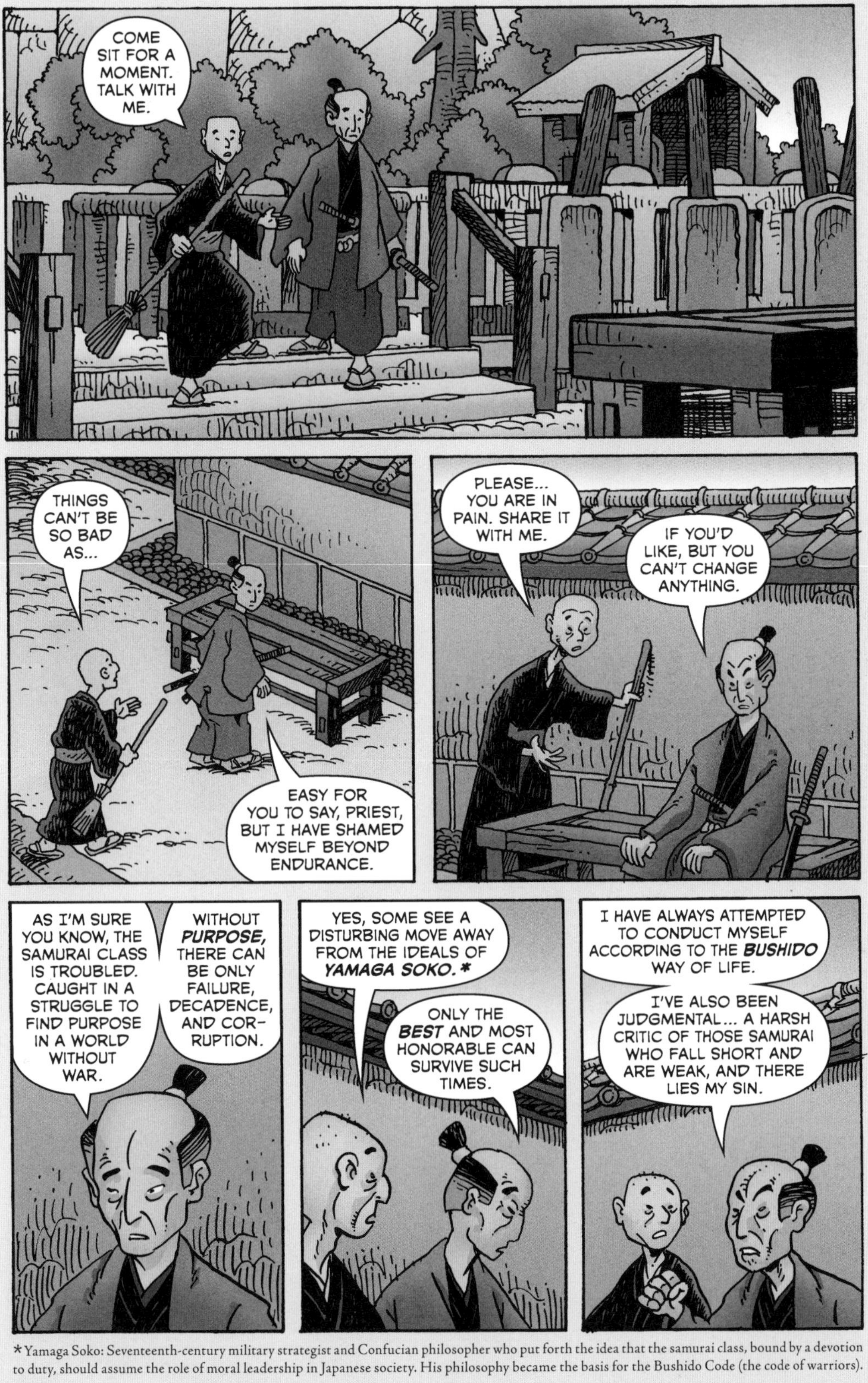
COME SIT FOR A MOMENT. TALK WITH ME.
THINGS CAN'T BE SO BAD AS...
EASY FOR YOU TO SAY, PRIEST, BUT I HAVE SHAMED MYSELF BEYOND ENDURANCE.
PLEASE... YOU ARE IN PAIN. SHARE IT WITH ME.
IF YOU'D LIKE, BUT YOU CAN'T CHANGE ANYTHING.
AS I'M SURE YOU KNOW, THE SAMURAI CLASS IS TROUBLED. CAUGHT IN A STRUGGLE TO FIND PURPOSE IN A WORLD WITHOUT WAR.
WITHOUT PURPOSE, THERE CAN BE ONLY FAILURE, DECADENCE, AND CORRUPTION.
YES, SOME SEE A DISTURBING MOVE AWAY FROM THE IDEALS OF YAMAGA SOKO.*
ONLY THE BEST AND MOST HONORABLE CAN SURVIVE SUCH TIMES.
I HAVE ALWAYS ATTEMPTED TO CONDUCT MYSELF ACCORDING TO THE BUSHIDO WAY OF LIFE.
I'VE ALSO BEEN JUDGMENTAL... A HARSH CRITIC OF THOSE SAMURAI WHO FALL SHORT AND ARE WEAK, AND THERE LIES MY SIN.

*Yamaga Soko: Seventeenth-century military strategist and Confucian philosopher who put forth the idea that the samurai class, bound by a devotion to duty, should assume the role of moral leadership in Japanese society. His philosophy became the basis for the Bushido Code (the code of warriors).

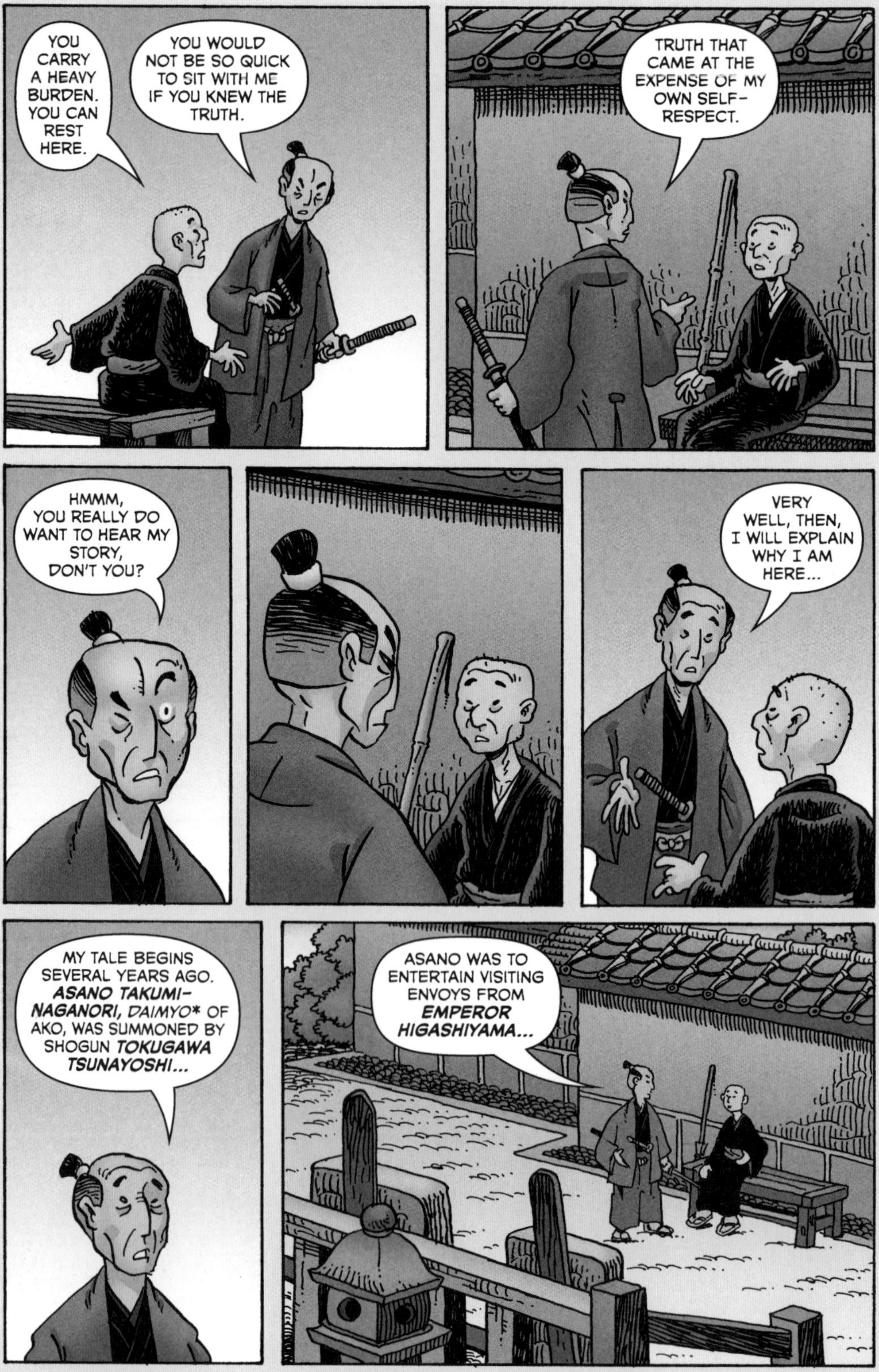
YOU CARRY A HEAVY BURDEN. YOU CAN REST HERE.
YOU WOULD NOT BE SO QUICK TO SIT WITH ME IF YOU KNEW THE TRUTH.
TRUTH THAT CAME AT THE EXPENSE OF MY OWN SELF-RESPECT.
HMMM, YOU REALLY DO WANT TO HEAR MY STORY, DON'T YOU?
VERY WELL, THEN, I WILL EXPLAIN WHY I AM HERE...
MY TALE BEGINS SEVERAL YEARS AGO. ***ASANO TAKUMI-NAGANORI,*** *DAIMYO** OF AKO, WAS SUMMONED BY SHOGUN ***TOKUGAWA TSUNAYOSHI...***
ASANO WAS TO ENTERTAIN VISITING ENVOYS FROM ***EMPEROR HIGASHIYAMA...***

* Daimyo: Powerful landholders who dominated Japan from the eleventh century until the nineteenth.

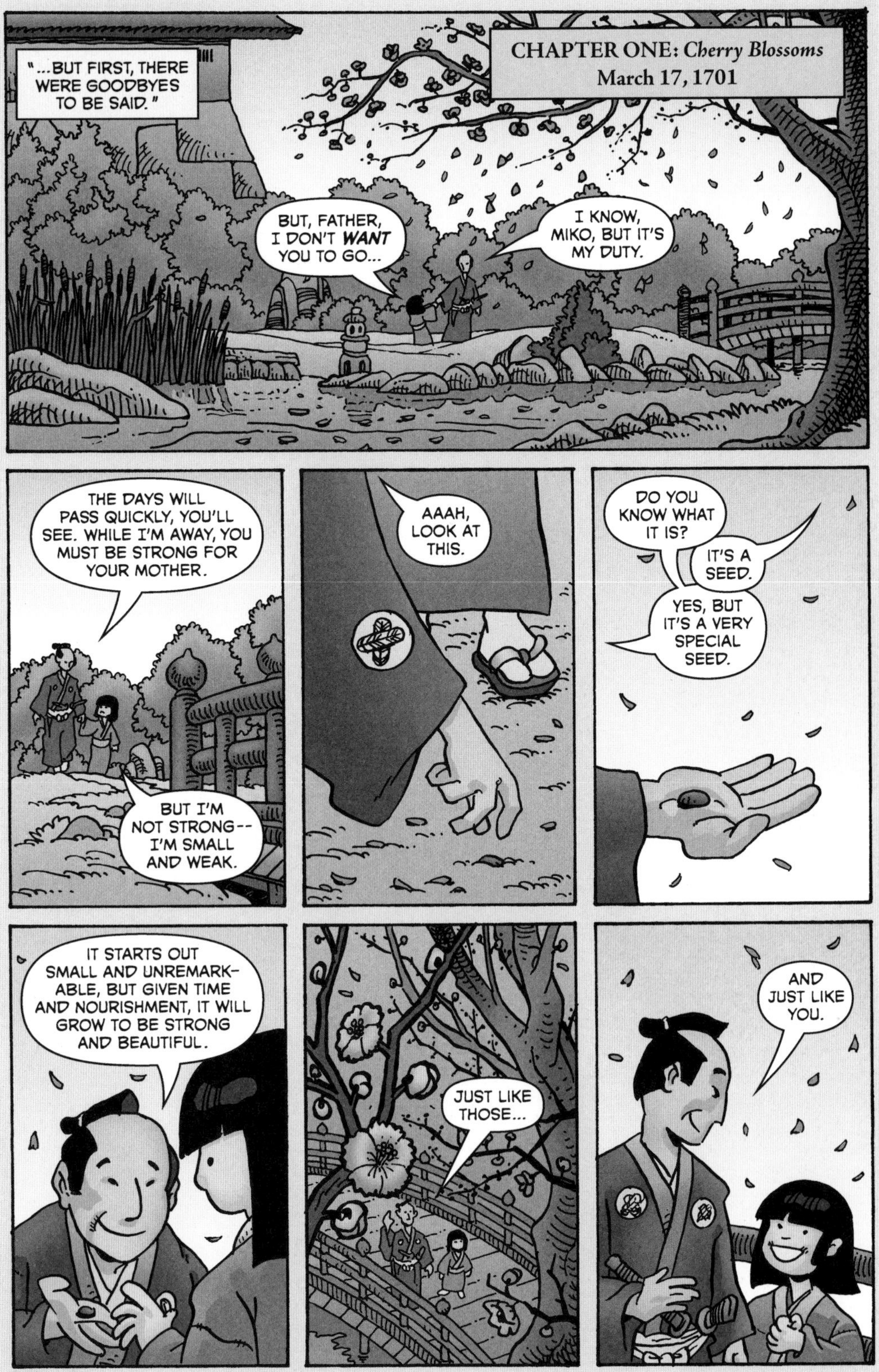
CHAPTER ONE: *Cherry Blossoms*
March 17, 1701
"...BUT FIRST, THERE WERE GOODBYES TO BE SAID."
BUT, FATHER, I DON'T **WANT** YOU TO GO...
I KNOW, MIKO, BUT IT'S MY DUTY.
THE DAYS WILL PASS QUICKLY, YOU'LL SEE. WHILE I'M AWAY, YOU MUST BE STRONG FOR YOUR MOTHER.
BUT I'M NOT STRONG-- I'M SMALL AND WEAK.
AAAH, LOOK AT THIS.
DO YOU KNOW WHAT IT IS?
IT'S A SEED.
YES, BUT IT'S A VERY SPECIAL SEED.
IT STARTS OUT SMALL AND UNREMARK-ABLE, BUT GIVEN TIME AND NOURISHMENT, IT WILL GROW TO BE STRONG AND BEAUTIFUL.
JUST LIKE THOSE...
AND JUST LIKE YOU.

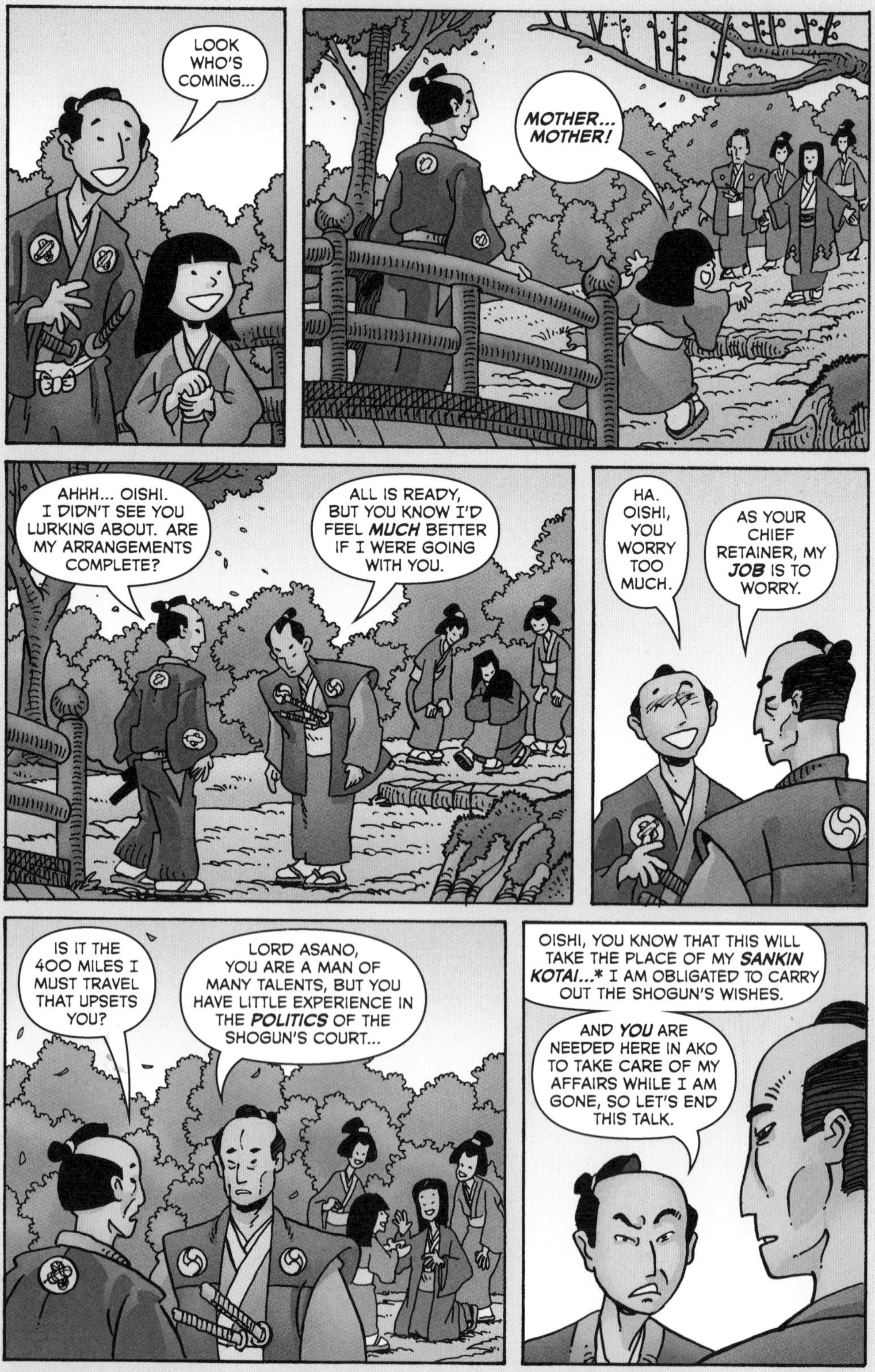
LOOK WHO'S COMING...
MOTHER... MOTHER!
AHHH... OISHI. I DIDN'T SEE YOU LURKING ABOUT. ARE MY ARRANGEMENTS COMPLETE?
ALL IS READY, BUT YOU KNOW I'D FEEL *MUCH* BETTER IF I WERE GOING WITH YOU.
HA. OISHI, YOU WORRY TOO MUCH.
AS YOUR CHIEF RETAINER, MY *JOB* IS TO WORRY.
IS IT THE 400 MILES I MUST TRAVEL THAT UPSETS YOU?
LORD ASANO, YOU ARE A MAN OF MANY TALENTS, BUT YOU HAVE LITTLE EXPERIENCE IN THE *POLITICS* OF THE SHOGUN'S COURT...
OISHI, YOU KNOW THAT THIS WILL TAKE THE PLACE OF MY *SANKIN KOTAI...** I AM OBLIGATED TO CARRY OUT THE SHOGUN'S WISHES.
AND *YOU* ARE NEEDED HERE IN AKO TO TAKE CARE OF MY AFFAIRS WHILE I AM GONE, SO LET'S END THIS TALK.

* Sankin Kotai: During Japan's Edo period, each daimyo and his family were periodically required by the shogunate to spend time in Edo, away from their own *hans*, or estates.

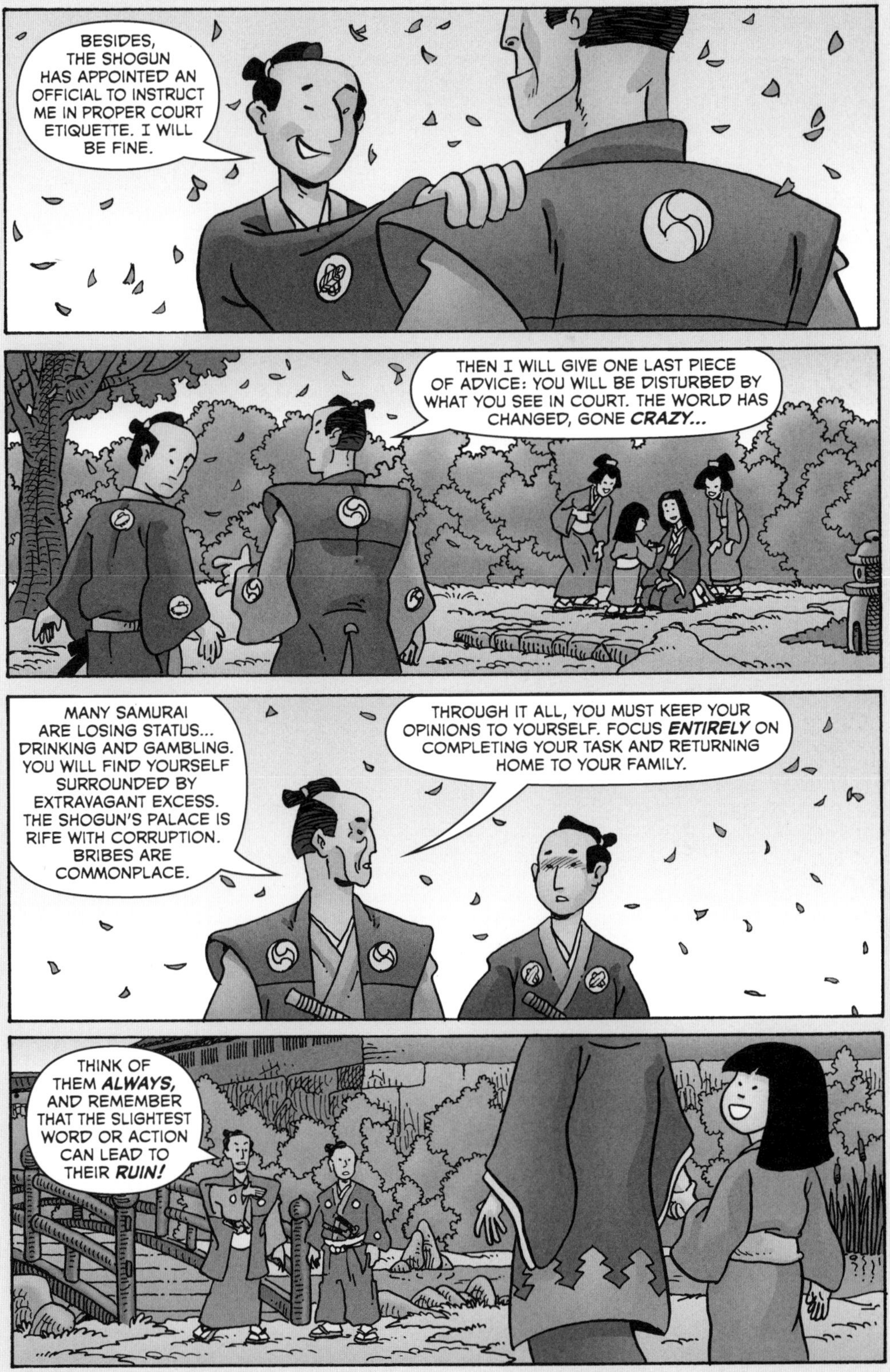
BESIDES, THE SHOGUN HAS APPOINTED AN OFFICIAL TO INSTRUCT ME IN PROPER COURT ETIQUETTE. I WILL BE FINE.
THEN I WILL GIVE ONE LAST PIECE OF ADVICE: YOU WILL BE DISTURBED BY WHAT YOU SEE IN COURT. THE WORLD HAS CHANGED, GONE CRAZY...
MANY SAMURAI ARE LOSING STATUS... DRINKING AND GAMBLING. YOU WILL FIND YOURSELF SURROUNDED BY EXTRAVAGANT EXCESS. THE SHOGUN'S PALACE IS RIFE WITH CORRUPTION. BRIBES ARE COMMONPLACE.
THROUGH IT ALL, YOU MUST KEEP YOUR OPINIONS TO YOURSELF. FOCUS ENTIRELY ON COMPLETING YOUR TASK AND RETURNING HOME TO YOUR FAMILY.
THINK OF THEM ALWAYS, AND REMEMBER THAT THE SLIGHTEST WORD OR ACTION CAN LEAD TO THEIR RUIN!

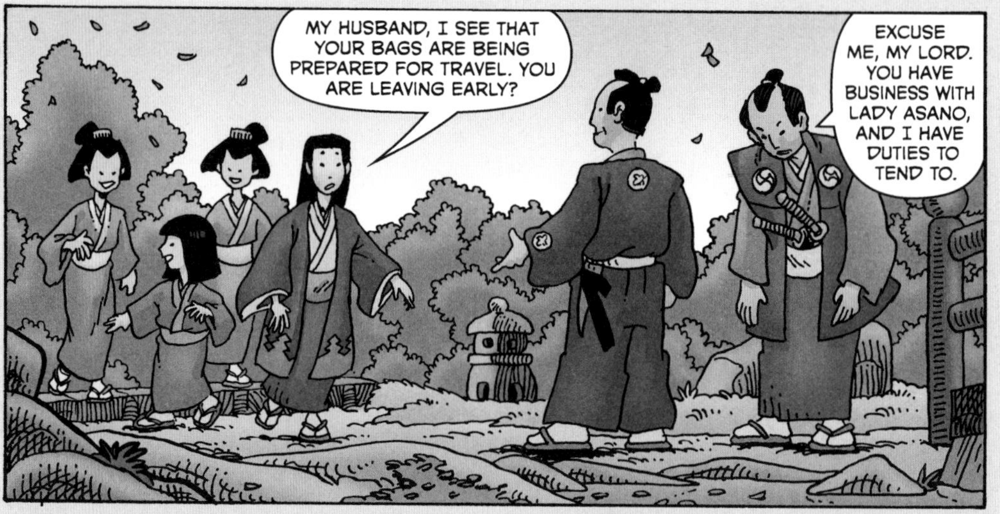
MY HUSBAND, I SEE THAT YOUR BAGS ARE BEING PREPARED FOR TRAVEL. YOU ARE LEAVING EARLY?
EXCUSE ME, MY LORD. YOU HAVE BUSINESS WITH LADY ASANO, AND I HAVE DUTIES TO TEND TO.

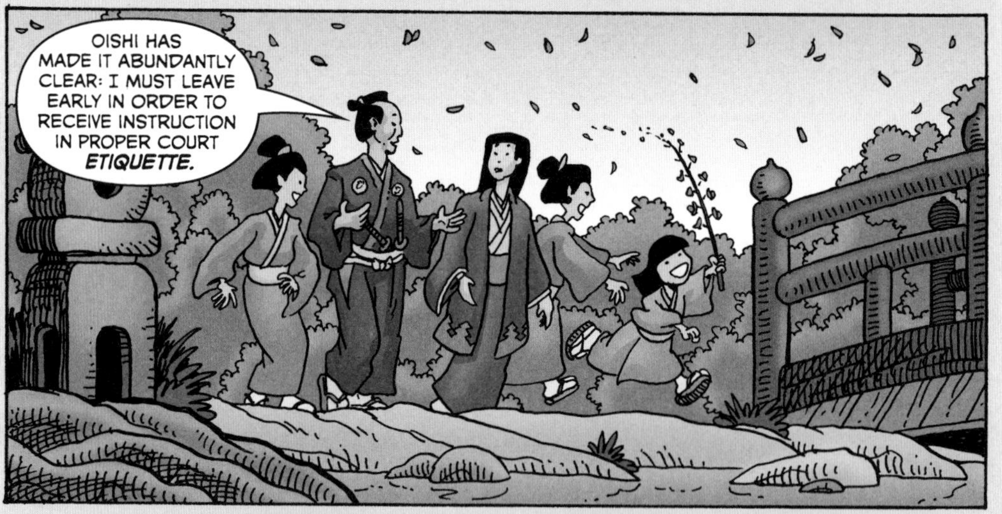
OISHI HAS MADE IT ABUNDANTLY CLEAR: I MUST LEAVE EARLY IN ORDER TO RECEIVE INSTRUCTION IN PROPER COURT *ETIQUETTE.*

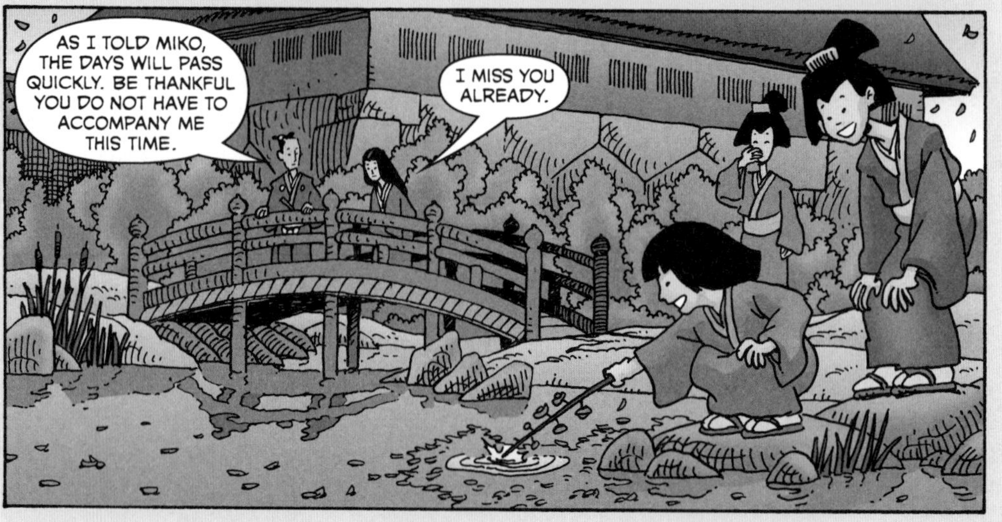
AS I TOLD MIKO, THE DAYS WILL PASS QUICKLY. BE THANKFUL YOU DO NOT HAVE TO ACCOMPANY ME THIS TIME.
I MISS YOU ALREADY.

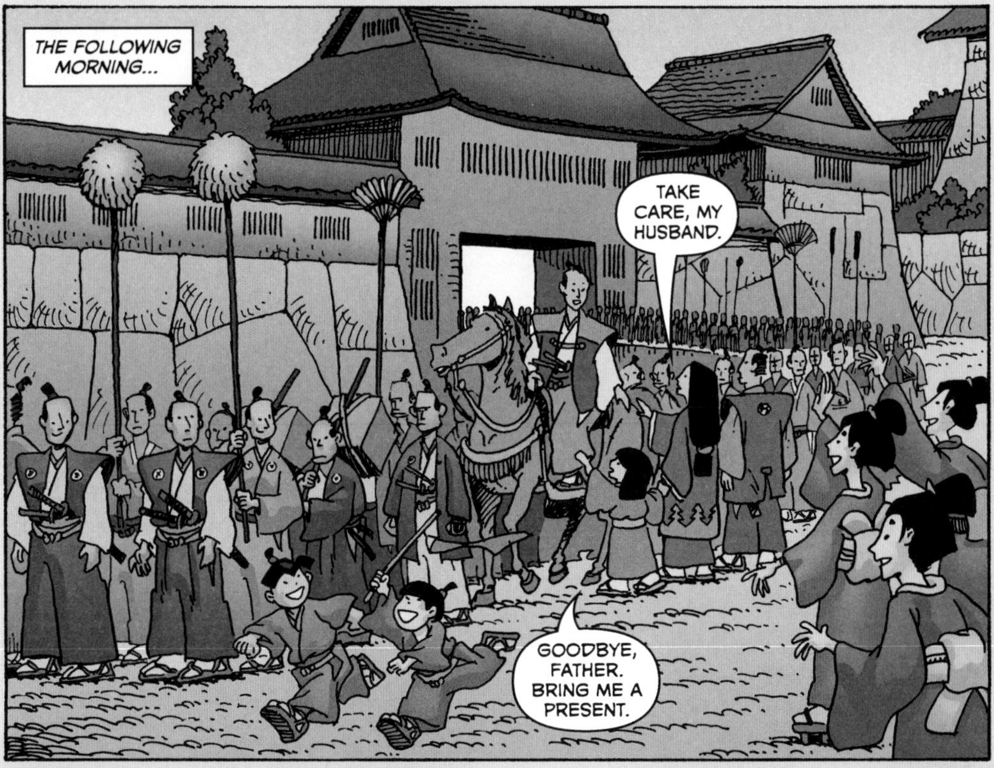
THE FOLLOWING MORNING...
TAKE CARE, MY HUSBAND.
GOODBYE, FATHER. BRING ME A PRESENT.

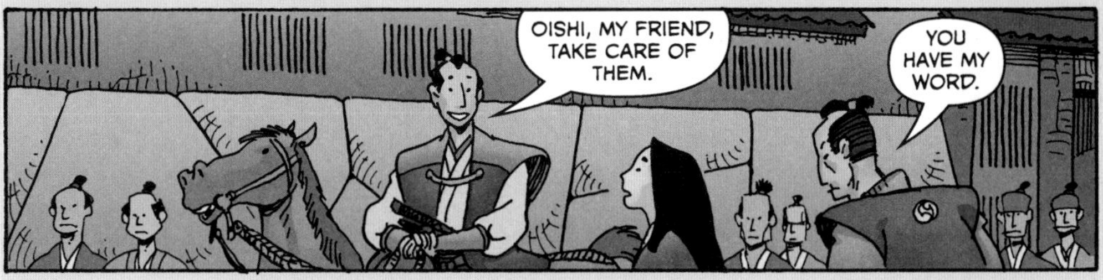
OISHI, MY FRIEND, TAKE CARE OF THEM.
YOU HAVE MY WORD.

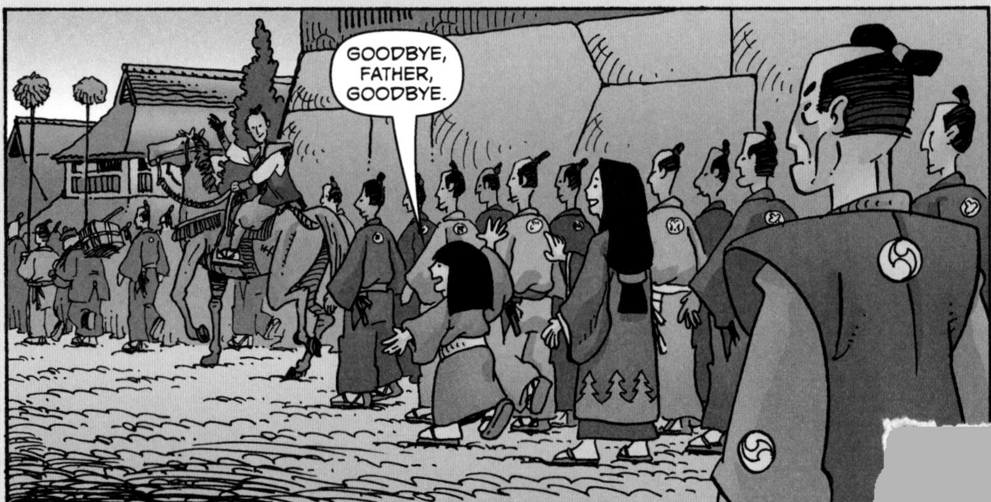
GOODBYE, FATHER, GOODBYE.

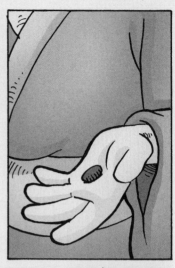

MOTHER, I WILL PLANT THE SEED FATHER GAVE ME IN THE GARDEN: A SURPRISE WHEN HE RETURNS.

THAT IS AN *EXCELLENT* IDEA. YOUR FATHER WILL BE VERY PLEASED.

THAT WILL BE A WONDERFUL SURPRISE, DON'T YOU THINK SO, OISHI?

YES. WONDERFUL... WHEN HE RETURNS.

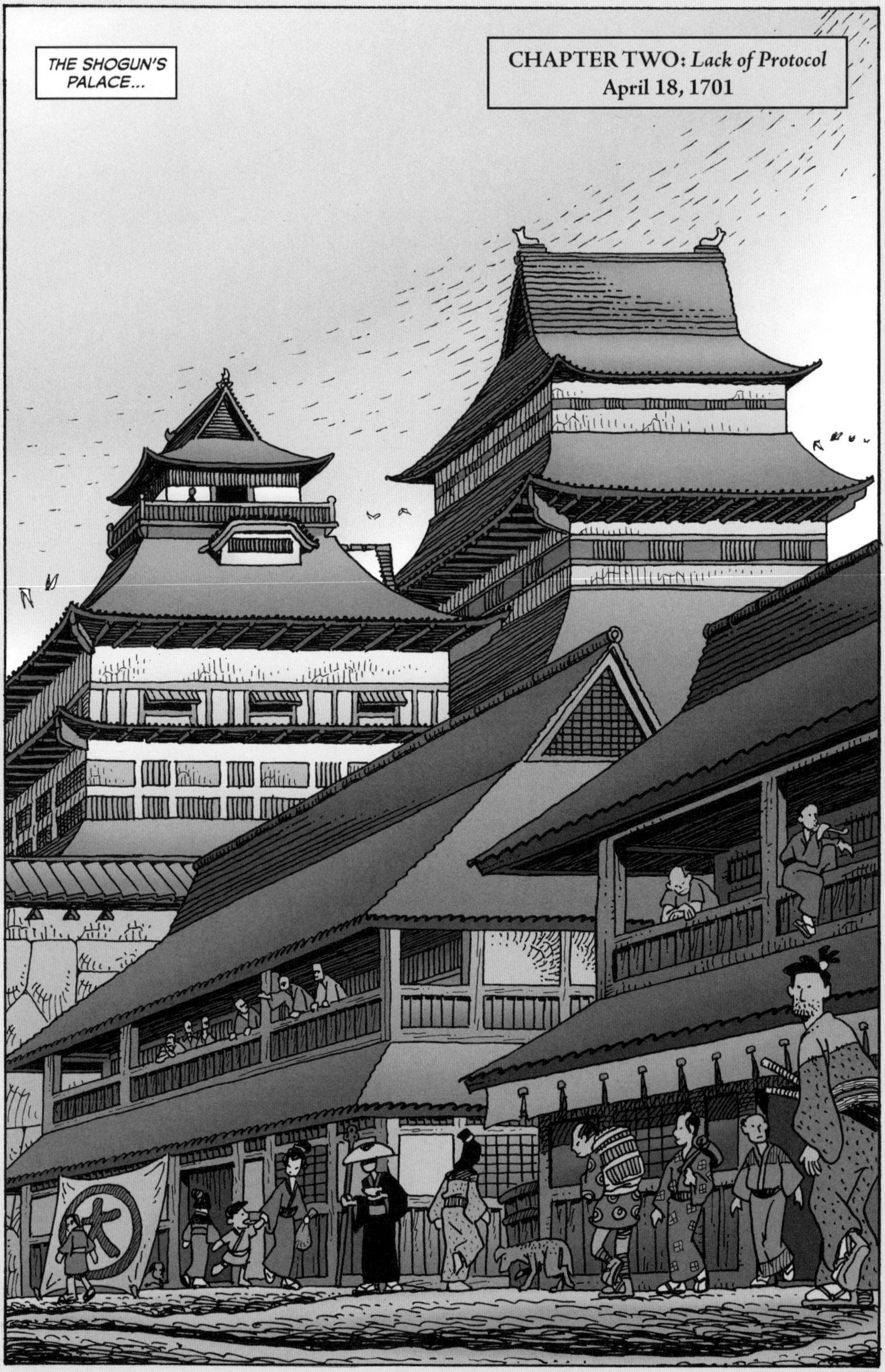
THE SHOGUN'S PALACE...
CHAPTER TWO: *Lack of Protocol*
April 18, 1701
大

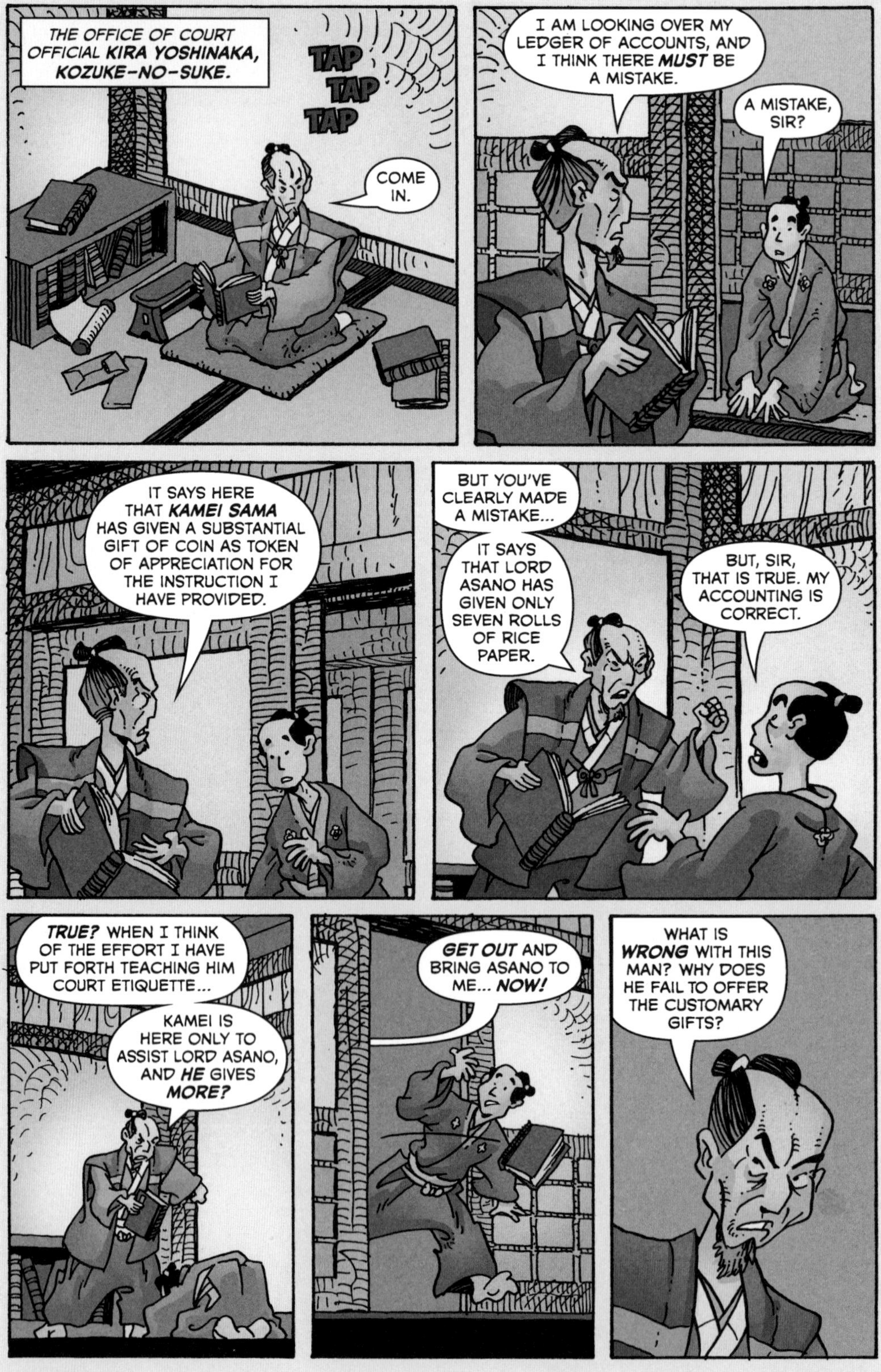
THE OFFICE OF COURT OFFICIAL KIRA YOSHINAKA, KOZUKE-NO-SUKE.
TAP TAP TAP
COME IN.
I AM LOOKING OVER MY LEDGER OF ACCOUNTS, AND I THINK THERE MUST BE A MISTAKE.
A MISTAKE, SIR?
IT SAYS HERE THAT KAMEI SAMA HAS GIVEN A SUBSTANTIAL GIFT OF COIN AS TOKEN OF APPRECIATION FOR THE INSTRUCTION I HAVE PROVIDED.
BUT YOU'VE CLEARLY MADE A MISTAKE...
IT SAYS THAT LORD ASANO HAS GIVEN ONLY SEVEN ROLLS OF RICE PAPER.
BUT, SIR, THAT IS TRUE. MY ACCOUNTING IS CORRECT.
TRUE? WHEN I THINK OF THE EFFORT I HAVE PUT FORTH TEACHING HIM COURT ETIQUETTE...
KAMEI IS HERE ONLY TO ASSIST LORD ASANO, AND HE GIVES MORE?
GET OUT AND BRING ASANO TO ME... NOW!
WHAT IS WRONG WITH THIS MAN? WHY DOES HE FAIL TO OFFER THE CUSTOMARY GIFTS?

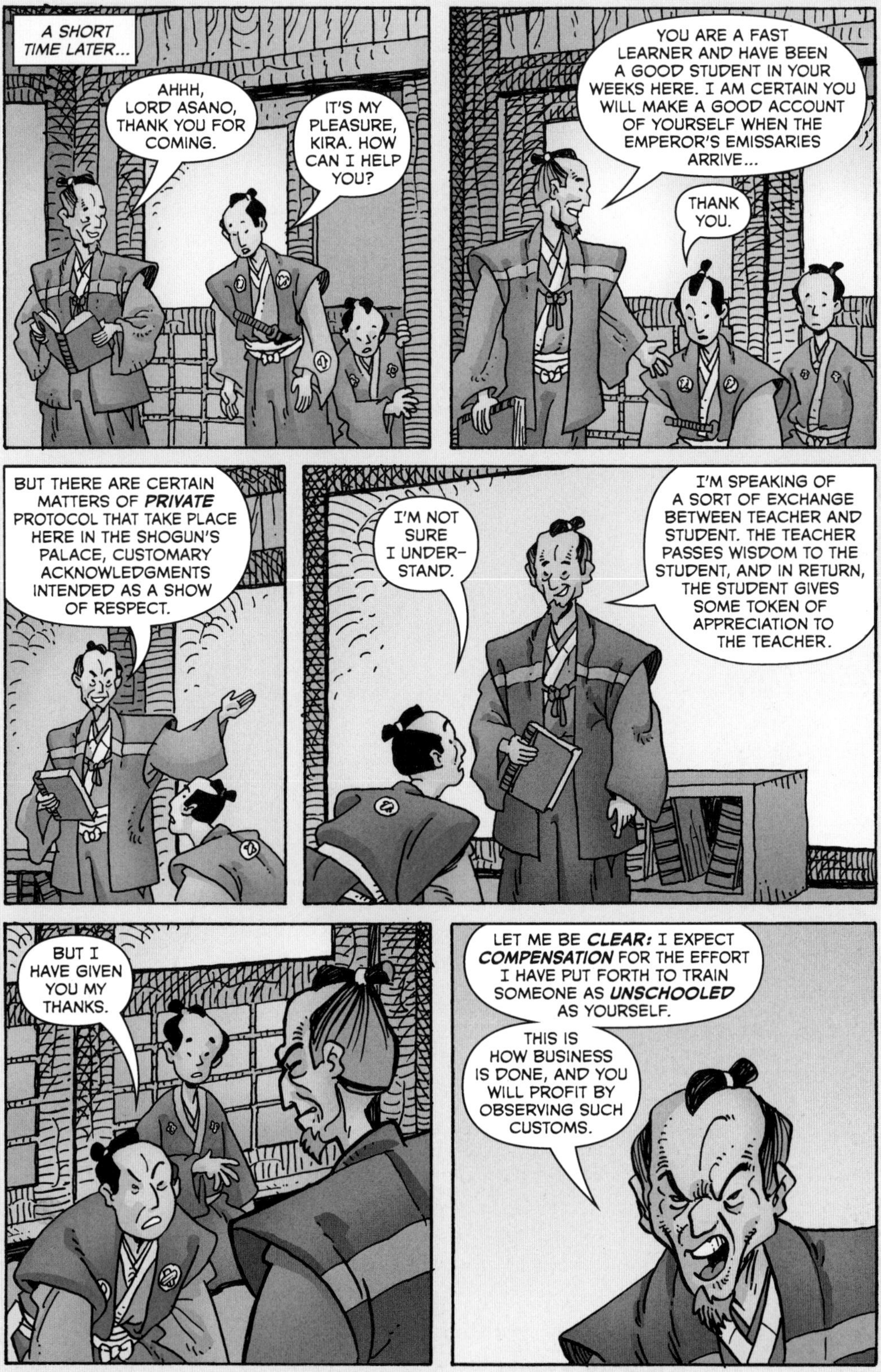
A SHORT TIME LATER...
AHHH, LORD ASANO, THANK YOU FOR COMING.
IT'S MY PLEASURE, KIRA. HOW CAN I HELP YOU?
YOU ARE A FAST LEARNER AND HAVE BEEN A GOOD STUDENT IN YOUR WEEKS HERE. I AM CERTAIN YOU WILL MAKE A GOOD ACCOUNT OF YOURSELF WHEN THE EMPEROR'S EMISSARIES ARRIVE...
THANK YOU.
BUT THERE ARE CERTAIN MATTERS OF *PRIVATE* PROTOCOL THAT TAKE PLACE HERE IN THE SHOGUN'S PALACE, CUSTOMARY ACKNOWLEDGMENTS INTENDED AS A SHOW OF RESPECT.
I'M NOT SURE I UNDER-STAND.
I'M SPEAKING OF A SORT OF EXCHANGE BETWEEN TEACHER AND STUDENT. THE TEACHER PASSES WISDOM TO THE STUDENT, AND IN RETURN, THE STUDENT GIVES SOME TOKEN OF APPRECIATION TO THE TEACHER.
BUT I HAVE GIVEN YOU MY THANKS.
LET ME BE *CLEAR:* I EXPECT *COMPENSATION* FOR THE EFFORT I HAVE PUT FORTH TO TRAIN SOMEONE AS *UNSCHOOLED* AS YOURSELF.
THIS IS HOW BUSINESS IS DONE, AND YOU WILL PROFIT BY OBSERVING SUCH CUSTOMS.

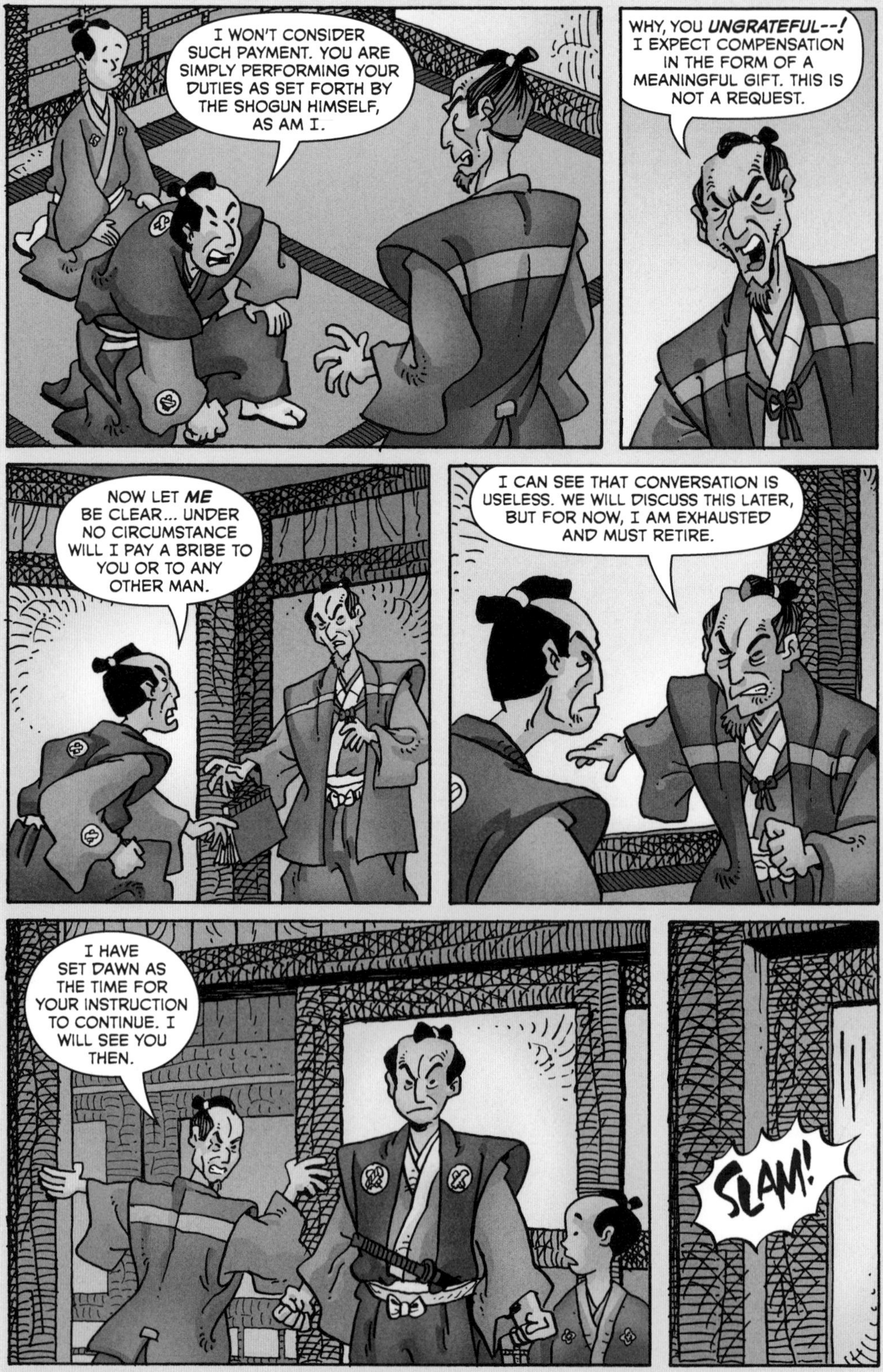
I WON'T CONSIDER SUCH PAYMENT. YOU ARE SIMPLY PERFORMING YOUR DUTIES AS SET FORTH BY THE SHOGUN HIMSELF, AS AM I.
WHY, YOU *UNGRATEFUL--!* I EXPECT COMPENSATION IN THE FORM OF A MEANINGFUL GIFT. THIS IS NOT A REQUEST.
NOW LET *ME* BE CLEAR... UNDER NO CIRCUMSTANCE WILL I PAY A BRIBE TO YOU OR TO ANY OTHER MAN.
I CAN SEE THAT CONVERSATION IS USELESS. WE WILL DISCUSS THIS LATER, BUT FOR NOW, I AM EXHAUSTED AND MUST RETIRE.
I HAVE SET DAWN AS THE TIME FOR YOUR INSTRUCTION TO CONTINUE. I WILL SEE YOU THEN.
SLAM!

LORD ASANO, WITH ALL DUE RESPECT, WAS IT WISE TO REFUSE KIRA? YOU HAVE MADE AN ENEMY OF HIM IN THE PROCESS.

I HAVE SEEN THIS SITUATION BEFORE, AND YOU WILL SAVE YOUR- SELF A GREAT DEAL OF TROUBLE BY RELENTING AND GIVING KIRA THE BRIBE THAT HE WANTS.

I WILL NOT OFFER GIFTS OR BRIBES TO A COURT OFFICIAL, ESPECIALLY NOT ONE AS OBVIOUSLY *CORRUPT* AS KIRA.

TELL ME, ACCOUNTANT... ANOTHER *DAIMYO*, KAMEI SAMA, IS TAKING THE SAME INSTRUCTION. DID HE OFFER A "GIFT"?

YES, BUT I BELIEVE HIS AIDES TOOK ACTION ON THEIR OWN AND WITHOUT THEIR MASTER'S KNOWLEDGE.

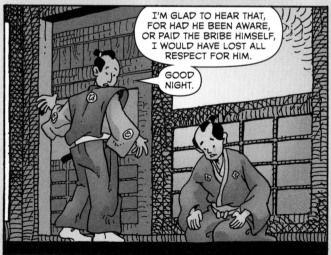

I'M GLAD TO HEAR THAT, FOR HAD HE BEEN AWARE, OR PAID THE BRIBE HIMSELF, I WOULD HAVE LOST ALL RESPECT FOR HIM.

GOOD NIGHT.

THIS WILL NOT TURN OUT WELL.

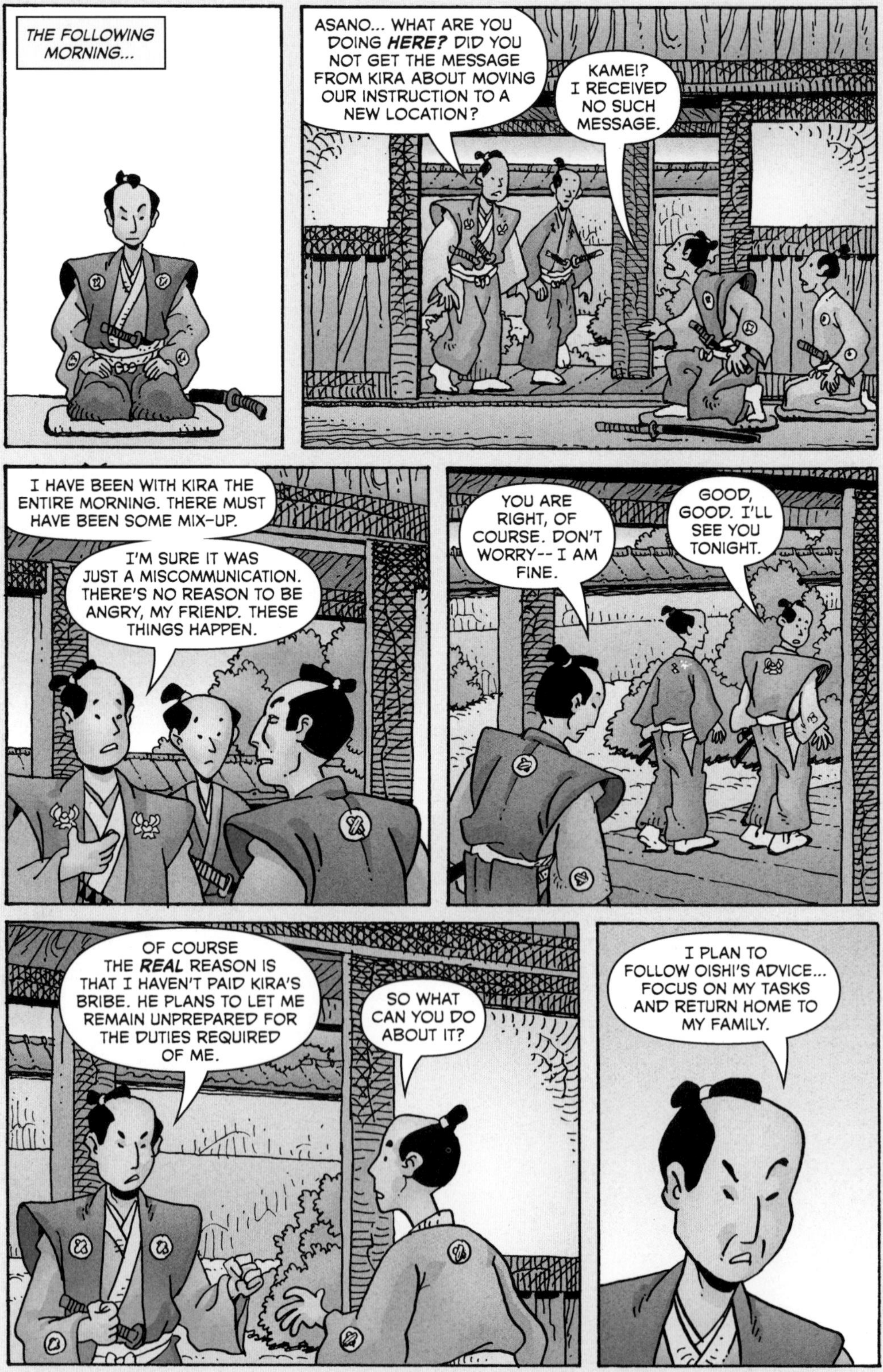
THE FOLLOWING MORNING...
ASANO... WHAT ARE YOU DOING HERE? DID YOU NOT GET THE MESSAGE FROM KIRA ABOUT MOVING OUR INSTRUCTION TO A NEW LOCATION?
KAMEI? I RECEIVED NO SUCH MESSAGE.
I HAVE BEEN WITH KIRA THE ENTIRE MORNING. THERE MUST HAVE BEEN SOME MIX-UP.
I'M SURE IT WAS JUST A MISCOMMUNICATION. THERE'S NO REASON TO BE ANGRY, MY FRIEND. THESE THINGS HAPPEN.
YOU ARE RIGHT, OF COURSE. DON'T WORRY-- I AM FINE.
GOOD, GOOD. I'LL SEE YOU TONIGHT.
OF COURSE THE REAL REASON IS THAT I HAVEN'T PAID KIRA'S BRIBE. HE PLANS TO LET ME REMAIN UNPREPARED FOR THE DUTIES REQUIRED OF ME.
SO WHAT CAN YOU DO ABOUT IT?
I PLAN TO FOLLOW OISHI'S ADVICE... FOCUS ON MY TASKS AND RETURN HOME TO MY FAMILY.

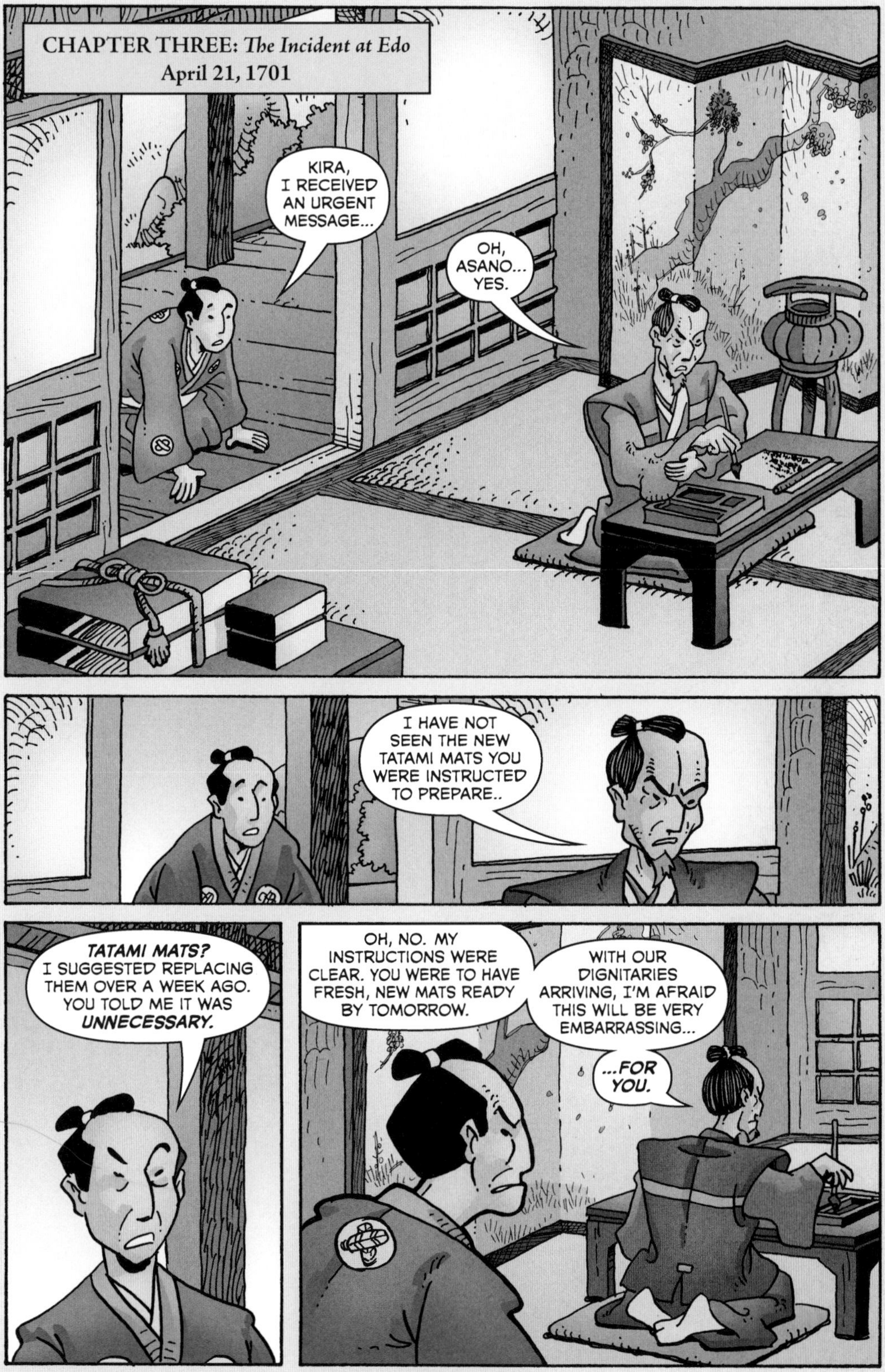
CHAPTER THREE: *The Incident at Edo*
April 21, 1701
KIRA, I RECEIVED AN URGENT MESSAGE...
OH, ASANO... YES.
I HAVE NOT SEEN THE NEW TATAMI MATS YOU WERE INSTRUCTED TO PREPARE..
TATAMI MATS? I SUGGESTED REPLACING THEM OVER A WEEK AGO. YOU TOLD ME IT WAS *UNNECESSARY.*
OH, NO. MY INSTRUCTIONS WERE CLEAR. YOU WERE TO HAVE FRESH, NEW MATS READY BY TOMORROW.
WITH OUR DIGNITARIES ARRIVING, I'M AFRAID THIS WILL BE VERY EMBARRASSING...
...FOR YOU.

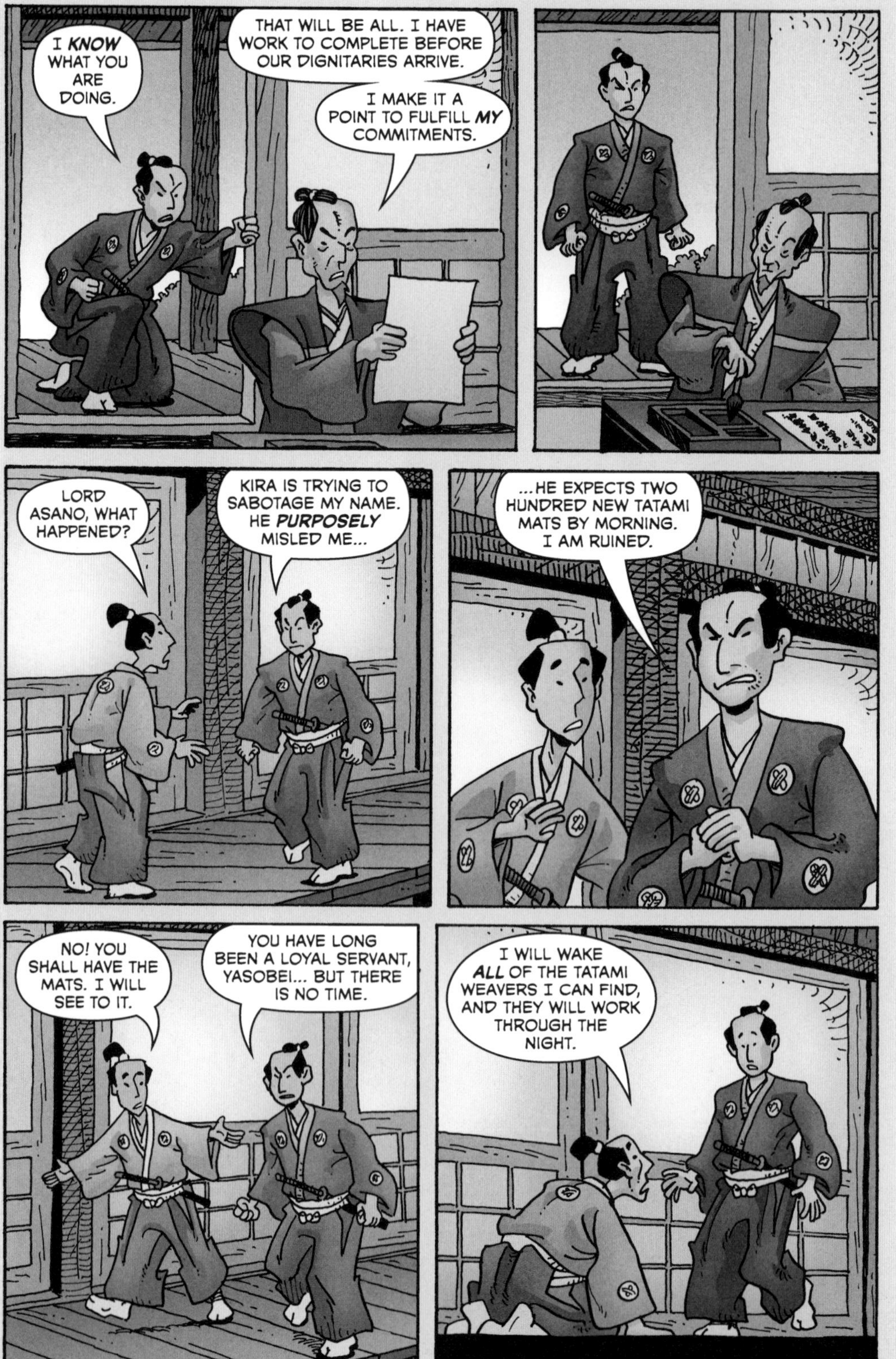
I *KNOW* WHAT YOU ARE DOING.
THAT WILL BE ALL. I HAVE WORK TO COMPLETE BEFORE OUR DIGNITARIES ARRIVE.
I MAKE IT A POINT TO FULFILL *MY* COMMITMENTS.
LORD ASANO, WHAT HAPPENED?
KIRA IS TRYING TO SABOTAGE MY NAME. HE *PURPOSELY* MISLED ME...
...HE EXPECTS TWO HUNDRED NEW TATAMI MATS BY MORNING. I AM RUINED.
NO! YOU SHALL HAVE THE MATS. I WILL SEE TO IT.
YOU HAVE LONG BEEN A LOYAL SERVANT, YASOBEI... BUT THERE IS NO TIME.
I WILL WAKE *ALL* OF THE TATAMI WEAVERS I CAN FIND, AND THEY WILL WORK THROUGH THE NIGHT.

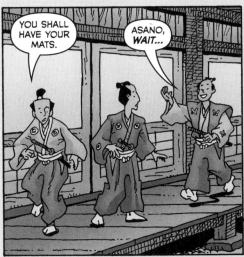

YOU SHALL HAVE YOUR MATS.

ASANO, *WAIT*...

WE HAVE A FREE NIGHT. WHY NOT SHARE A MEAL BEFORE THE EMPEROR'S GROUP ARRIVES TOMORROW?

THERE WILL BE NO NIGHT OFF FOR ME, KAMEI...

KIRA WANTS TWO HUNDRED TATAMI MATS BEFORE MORNING.

NEW TATAMI MATS? I WAS THERE WHEN HE TOLD YOU THEY WEREN'T NECESSARY.

I'VE HAD *ENOUGH* OF HIS INSULTS AND BAITING. YOU ARE *DAIMYO* OF CASTLE AKO.

HE NEEDS TO BE *TAUGHT* THE MEANING OF RESPECT!

NO, MY FRIEND. YASOBEI IS CONFIDENT THAT HE CAN DELIVER THE MATS ON TIME. LET IT PASS.

WE WILL SOON BE FINISHED HERE AND CAN RETURN TO OUR FAMILIES.

KIRA WILL BE OUT OF OUR LIVES SOON ENOUGH.

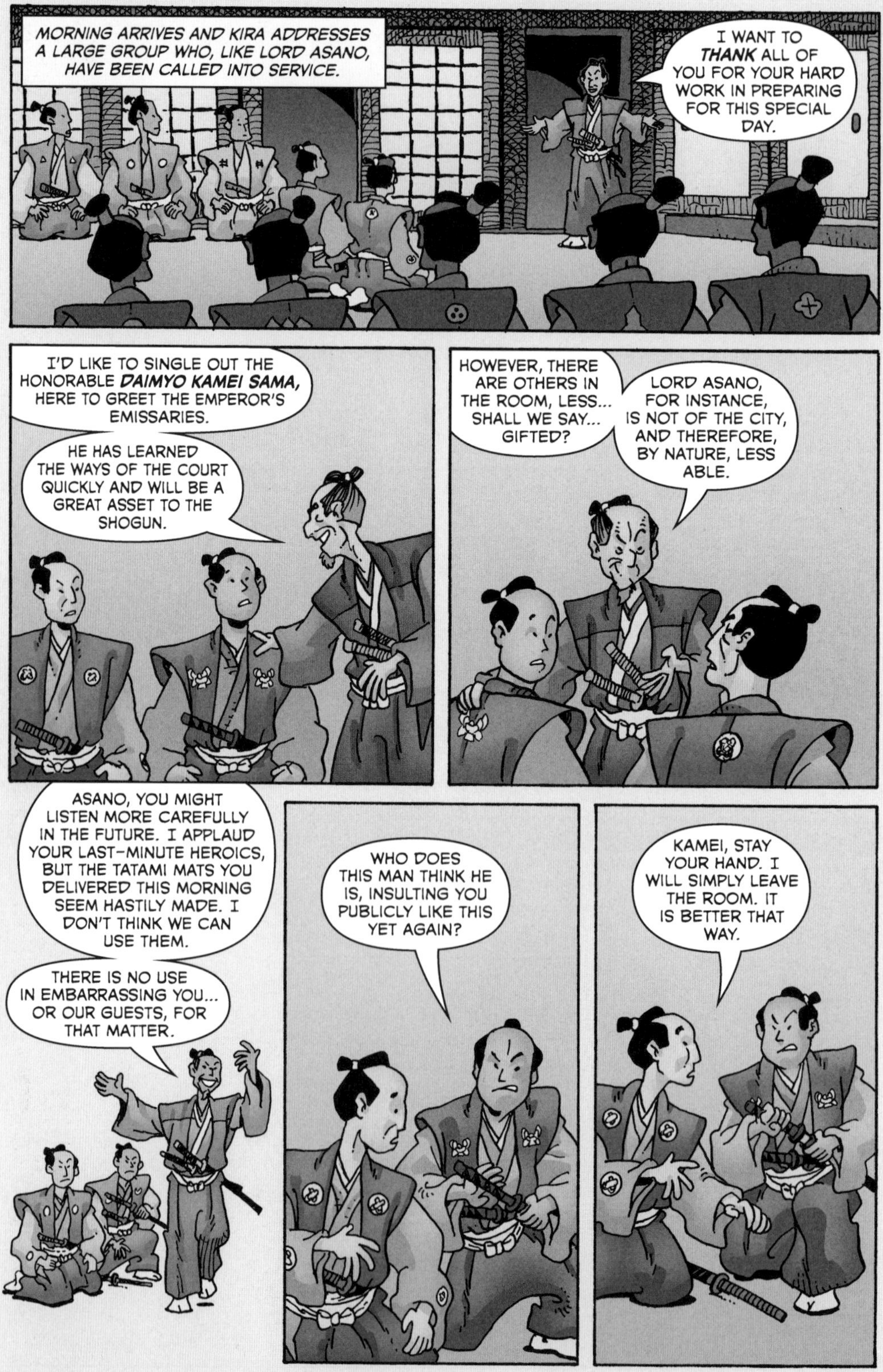
MORNING ARRIVES AND KIRA ADDRESSES A LARGE GROUP WHO, LIKE LORD ASANO, HAVE BEEN CALLED INTO SERVICE.
I WANT TO THANK ALL OF YOU FOR YOUR HARD WORK IN PREPARING FOR THIS SPECIAL DAY.
I'D LIKE TO SINGLE OUT THE HONORABLE DAIMYO KAMEI SAMA, HERE TO GREET THE EMPEROR'S EMISSARIES.
HE HAS LEARNED THE WAYS OF THE COURT QUICKLY AND WILL BE A GREAT ASSET TO THE SHOGUN.
HOWEVER, THERE ARE OTHERS IN THE ROOM, LESS... SHALL WE SAY... GIFTED?
LORD ASANO, FOR INSTANCE, IS NOT OF THE CITY, AND THEREFORE, BY NATURE, LESS ABLE.
ASANO, YOU MIGHT LISTEN MORE CAREFULLY IN THE FUTURE. I APPLAUD YOUR LAST-MINUTE HEROICS, BUT THE TATAMI MATS YOU DELIVERED THIS MORNING SEEM HASTILY MADE. I DON'T THINK WE CAN USE THEM.
THERE IS NO USE IN EMBARRASSING YOU... OR OUR GUESTS, FOR THAT MATTER.
WHO DOES THIS MAN THINK HE IS, INSULTING YOU PUBLICLY LIKE THIS YET AGAIN?
KAMEI, STAY YOUR HAND. I WILL SIMPLY LEAVE THE ROOM. IT IS BETTER THAT WAY.

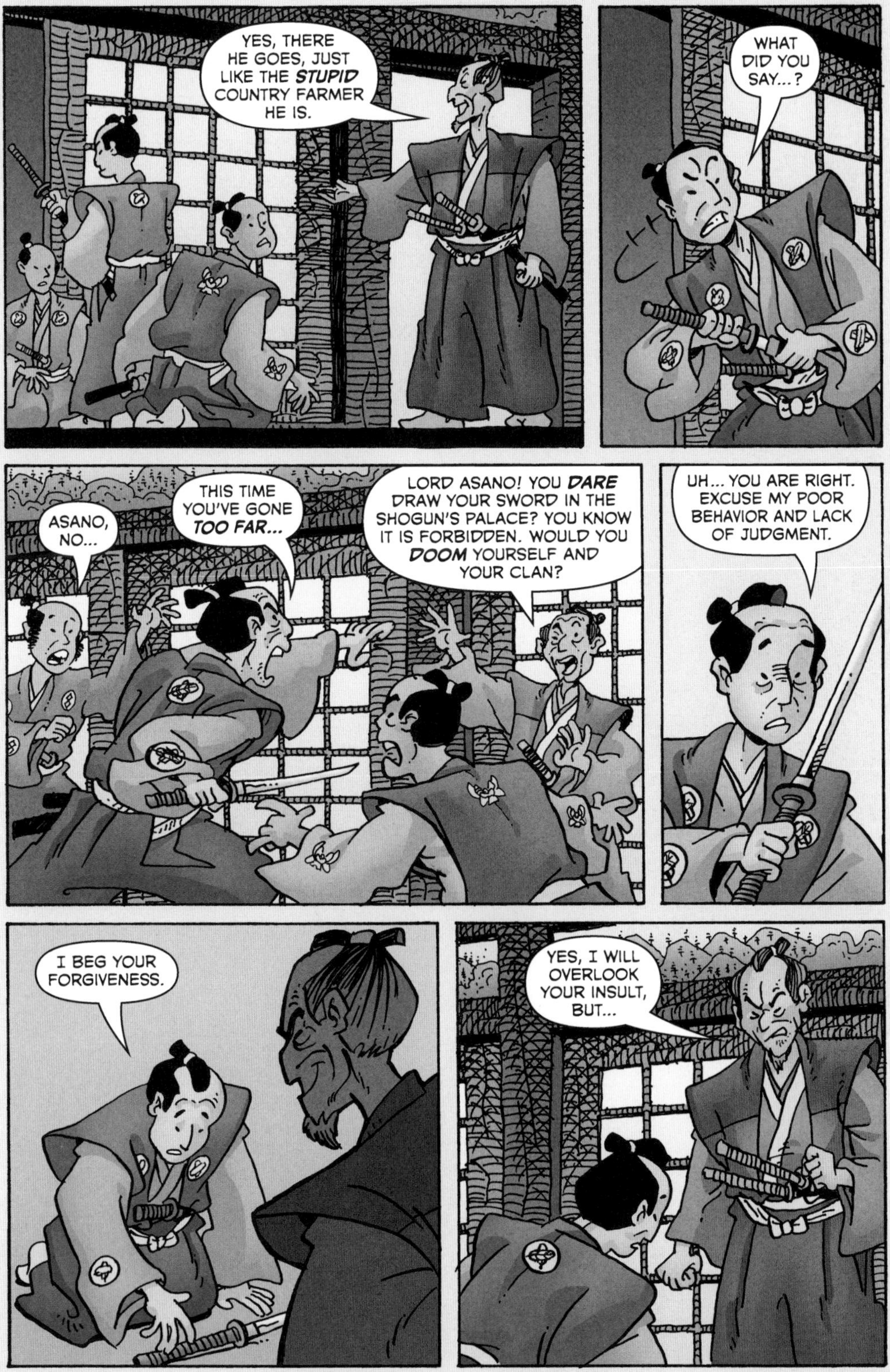
YES, THERE HE GOES, JUST LIKE THE STUPID COUNTRY FARMER HE IS.
WHAT DID YOU SAY...?
ASANO, NO...
THIS TIME YOU'VE GONE TOO FAR...
LORD ASANO! YOU DARE DRAW YOUR SWORD IN THE SHOGUN'S PALACE? YOU KNOW IT IS FORBIDDEN. WOULD YOU DOOM YOURSELF AND YOUR CLAN?
UH... YOU ARE RIGHT. EXCUSE MY POOR BEHAVIOR AND LACK OF JUDGMENT.
I BEG YOUR FORGIVENESS.
YES, I WILL OVERLOOK YOUR INSULT, BUT...

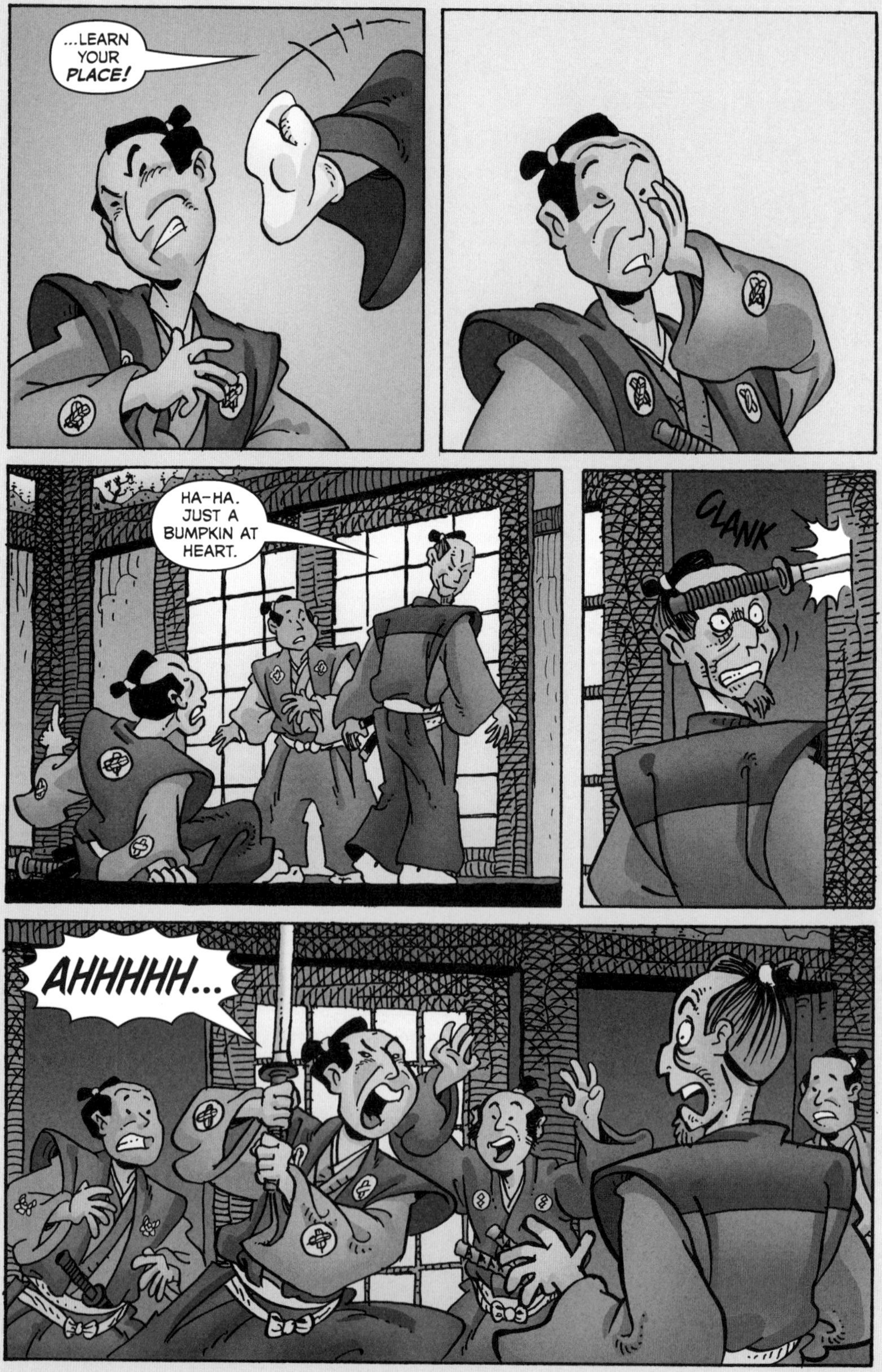
...LEARN YOUR PLACE!
HA-HA. JUST A BUMPKIN AT HEART.
CLANK
AHHHHH...

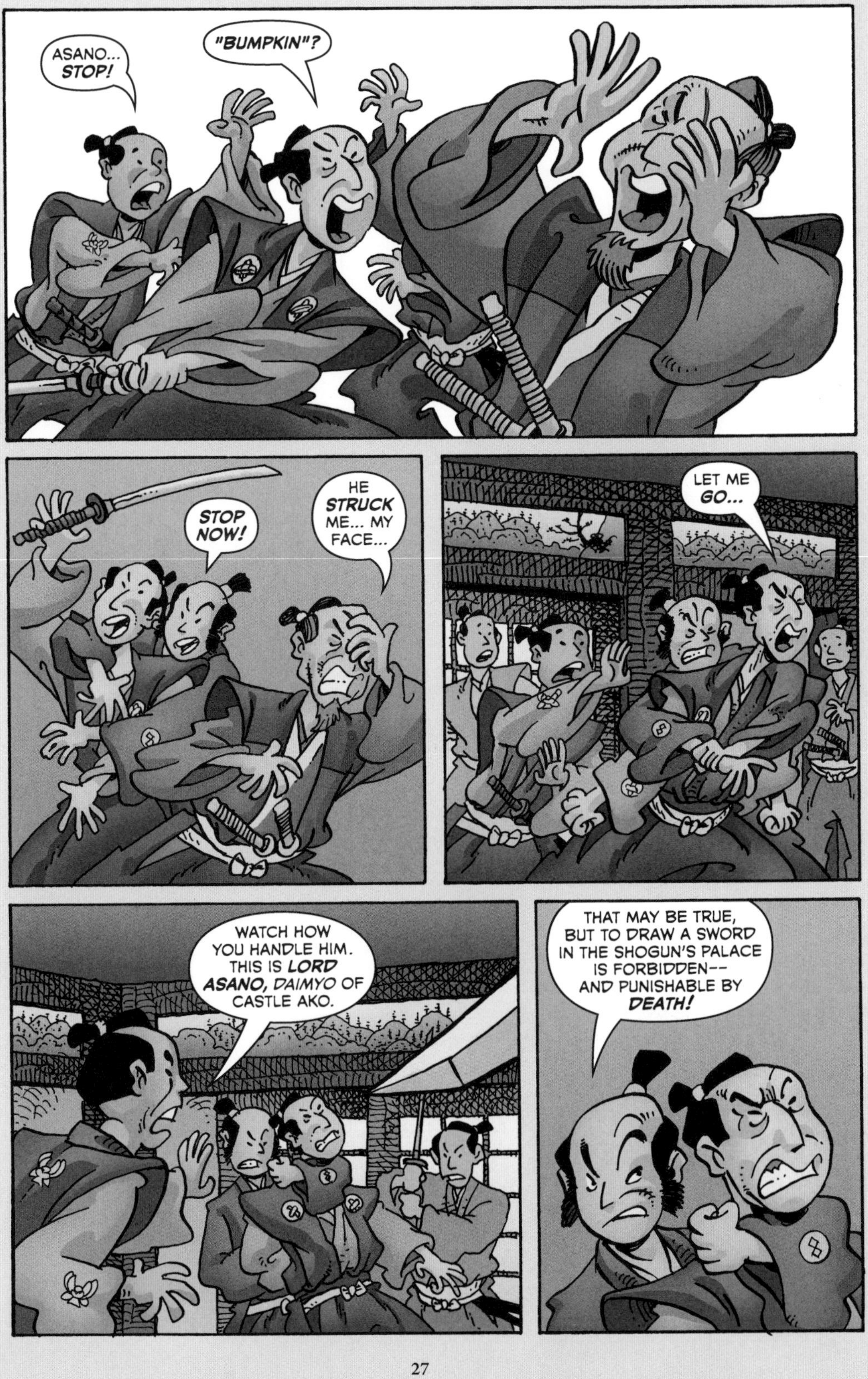
ASANO... STOP!
"BUMPKIN"?
STOP NOW!
HE STRUCK ME... MY FACE...
LET ME GO...
WATCH HOW YOU HANDLE HIM. THIS IS LORD ASANO, DAIMYO OF CASTLE AKO.
THAT MAY BE TRUE, BUT TO DRAW A SWORD IN THE SHOGUN'S PALACE IS FORBIDDEN-- AND PUNISHABLE BY DEATH!

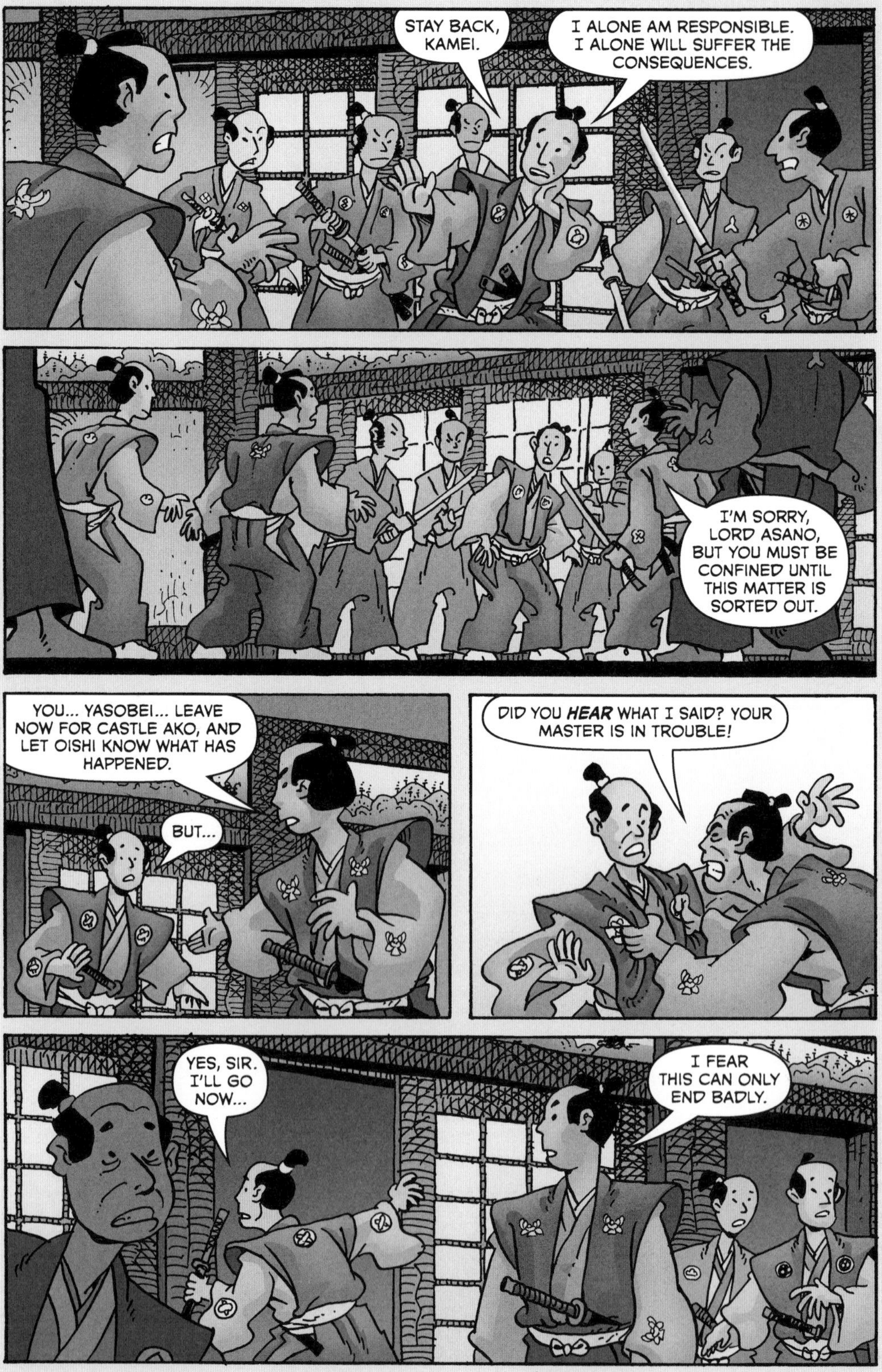
STAY BACK, KAMEI.
I ALONE AM RESPONSIBLE. I ALONE WILL SUFFER THE CONSEQUENCES.
I'M SORRY, LORD ASANO, BUT YOU MUST BE CONFINED UNTIL THIS MATTER IS SORTED OUT.
YOU... YASOBEI... LEAVE NOW FOR CASTLE AKO, AND LET OISHI KNOW WHAT HAS HAPPENED.
BUT...
DID YOU **HEAR** WHAT I SAID? YOUR MASTER IS IN TROUBLE!
YES, SIR. I'LL GO NOW...
I FEAR THIS CAN ONLY END BADLY.

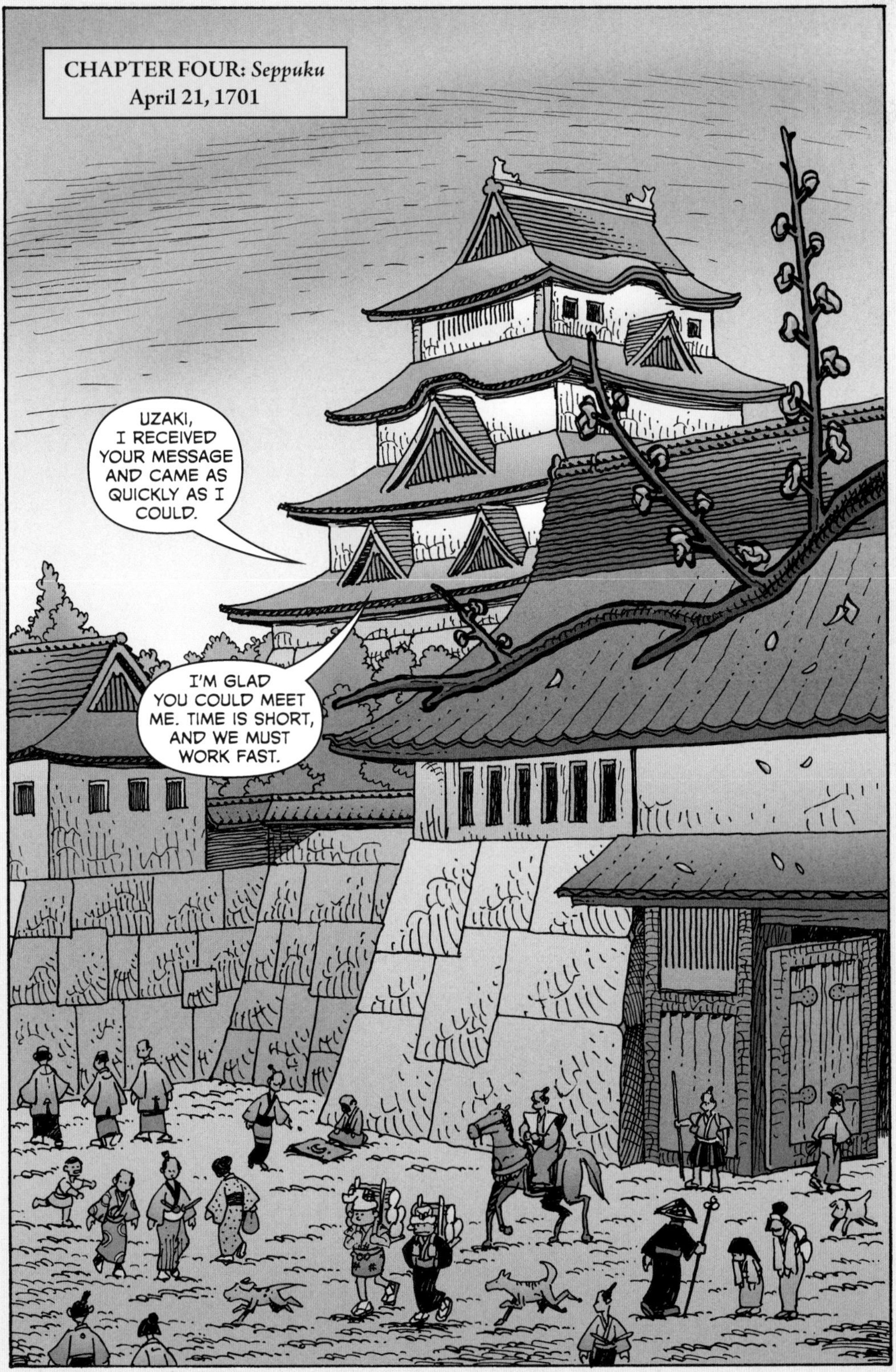
CHAPTER FOUR: *Seppuku*
April 21, 1701
UZAKI, I RECEIVED YOUR MESSAGE AND CAME AS QUICKLY AS I COULD.
I'M GLAD YOU COULD MEET ME. TIME IS SHORT, AND WE MUST WORK FAST.

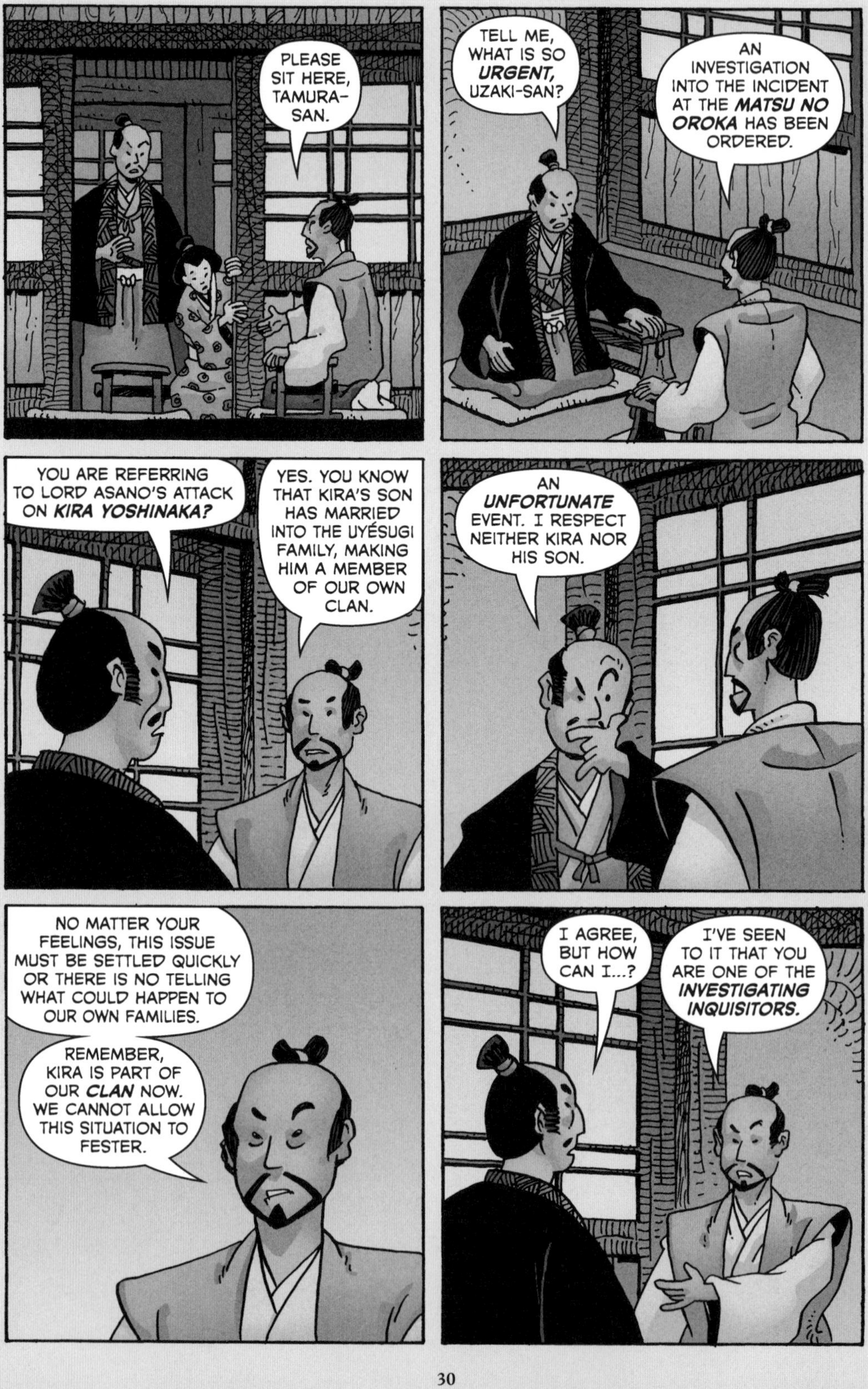
PLEASE SIT HERE, TAMURA-SAN.
TELL ME, WHAT IS SO URGENT, UZAKI-SAN?
AN INVESTIGATION INTO THE INCIDENT AT THE MATSU NO OROKA HAS BEEN ORDERED.
YOU ARE REFERRING TO LORD ASANO'S ATTACK ON KIRA YOSHINAKA?
YES. YOU KNOW THAT KIRA'S SON HAS MARRIED INTO THE UYÉSUGI FAMILY, MAKING HIM A MEMBER OF OUR OWN CLAN.
AN UNFORTUNATE EVENT. I RESPECT NEITHER KIRA NOR HIS SON.
NO MATTER YOUR FEELINGS, THIS ISSUE MUST BE SETTLED QUICKLY OR THERE IS NO TELLING WHAT COULD HAPPEN TO OUR OWN FAMILIES.
REMEMBER, KIRA IS PART OF OUR CLAN NOW. WE CANNOT ALLOW THIS SITUATION TO FESTER.
I AGREE, BUT HOW CAN I...?
I'VE SEEN TO IT THAT YOU ARE ONE OF THE INVESTIGATING INQUISITORS.

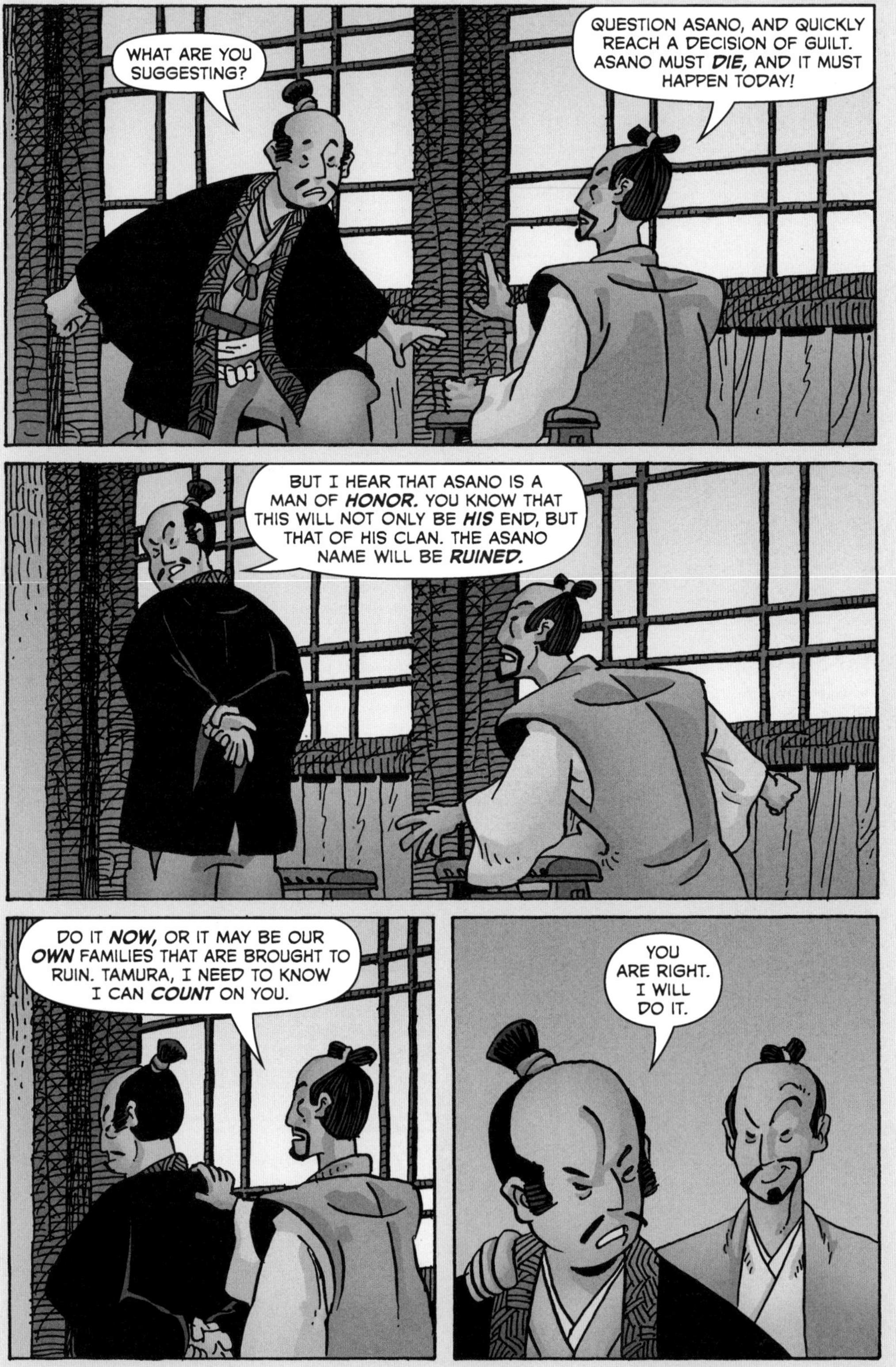
WHAT ARE YOU SUGGESTING?
QUESTION ASANO, AND QUICKLY REACH A DECISION OF GUILT. ASANO MUST DIE, AND IT MUST HAPPEN TODAY!
BUT I HEAR THAT ASANO IS A MAN OF HONOR. YOU KNOW THAT THIS WILL NOT ONLY BE HIS END, BUT THAT OF HIS CLAN. THE ASANO NAME WILL BE RUINED.
DO IT NOW, OR IT MAY BE OUR OWN FAMILIES THAT ARE BROUGHT TO RUIN. TAMURA, I NEED TO KNOW I CAN COUNT ON YOU.
YOU ARE RIGHT. I WILL DO IT.

A SHORT TIME LATER.

HE IS WAITING INSIDE.

EXCUSE US, LORD ASANO. WE HAVE BEEN ASSIGNED TO INVESTIGATE TODAY'S INCIDENT.

I AM *MATSUKI SADAMORI*, AND THIS IS *TAMURA UKIYŌ*. WE WOULD KNOW THE REASONS YOU DREW YOUR WEAPON AGAINST A COURT OFFICIAL...?

YES, YOU MUST HAVE KNOWN THAT PULLING A SWORD IN THE SHOGUN'S PALACE WOULD RESULT IN *SEVERE* PUNISHMENT.

UNDER THE SAME CIRCUMSTANCES, I WOULD DO IT AGAIN.

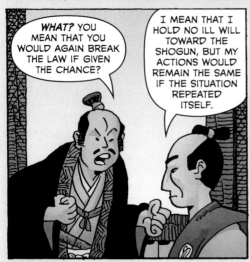

WHAT? YOU MEAN THAT YOU WOULD AGAIN BREAK THE LAW IF GIVEN THE CHANCE?

I MEAN THAT I HOLD NO ILL WILL TOWARD THE SHOGUN, BUT MY ACTIONS WOULD REMAIN THE SAME IF THE SITUATION REPEATED ITSELF.

LORD ASANO, THIS IS YOUR CHANCE TO *DEFEND* YOUR ACTIONS. IS IT NOT TRUE THAT YOU WERE *PROVOKED?*

AS I SAID, I MEAN NO ILL WILL OR HARM TOWARD THE SHOGUN. MY ONLY REGRET IS THAT I WAS UNABLE TO *KILL* KIRA.

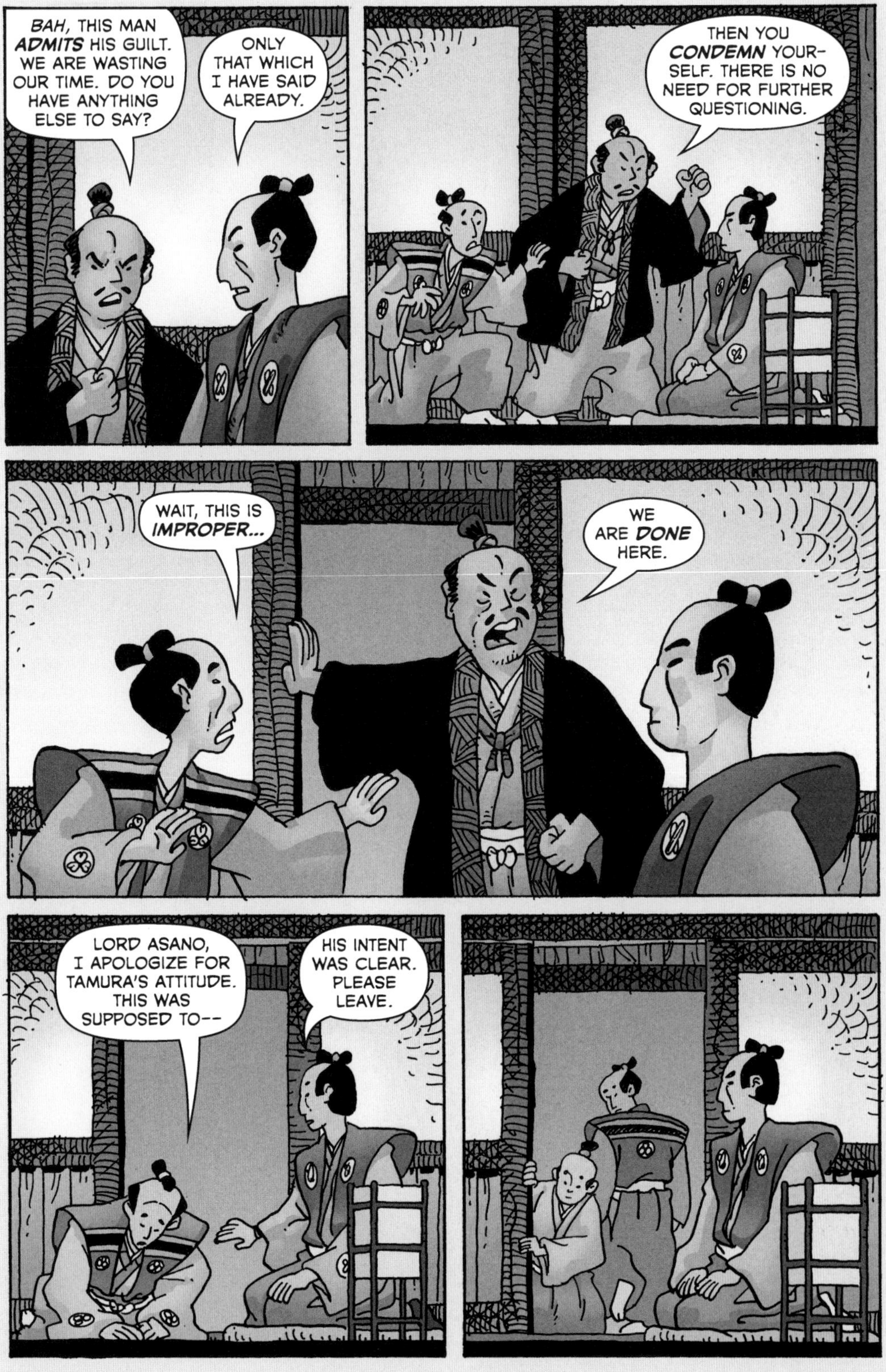
BAH, THIS MAN ADMITS HIS GUILT. WE ARE WASTING OUR TIME. DO YOU HAVE ANYTHING ELSE TO SAY?
ONLY THAT WHICH I HAVE SAID ALREADY.
THEN YOU CONDEMN YOURSELF. THERE IS NO NEED FOR FURTHER QUESTIONING.
WAIT, THIS IS IMPROPER...
WE ARE DONE HERE.
LORD ASANO, I APOLOGIZE FOR TAMURA'S ATTITUDE. THIS WAS SUPPOSED TO--
HIS INTENT WAS CLEAR. PLEASE LEAVE.

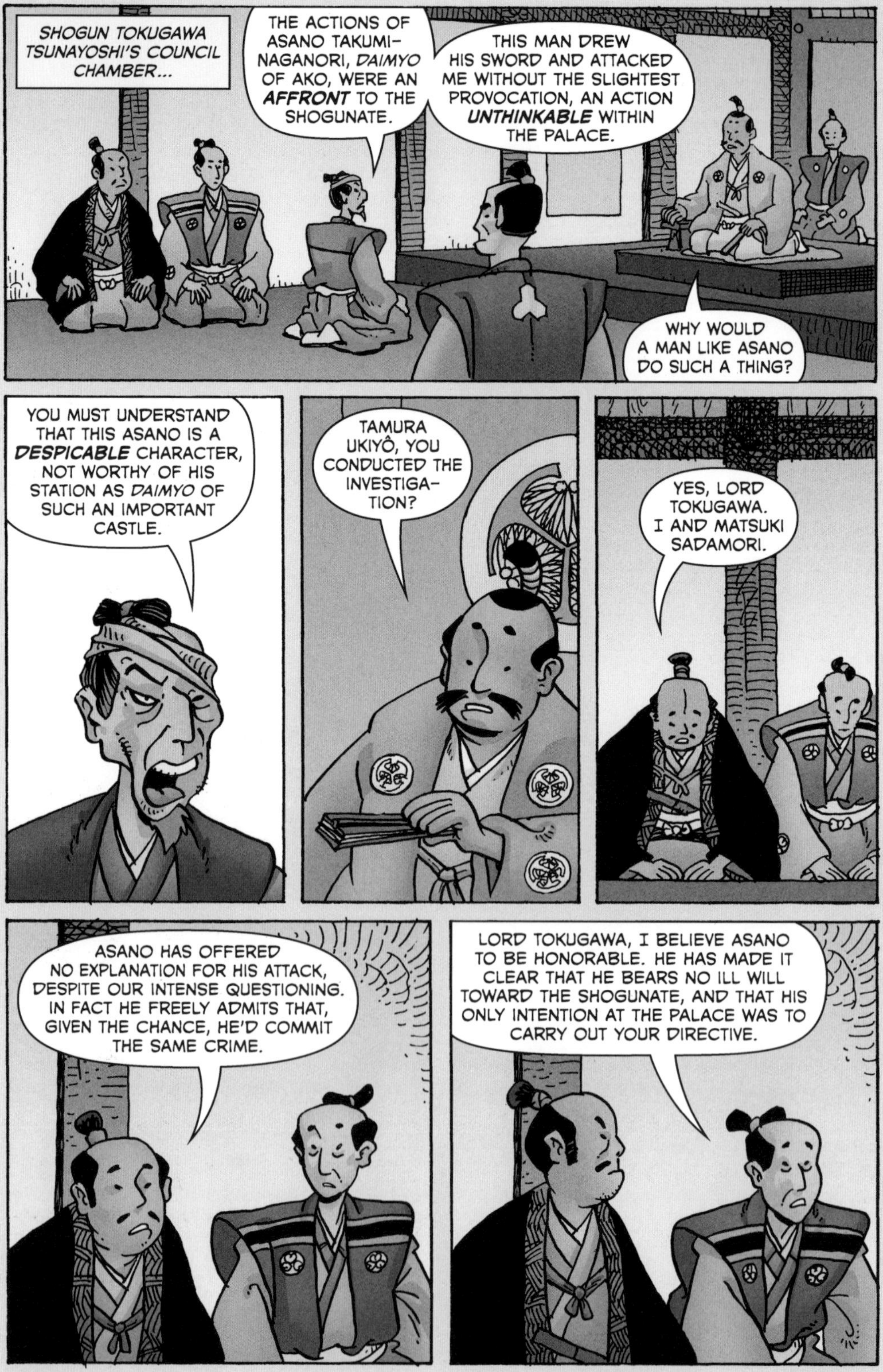
SHOGUN TOKUGAWA TSUNAYOSHI'S COUNCIL CHAMBER...
THE ACTIONS OF ASANO TAKUMI-NAGANORI, *DAIMYO* OF AKO, WERE AN ***AFFRONT*** TO THE SHOGUNATE.
THIS MAN DREW HIS SWORD AND ATTACKED ME WITHOUT THE SLIGHTEST PROVOCATION, AN ACTION ***UNTHINKABLE*** WITHIN THE PALACE.
WHY WOULD A MAN LIKE ASANO DO SUCH A THING?
YOU MUST UNDERSTAND THAT THIS ASANO IS A ***DESPICABLE*** CHARACTER, NOT WORTHY OF HIS STATION AS *DAIMYO* OF SUCH AN IMPORTANT CASTLE.
TAMURA UKIYÔ, YOU CONDUCTED THE INVESTIGA-TION?
YES, LORD TOKUGAWA. I AND MATSUKI SADAMORI.
ASANO HAS OFFERED NO EXPLANATION FOR HIS ATTACK, DESPITE OUR INTENSE QUESTIONING. IN FACT HE FREELY ADMITS THAT, GIVEN THE CHANCE, HE'D COMMIT THE SAME CRIME.
LORD TOKUGAWA, I BELIEVE ASANO TO BE HONORABLE. HE HAS MADE IT CLEAR THAT HE BEARS NO ILL WILL TOWARD THE SHOGUNATE, AND THAT HIS ONLY INTENTION AT THE PALACE WAS TO CARRY OUT YOUR DIRECTIVE.

DID ASANO GIVE ANY REASON FOR HIS ATTACK ON KIRA, OR FOR THAT MATTER, ANY EXPLANATION AT ALL?

NO, LORD TOKUGAWA.

I AM TOLD THAT WE HAVE A WITNESS?

YES, *KAJIKAWA YASOBEI* WAS AN EYEWITNESS TO THE EVENT.

BRING HIM FORWARD.

LORD TOKUGAWA, IT IS TRUE THAT I SAW ASANO ATTACK KIRA. I DID NOT SEE THE EVENTS LEADING UP TO HIS ATTACK, BUT A WEAPON WAS DRAWN AND....

THANK YOU, YASOBEI.

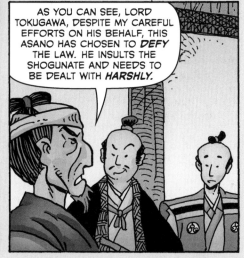

AS YOU CAN SEE, LORD TOKUGAWA, DESPITE MY CAREFUL EFFORTS ON HIS BEHALF, THIS ASANO HAS CHOSEN TO *DEFY* THE LAW. HE INSULTS THE SHOGUNATE AND NEEDS TO BE DEALT WITH *HARSHLY.*

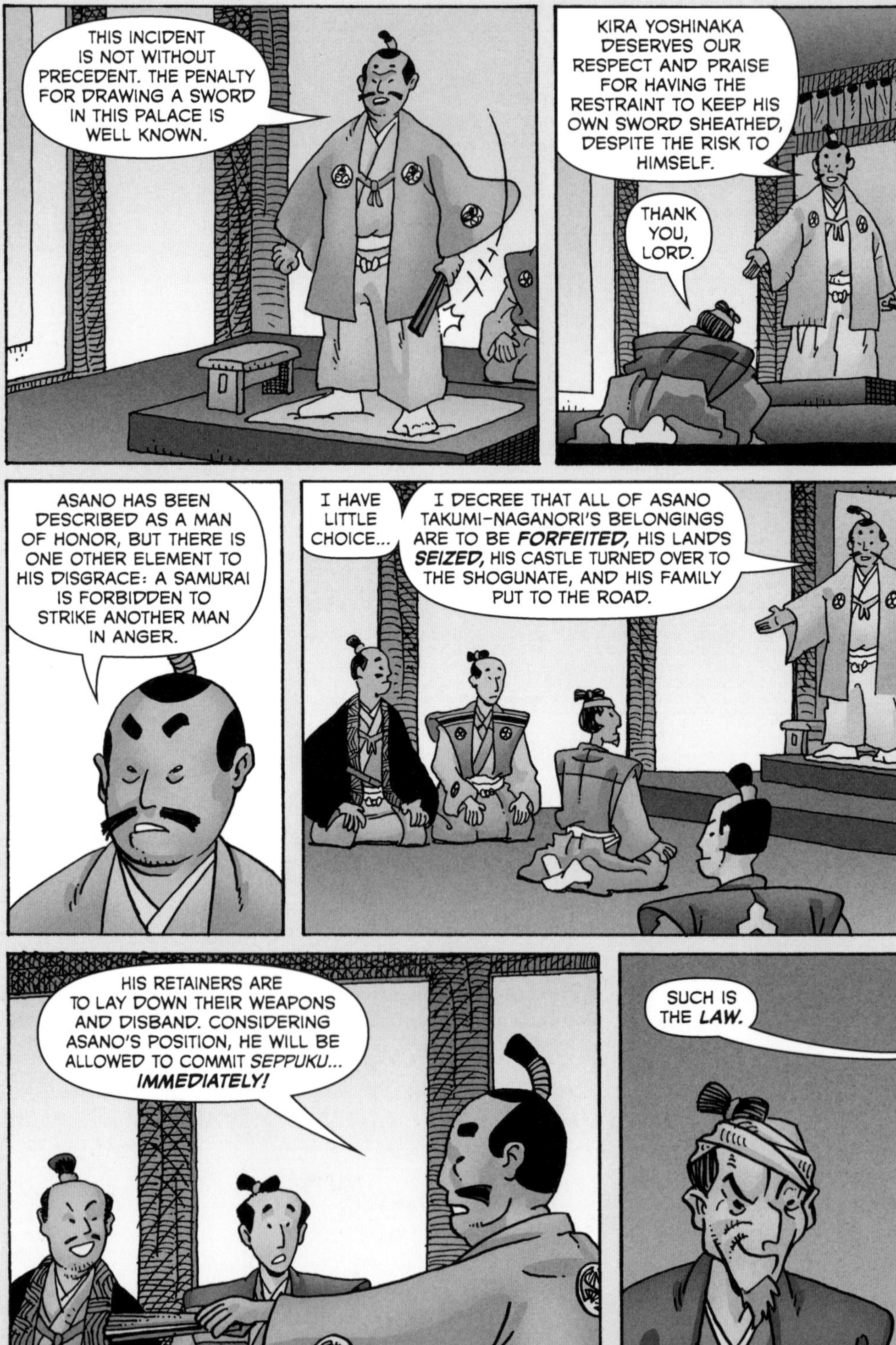
THIS INCIDENT IS NOT WITHOUT PRECEDENT. THE PENALTY FOR DRAWING A SWORD IN THIS PALACE IS WELL KNOWN.
KIRA YOSHINAKA DESERVES OUR RESPECT AND PRAISE FOR HAVING THE RESTRAINT TO KEEP HIS OWN SWORD SHEATHED, DESPITE THE RISK TO HIMSELF.
THANK YOU, LORD.
ASANO HAS BEEN DESCRIBED AS A MAN OF HONOR, BUT THERE IS ONE OTHER ELEMENT TO HIS DISGRACE: A SAMURAI IS FORBIDDEN TO STRIKE ANOTHER MAN IN ANGER.
I HAVE LITTLE CHOICE...
I DECREE THAT ALL OF ASANO TAKUMI-NAGANORI'S BELONGINGS ARE TO BE *FORFEITED,* HIS LANDS *SEIZED,* HIS CASTLE TURNED OVER TO THE SHOGUNATE, AND HIS FAMILY PUT TO THE ROAD.
HIS RETAINERS ARE TO LAY DOWN THEIR WEAPONS AND DISBAND. CONSIDERING ASANO'S POSITION, HE WILL BE ALLOWED TO COMMIT *SEPPUKU*... ***IMMEDIATELY!***
SUCH IS THE ***LAW.***

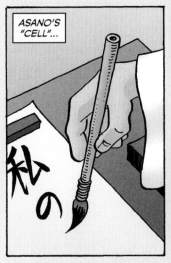

ASANO'S "CELL"...

LORD ASANO, IT IS TIME.

ASANO TAKUMI-NAGANORI, *DAIMYO* OF AKO, YOUR PROPERTY AND TITLE ARE FORFEIT, YOUR FAMILY DISINHERITED, YOUR RETAINERS DISBANDED. BY ORDER OF SHOGUN TOKUGAWA TSUNAYOSHI.

FURTHER, RECOGNIZING YOUR POSITION, THE SHOGUN HAS GRACIOUSLY OFFERED YOU THE OPPORTUNITY TO DIE WITH HONOR, AS BEFITS...

THERE IS NO NEED TO CONTINUE. *SEPPUKU.* WHEN?

IMMEDIATELY. WE WILL ESCORT YOU TO THE PROPER LOCATION. A *SECOND* HAS BEEN SECURED.

SO QUICKLY? I HAD HOPED TO SEE MY WIFE AND CHILDREN ONE LAST TIME.

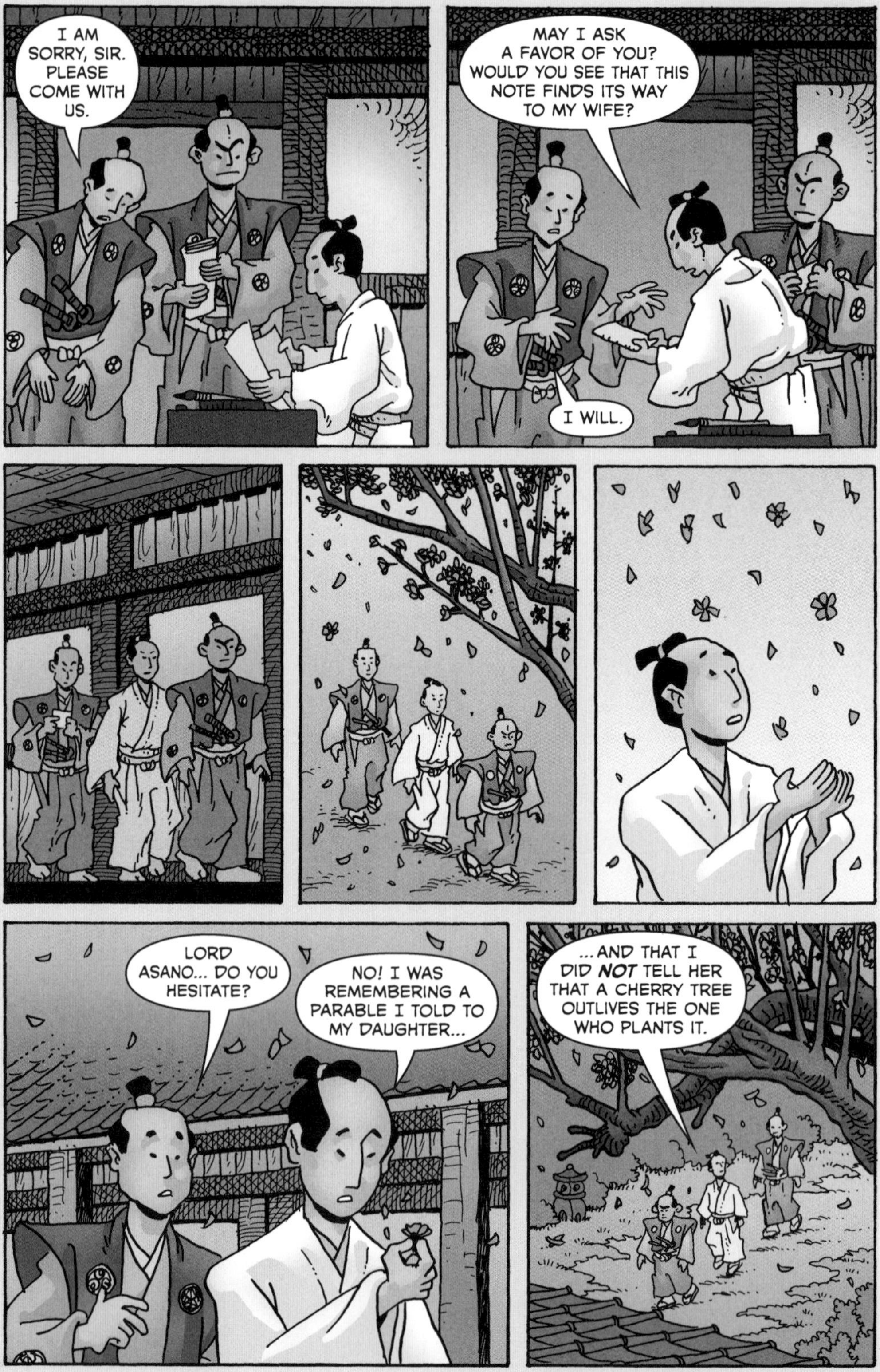
I AM SORRY, SIR. PLEASE COME WITH US.
MAY I ASK A FAVOR OF YOU? WOULD YOU SEE THAT THIS NOTE FINDS ITS WAY TO MY WIFE?
I WILL.
LORD ASANO... DO YOU HESITATE?
NO! I WAS REMEMBERING A PARABLE I TOLD TO MY DAUGHTER...
...AND THAT I DID **NOT** TELL HER THAT A CHERRY TREE OUTLIVES THE ONE WHO PLANTS IT.

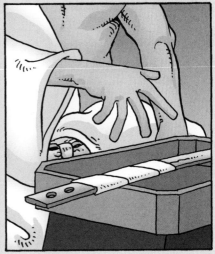

AAAGGHH...

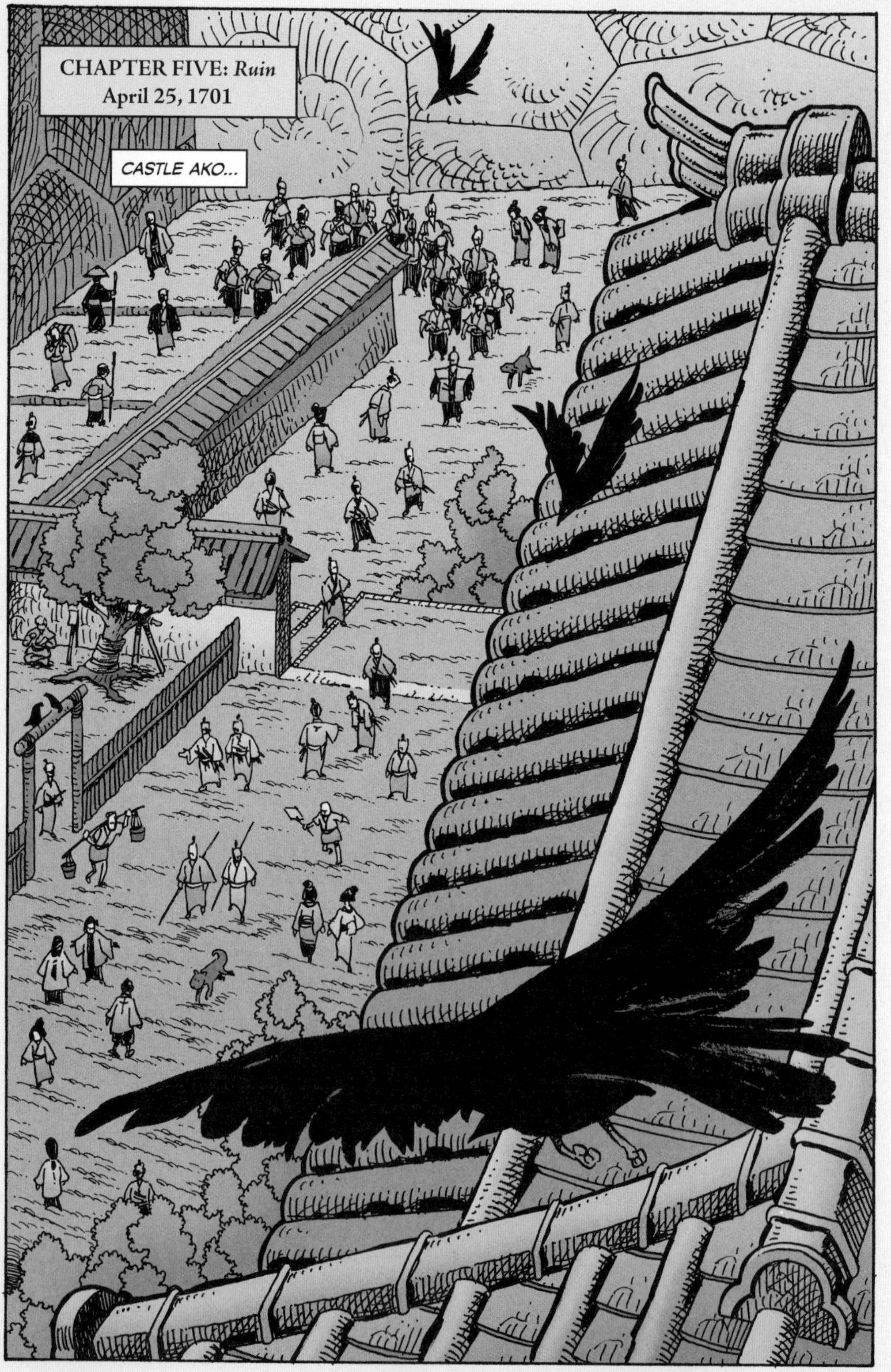
CHAPTER FIVE: *Ruin*
April 25, 1701
CASTLE AKO...

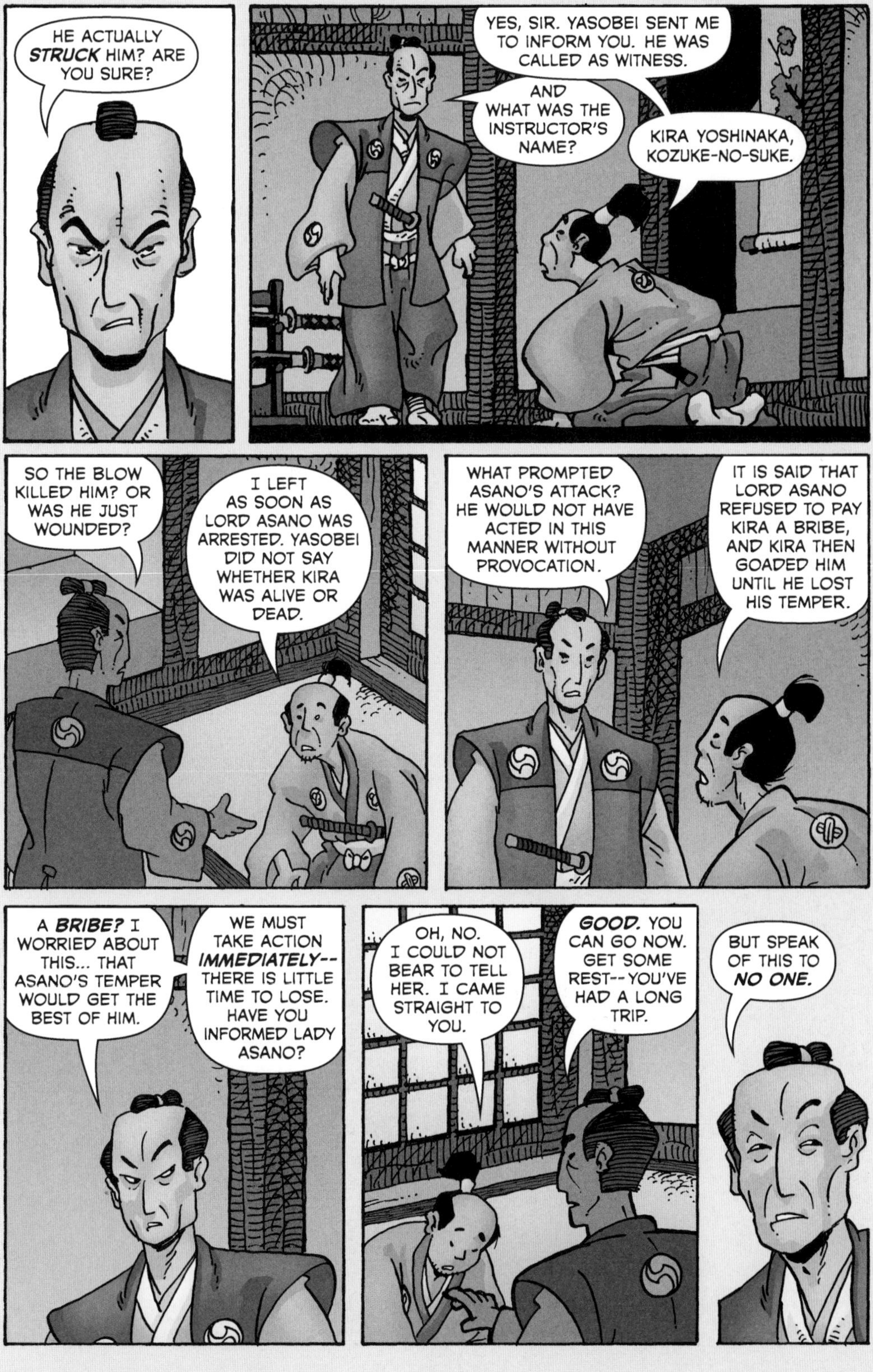
HE ACTUALLY STRUCK HIM? ARE YOU SURE?
YES, SIR. YASOBEI SENT ME TO INFORM YOU. HE WAS CALLED AS WITNESS.
AND WHAT WAS THE INSTRUCTOR'S NAME?
KIRA YOSHINAKA, KOZUKE-NO-SUKE.
SO THE BLOW KILLED HIM? OR WAS HE JUST WOUNDED?
I LEFT AS SOON AS LORD ASANO WAS ARRESTED. YASOBEI DID NOT SAY WHETHER KIRA WAS ALIVE OR DEAD.
WHAT PROMPTED ASANO'S ATTACK? HE WOULD NOT HAVE ACTED IN THIS MANNER WITHOUT PROVOCATION.
IT IS SAID THAT LORD ASANO REFUSED TO PAY KIRA A BRIBE, AND KIRA THEN GOADED HIM UNTIL HE LOST HIS TEMPER.
A BRIBE? I WORRIED ABOUT THIS... THAT ASANO'S TEMPER WOULD GET THE BEST OF HIM.
WE MUST TAKE ACTION IMMEDIATELY-- THERE IS LITTLE TIME TO LOSE. HAVE YOU INFORMED LADY ASANO?
OH, NO. I COULD NOT BEAR TO TELL HER. I CAME STRAIGHT TO YOU.
GOOD. YOU CAN GO NOW. GET SOME REST--YOU'VE HAD A LONG TRIP.
BUT SPEAK OF THIS TO NO ONE.

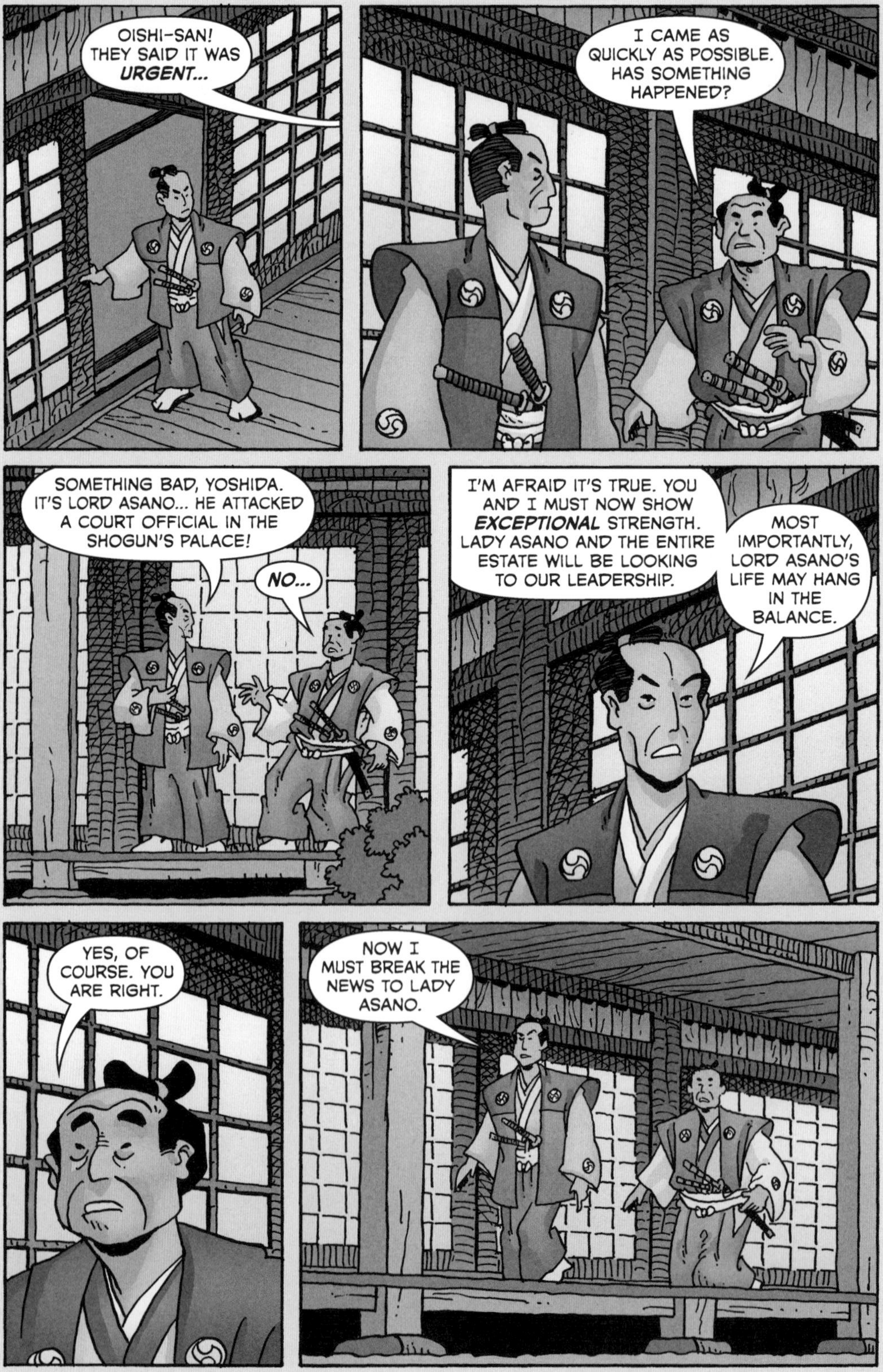
OISHI-SAN! THEY SAID IT WAS URGENT...
I CAME AS QUICKLY AS POSSIBLE. HAS SOMETHING HAPPENED?
SOMETHING BAD, YOSHIDA. IT'S LORD ASANO... HE ATTACKED A COURT OFFICIAL IN THE SHOGUN'S PALACE!
NO...
I'M AFRAID IT'S TRUE. YOU AND I MUST NOW SHOW EXCEPTIONAL STRENGTH. LADY ASANO AND THE ENTIRE ESTATE WILL BE LOOKING TO OUR LEADERSHIP.
MOST IMPORTANTLY, LORD ASANO'S LIFE MAY HANG IN THE BALANCE.
YES, OF COURSE. YOU ARE RIGHT.
NOW I MUST BREAK THE NEWS TO LADY ASANO.

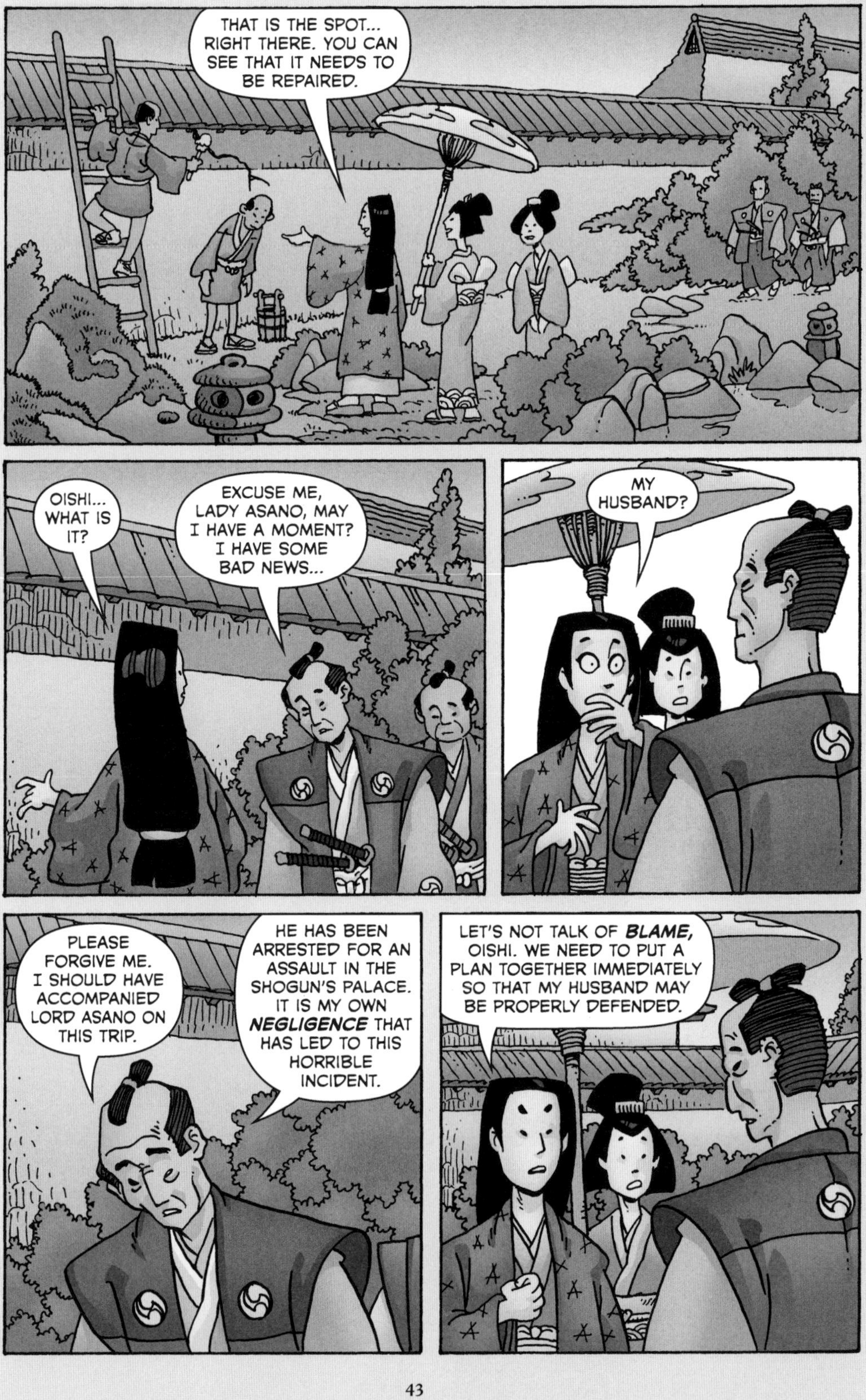
THAT IS THE SPOT... RIGHT THERE. YOU CAN SEE THAT IT NEEDS TO BE REPAIRED.
OISHI... WHAT IS IT?
EXCUSE ME, LADY ASANO, MAY I HAVE A MOMENT? I HAVE SOME BAD NEWS...
MY HUSBAND?
PLEASE FORGIVE ME. I SHOULD HAVE ACCOMPANIED LORD ASANO ON THIS TRIP.
HE HAS BEEN ARRESTED FOR AN ASSAULT IN THE SHOGUN'S PALACE. IT IS MY OWN ***NEGLIGENCE*** THAT HAS LED TO THIS HORRIBLE INCIDENT.
LET'S NOT TALK OF ***BLAME,*** OISHI. WE NEED TO PUT A PLAN TOGETHER IMMEDIATELY SO THAT MY HUSBAND MAY BE PROPERLY DEFENDED.

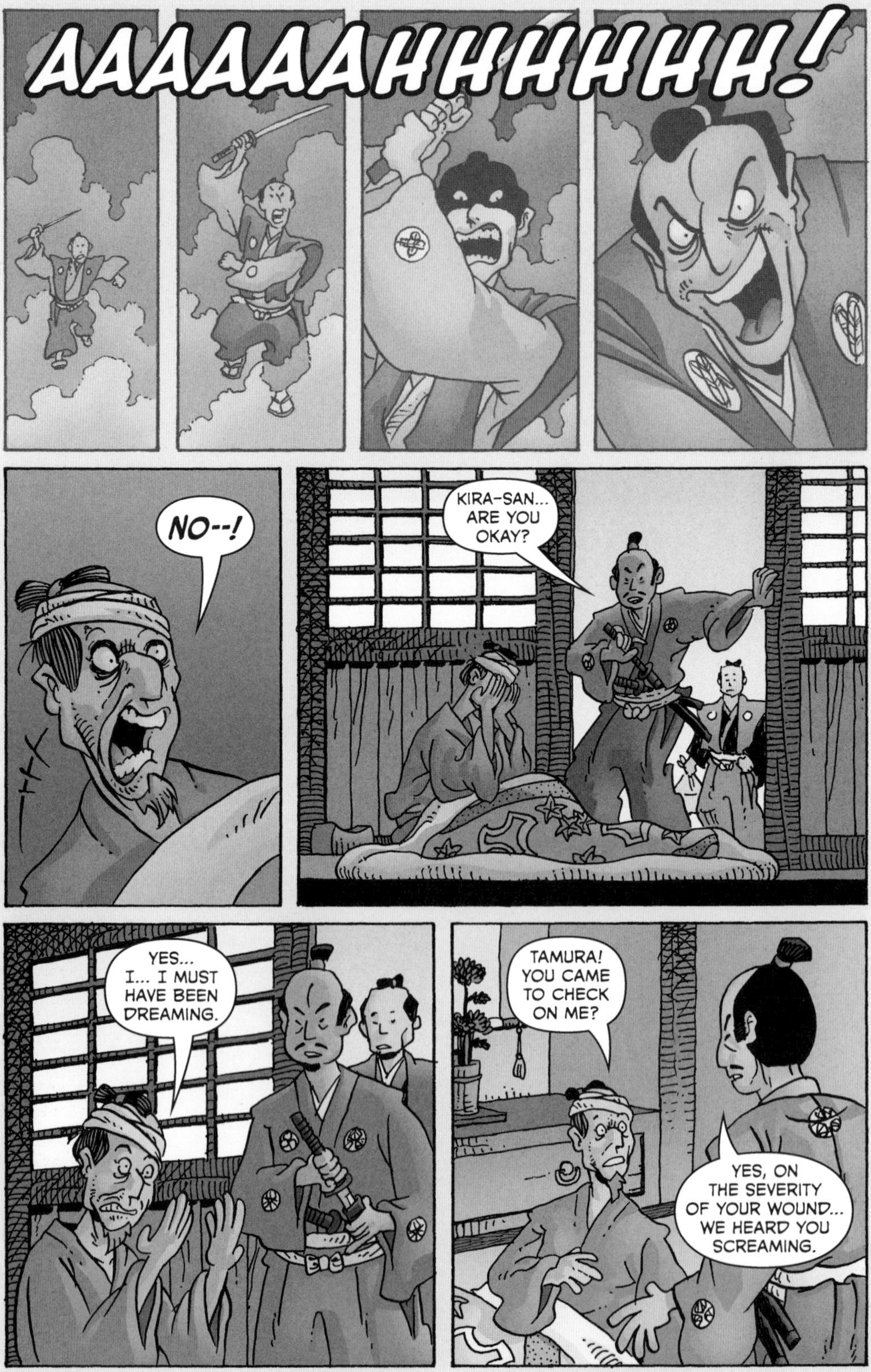
AAAAAAHHHHHHH!
NO--!
KIRA-SAN... ARE YOU OKAY?
YES... I... I MUST HAVE BEEN DREAMING.
TAMURA! YOU CAME TO CHECK ON ME?
YES, ON THE SEVERITY OF YOUR WOUND... WE HEARD YOU SCREAMING.

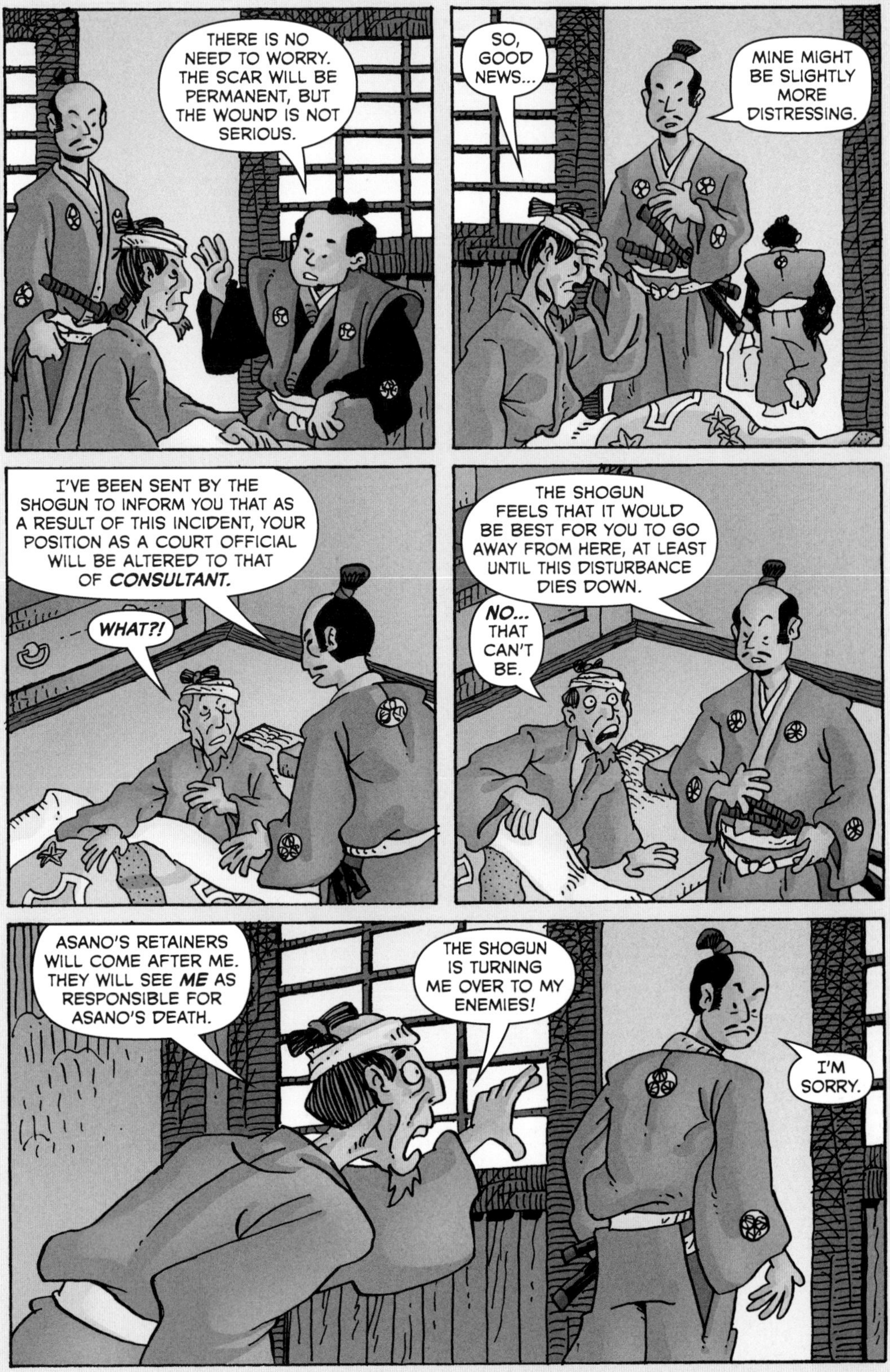
THERE IS NO NEED TO WORRY. THE SCAR WILL BE PERMANENT, BUT THE WOUND IS NOT SERIOUS.
SO, GOOD NEWS...
MINE MIGHT BE SLIGHTLY MORE DISTRESSING.
I'VE BEEN SENT BY THE SHOGUN TO INFORM YOU THAT AS A RESULT OF THIS INCIDENT, YOUR POSITION AS A COURT OFFICIAL WILL BE ALTERED TO THAT OF ***CONSULTANT.***
WHAT?!
THE SHOGUN FEELS THAT IT WOULD BE BEST FOR YOU TO GO AWAY FROM HERE, AT LEAST UNTIL THIS DISTURBANCE DIES DOWN.
NO... THAT CAN'T BE.
ASANO'S RETAINERS WILL COME AFTER ME. THEY WILL SEE ***ME*** AS RESPONSIBLE FOR ASANO'S DEATH.
THE SHOGUN IS TURNING ME OVER TO MY ENEMIES!
I'M SORRY.

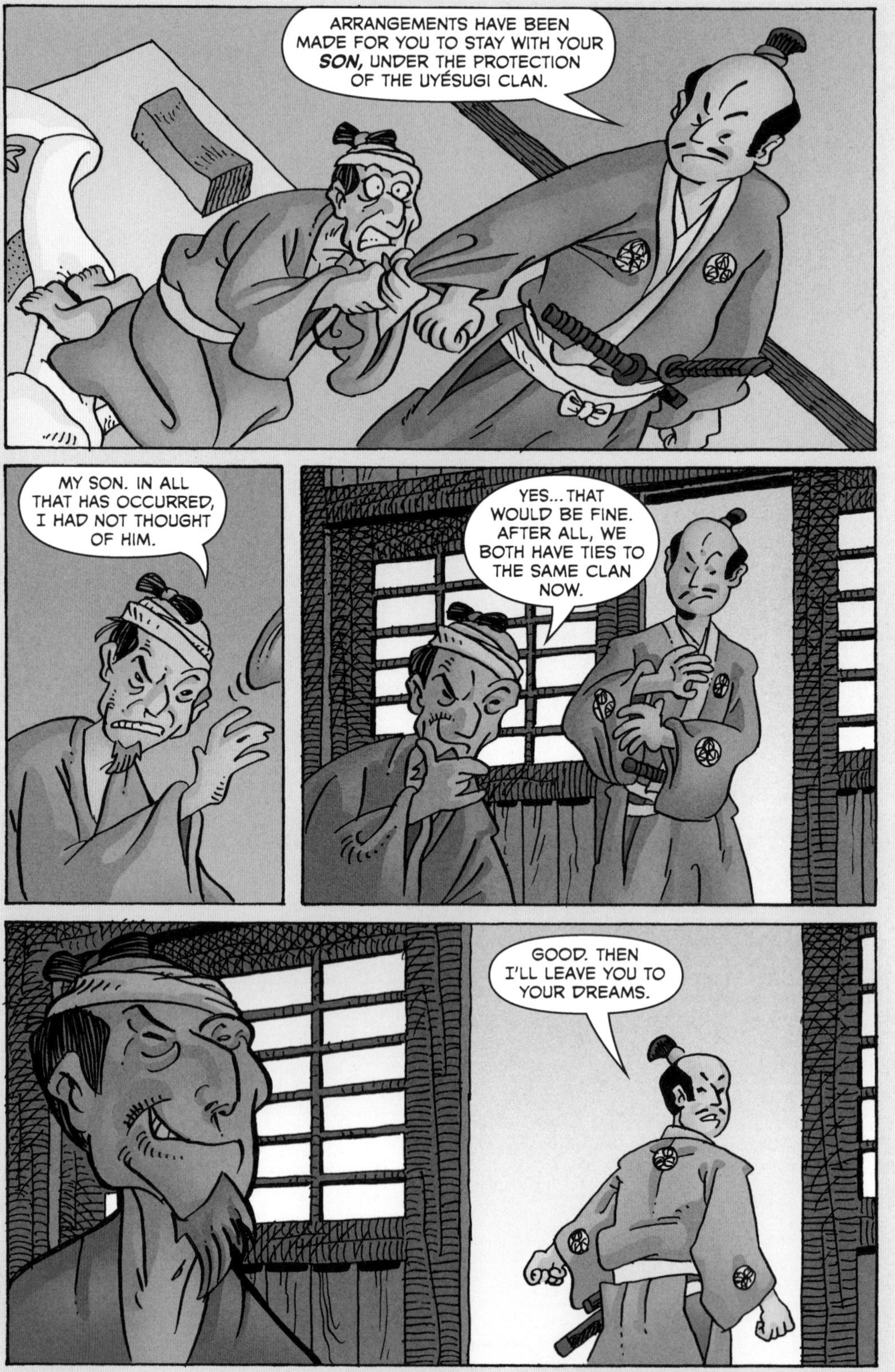
ARRANGEMENTS HAVE BEEN MADE FOR YOU TO STAY WITH YOUR ***SON,*** UNDER THE PROTECTION OF THE UYÉSUGI CLAN.
MY SON. IN ALL THAT HAS OCCURRED, I HAD NOT THOUGHT OF HIM.
YES... THAT WOULD BE FINE. AFTER ALL, WE BOTH HAVE TIES TO THE SAME CLAN NOW.
GOOD. THEN I'LL LEAVE YOU TO YOUR DREAMS.

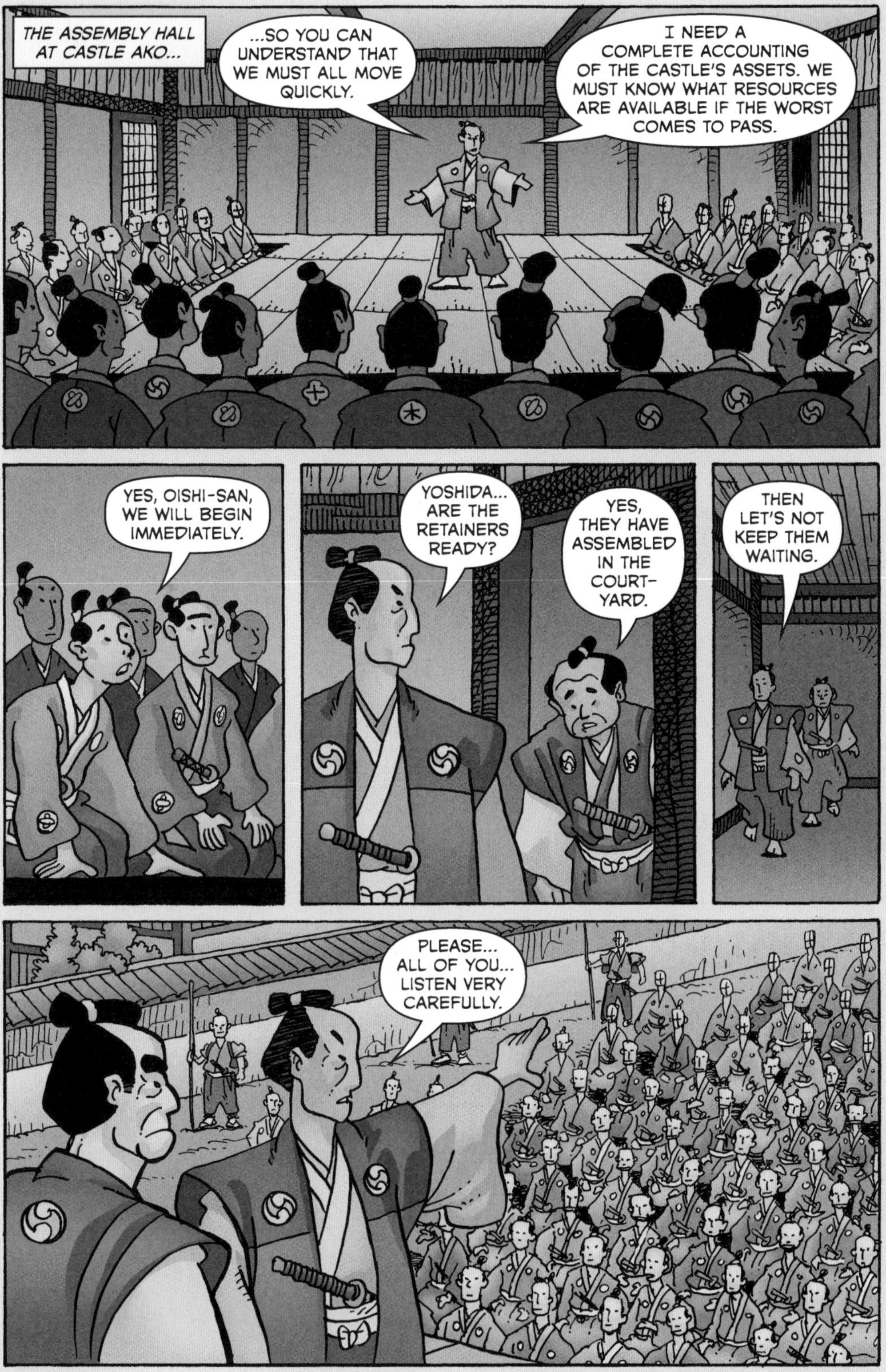
THE ASSEMBLY HALL AT CASTLE AKO...
...SO YOU CAN UNDERSTAND THAT WE MUST ALL MOVE QUICKLY.
I NEED A COMPLETE ACCOUNTING OF THE CASTLE'S ASSETS. WE MUST KNOW WHAT RESOURCES ARE AVAILABLE IF THE WORST COMES TO PASS.
YES, OISHI-SAN, WE WILL BEGIN IMMEDIATELY.
YOSHIDA... ARE THE RETAINERS READY?
YES, THEY HAVE ASSEMBLED IN THE COURT-YARD.
THEN LET'S NOT KEEP THEM WAITING.
PLEASE... ALL OF YOU... LISTEN VERY CAREFULLY.

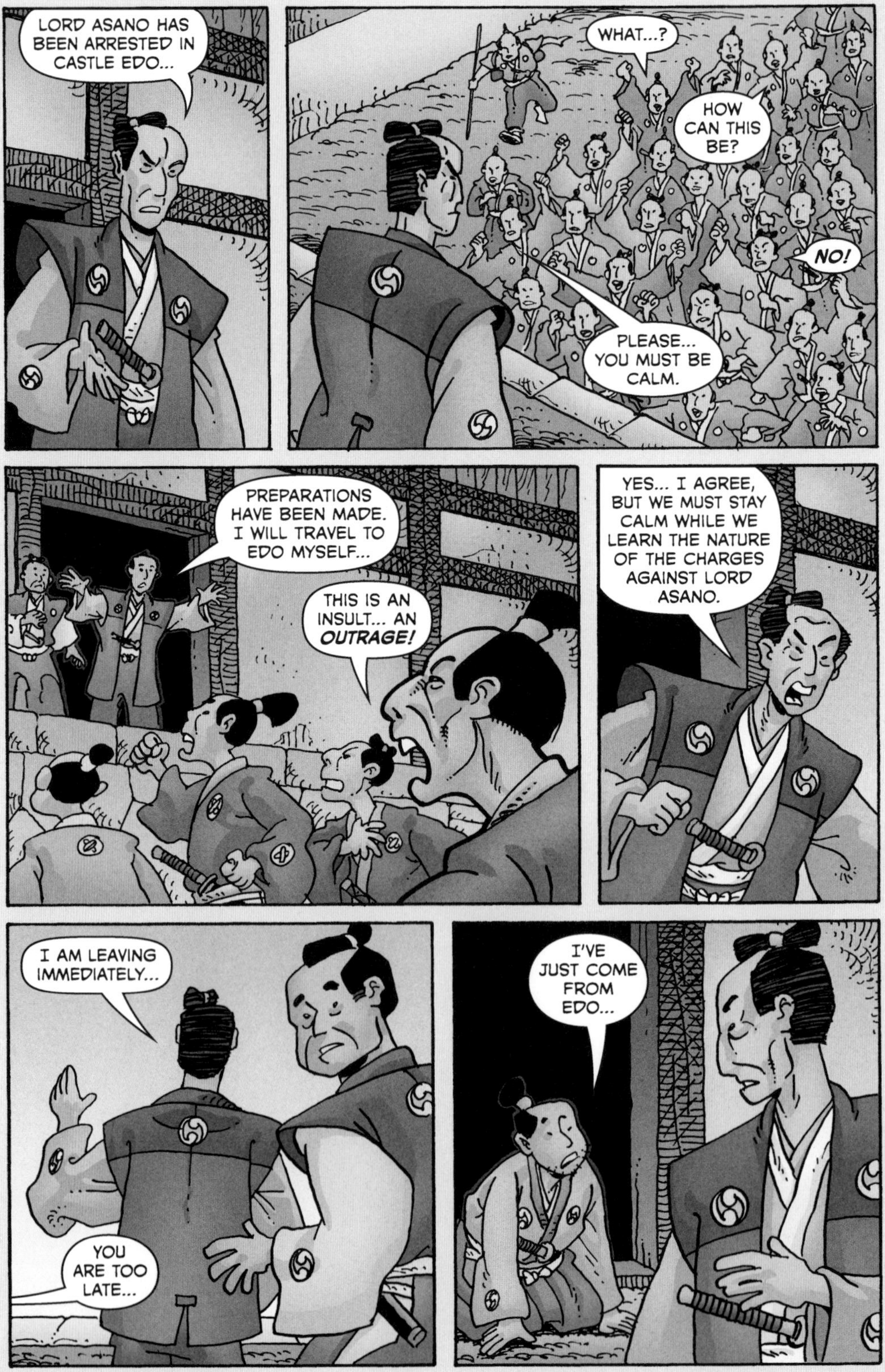
LORD ASANO HAS BEEN ARRESTED IN CASTLE EDO...
WHAT...?
HOW CAN THIS BE?
NO!
PLEASE... YOU MUST BE CALM.
PREPARATIONS HAVE BEEN MADE. I WILL TRAVEL TO EDO MYSELF...
THIS IS AN INSULT... AN *OUTRAGE!*
YES... I AGREE, BUT WE MUST STAY CALM WHILE WE LEARN THE NATURE OF THE CHARGES AGAINST LORD ASANO.
I AM LEAVING IMMEDIATELY...
YOU ARE TOO LATE...
I'VE JUST COME FROM EDO...

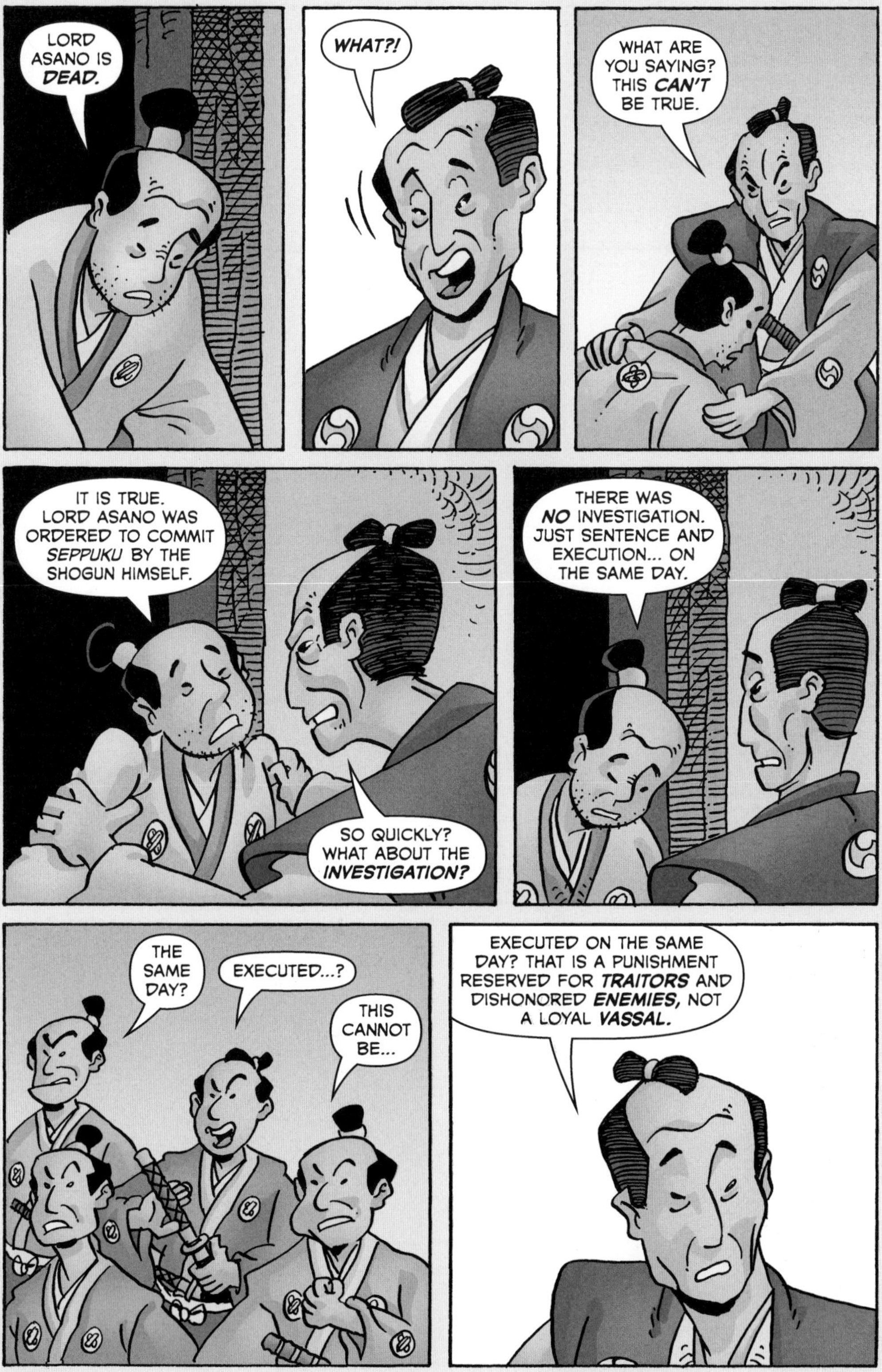
LORD ASANO IS DEAD.
WHAT?!
WHAT ARE YOU SAYING? THIS CAN'T BE TRUE.
IT IS TRUE. LORD ASANO WAS ORDERED TO COMMIT SEPPUKU BY THE SHOGUN HIMSELF.
SO QUICKLY? WHAT ABOUT THE INVESTIGATION?
THERE WAS NO INVESTIGATION. JUST SENTENCE AND EXECUTION... ON THE SAME DAY.
THE SAME DAY?
EXECUTED...?
THIS CANNOT BE...
EXECUTED ON THE SAME DAY? THAT IS A PUNISHMENT RESERVED FOR TRAITORS AND DISHONORED ENEMIES, NOT A LOYAL VASSAL.

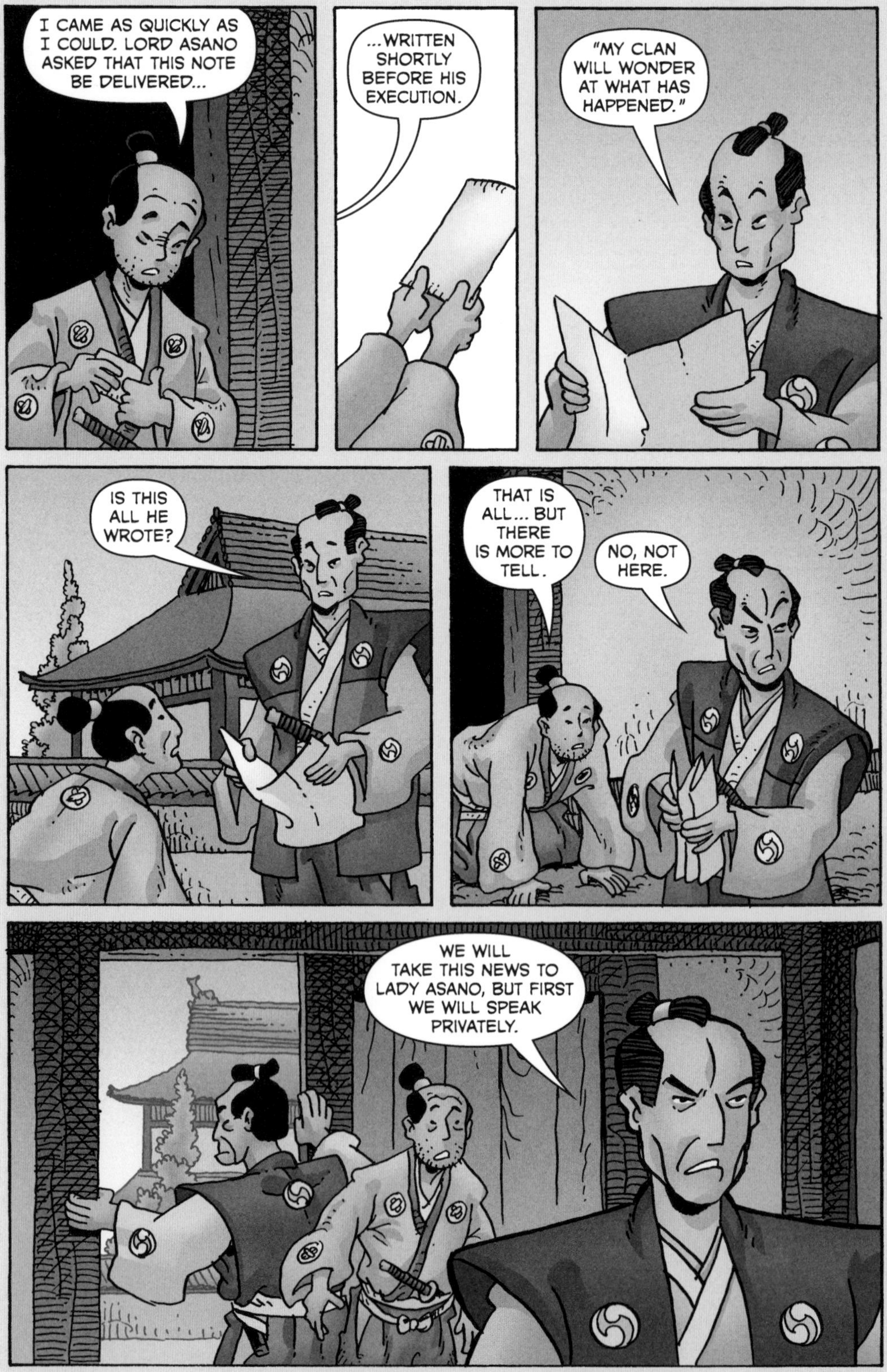
I CAME AS QUICKLY AS I COULD. LORD ASANO ASKED THAT THIS NOTE BE DELIVERED...
...WRITTEN SHORTLY BEFORE HIS EXECUTION.
"MY CLAN WILL WONDER AT WHAT HAS HAPPENED."
IS THIS ALL HE WROTE?
THAT IS ALL... BUT THERE IS MORE TO TELL.
NO, NOT HERE.
WE WILL TAKE THIS NEWS TO LADY ASANO, BUT FIRST WE WILL SPEAK PRIVATELY.

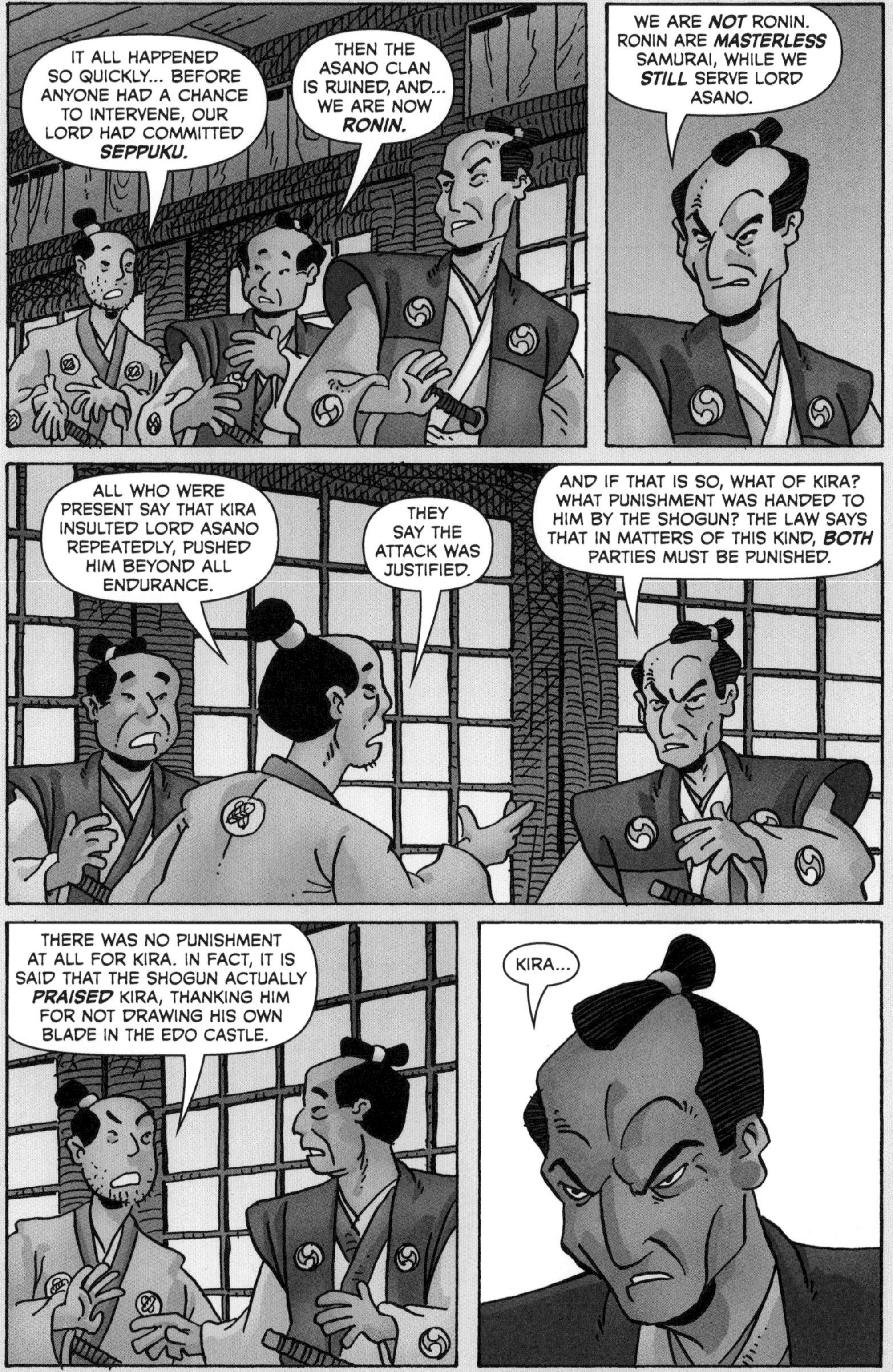
IT ALL HAPPENED SO QUICKLY... BEFORE ANYONE HAD A CHANCE TO INTERVENE, OUR LORD HAD COMMITTED ***SEPPUKU.***
THEN THE ASANO CLAN IS RUINED, AND... WE ARE NOW ***RONIN.***
WE ARE ***NOT*** RONIN. RONIN ARE ***MASTERLESS*** SAMURAI, WHILE WE ***STILL*** SERVE LORD ASANO.
ALL WHO WERE PRESENT SAY THAT KIRA INSULTED LORD ASANO REPEATEDLY, PUSHED HIM BEYOND ALL ENDURANCE.
THEY SAY THE ATTACK WAS JUSTIFIED.
AND IF THAT IS SO, WHAT OF KIRA? WHAT PUNISHMENT WAS HANDED TO HIM BY THE SHOGUN? THE LAW SAYS THAT IN MATTERS OF THIS KIND, ***BOTH*** PARTIES MUST BE PUNISHED.
THERE WAS NO PUNISHMENT AT ALL FOR KIRA. IN FACT, IT IS SAID THAT THE SHOGUN ACTUALLY ***PRAISED*** KIRA, THANKING HIM FOR NOT DRAWING HIS OWN BLADE IN THE EDO CASTLE.
KIRA...

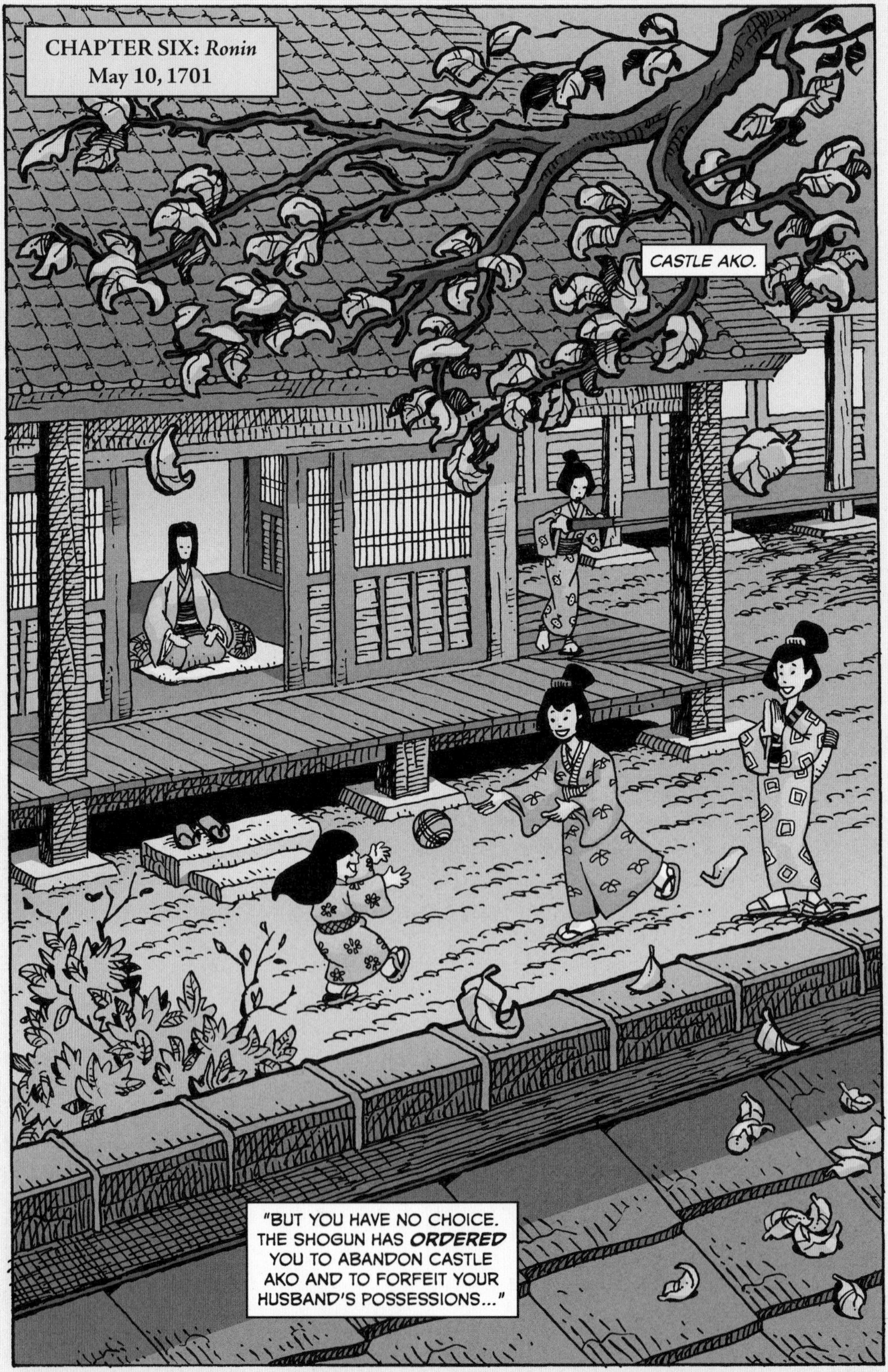
CHAPTER SIX: *Ronin*
May 10, 1701
CASTLE AKO.
"BUT YOU HAVE NO CHOICE. THE SHOGUN HAS ***ORDERED*** YOU TO ABANDON CASTLE AKO AND TO FORFEIT YOUR HUSBAND'S POSSESSIONS..."

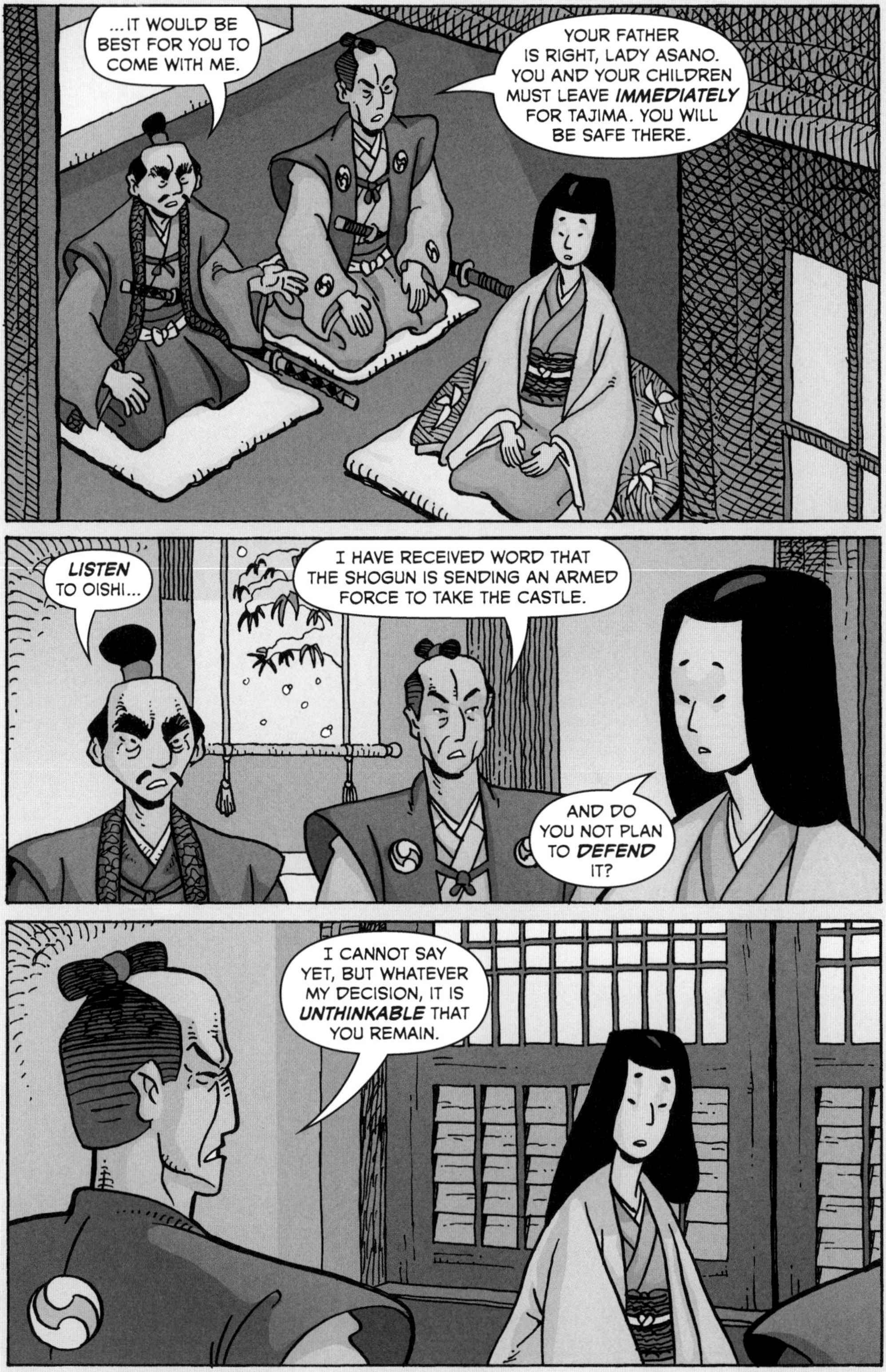
...IT WOULD BE BEST FOR YOU TO COME WITH ME.
YOUR FATHER IS RIGHT, LADY ASANO. YOU AND YOUR CHILDREN MUST LEAVE IMMEDIATELY FOR TAJIMA. YOU WILL BE SAFE THERE.
LISTEN TO OISHI...
I HAVE RECEIVED WORD THAT THE SHOGUN IS SENDING AN ARMED FORCE TO TAKE THE CASTLE.
AND DO YOU NOT PLAN TO DEFEND IT?
I CANNOT SAY YET, BUT WHATEVER MY DECISION, IT IS UNTHINKABLE THAT YOU REMAIN.

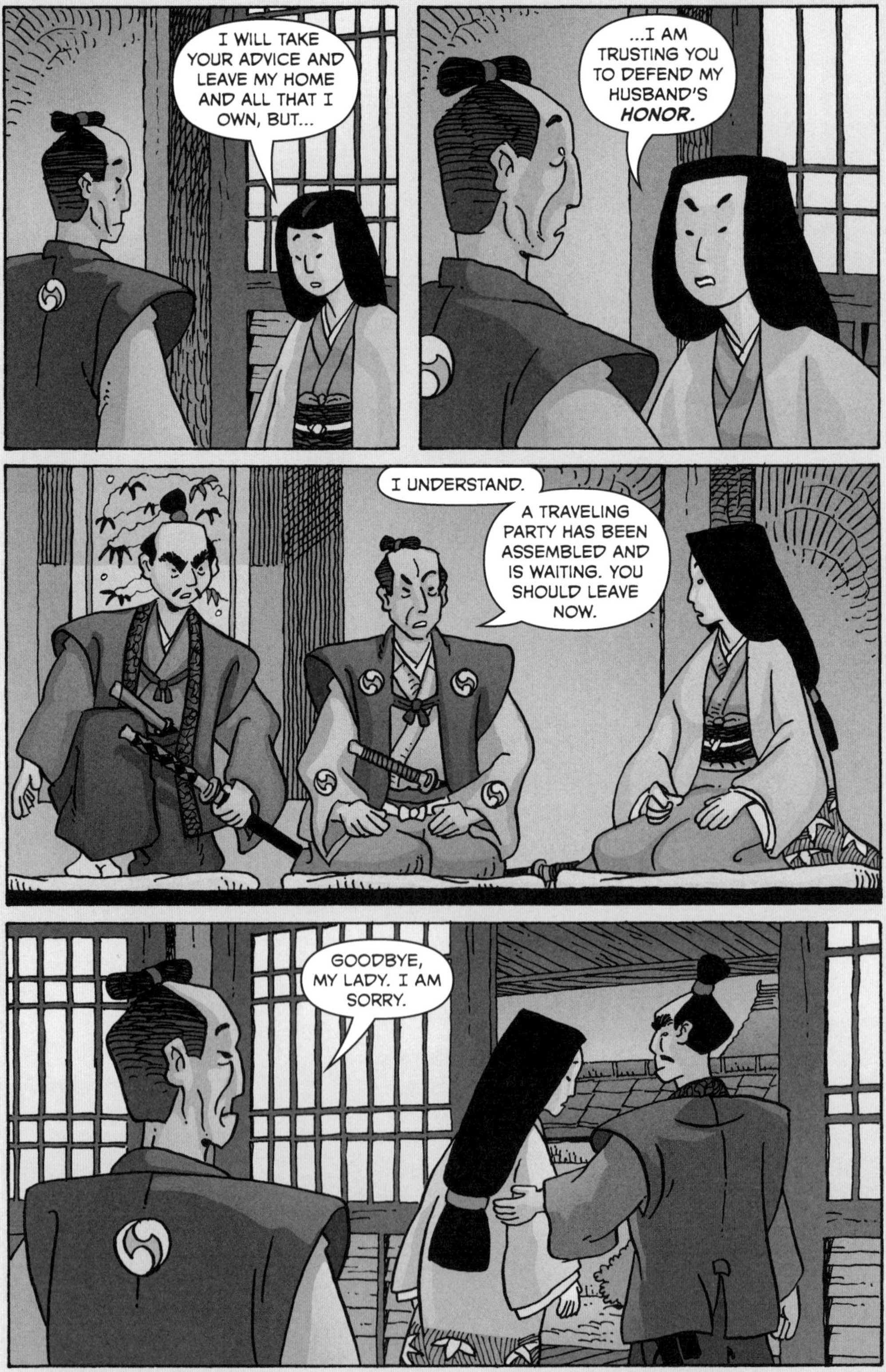
I WILL TAKE YOUR ADVICE AND LEAVE MY HOME AND ALL THAT I OWN, BUT...
...I AM TRUSTING YOU TO DEFEND MY HUSBAND'S **HONOR.**
I UNDERSTAND.
A TRAVELING PARTY HAS BEEN ASSEMBLED AND IS WAITING. YOU SHOULD LEAVE NOW.
GOODBYE, MY LADY. I AM SORRY.

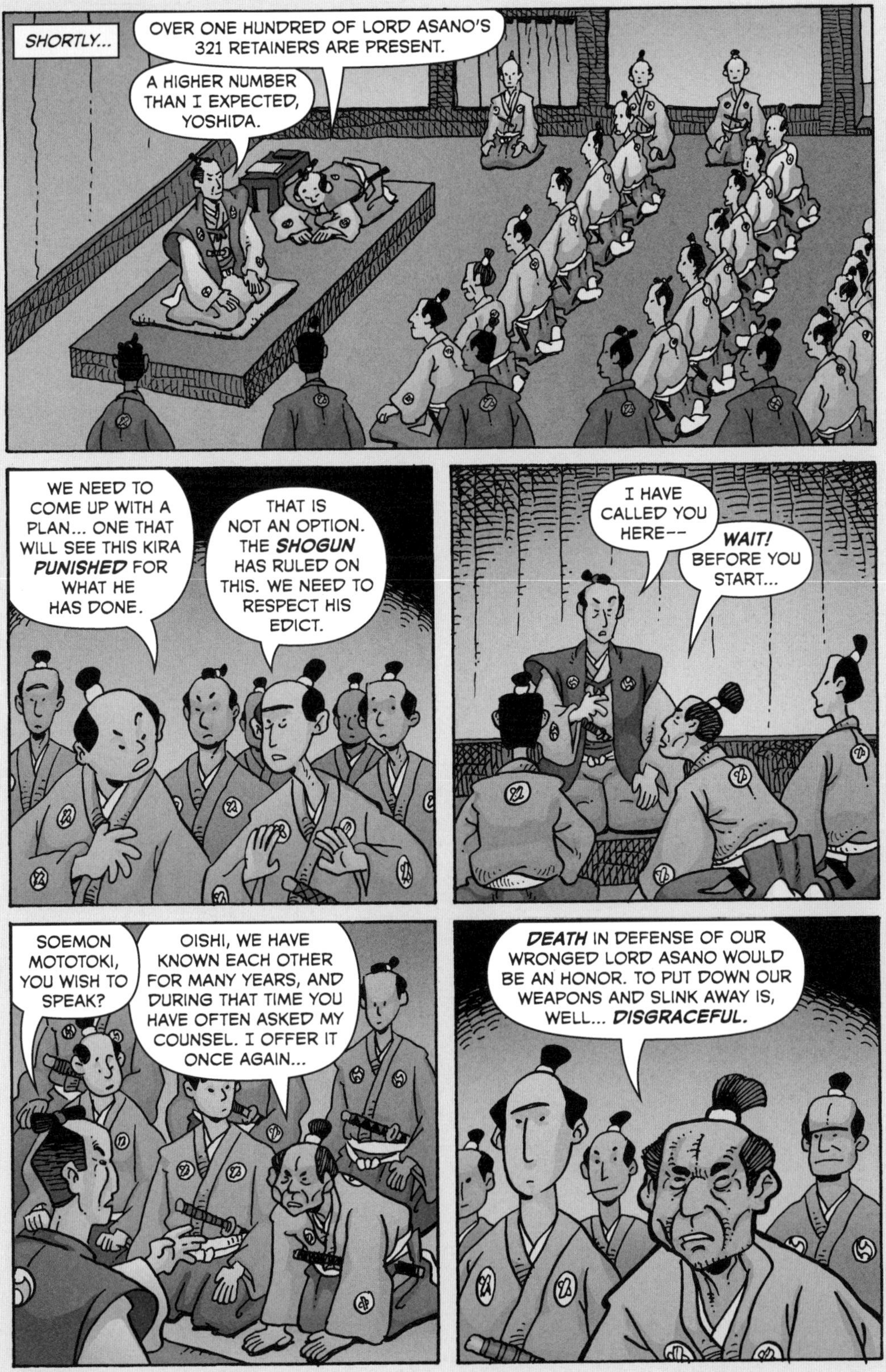
SHORTLY...
OVER ONE HUNDRED OF LORD ASANO'S 321 RETAINERS ARE PRESENT.
A HIGHER NUMBER THAN I EXPECTED, YOSHIDA.
WE NEED TO COME UP WITH A PLAN... ONE THAT WILL SEE THIS KIRA PUNISHED FOR WHAT HE HAS DONE.
THAT IS NOT AN OPTION. THE SHOGUN HAS RULED ON THIS. WE NEED TO RESPECT HIS EDICT.
I HAVE CALLED YOU HERE--
WAIT! BEFORE YOU START...
SOEMON MOTOTOKI, YOU WISH TO SPEAK?
OISHI, WE HAVE KNOWN EACH OTHER FOR MANY YEARS, AND DURING THAT TIME YOU HAVE OFTEN ASKED MY COUNSEL. I OFFER IT ONCE AGAIN...
DEATH IN DEFENSE OF OUR WRONGED LORD ASANO WOULD BE AN HONOR. TO PUT DOWN OUR WEAPONS AND SLINK AWAY IS, WELL... DISGRACEFUL.

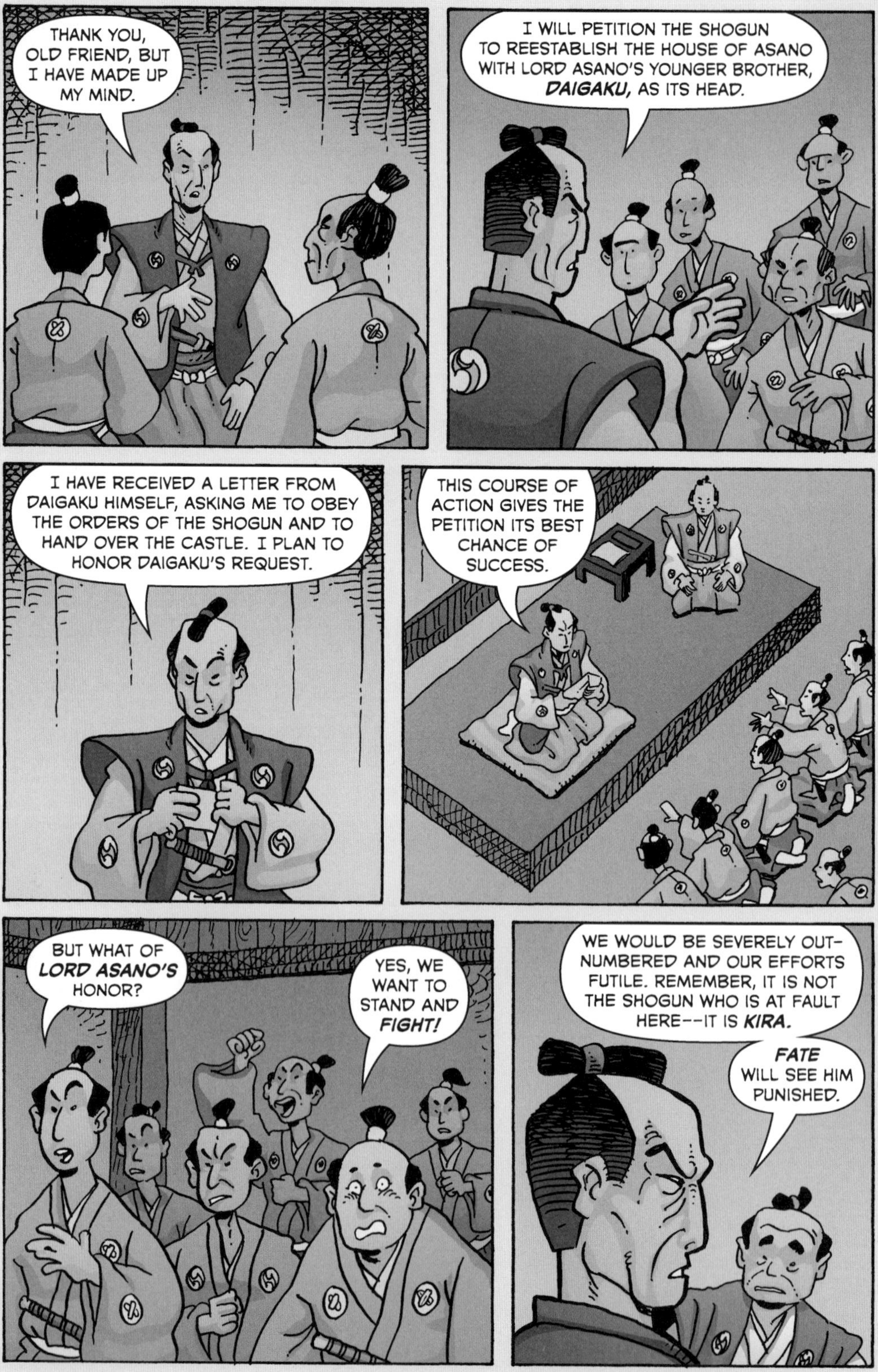
THANK YOU, OLD FRIEND, BUT I HAVE MADE UP MY MIND.
I WILL PETITION THE SHOGUN TO REESTABLISH THE HOUSE OF ASANO WITH LORD ASANO'S YOUNGER BROTHER, DAIGAKU, AS ITS HEAD.
I HAVE RECEIVED A LETTER FROM DAIGAKU HIMSELF, ASKING ME TO OBEY THE ORDERS OF THE SHOGUN AND TO HAND OVER THE CASTLE. I PLAN TO HONOR DAIGAKU'S REQUEST.
THIS COURSE OF ACTION GIVES THE PETITION ITS BEST CHANCE OF SUCCESS.
BUT WHAT OF LORD ASANO'S HONOR?
YES, WE WANT TO STAND AND FIGHT!
WE WOULD BE SEVERELY OUT-NUMBERED AND OUR EFFORTS FUTILE. REMEMBER, IT IS NOT THE SHOGUN WHO IS AT FAULT HERE--IT IS KIRA.
FATE WILL SEE HIM PUNISHED.

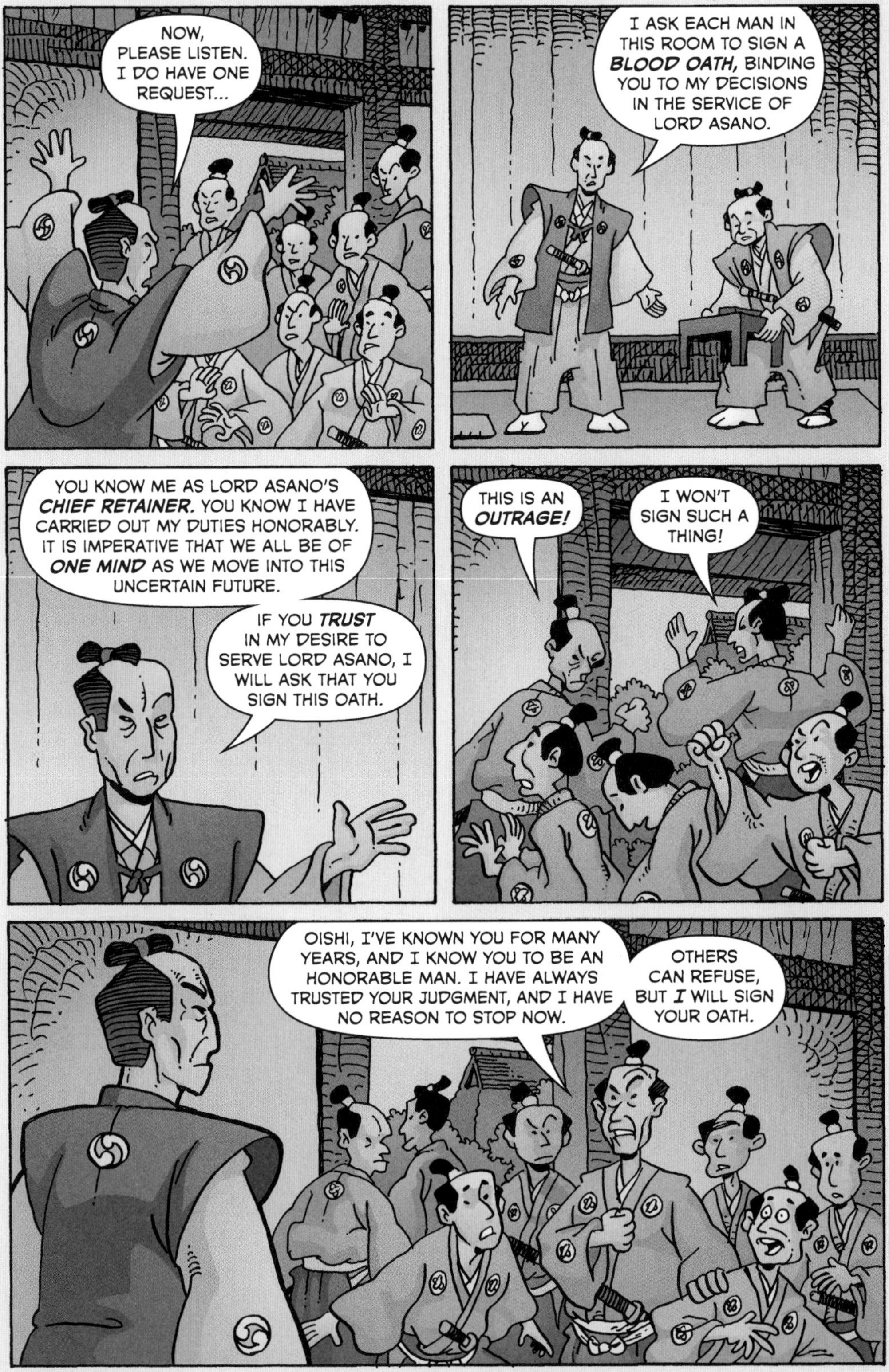
NOW, PLEASE LISTEN. I DO HAVE ONE REQUEST...
I ASK EACH MAN IN THIS ROOM TO SIGN A BLOOD OATH, BINDING YOU TO MY DECISIONS IN THE SERVICE OF LORD ASANO.
YOU KNOW ME AS LORD ASANO'S CHIEF RETAINER. YOU KNOW I HAVE CARRIED OUT MY DUTIES HONORABLY. IT IS IMPERATIVE THAT WE ALL BE OF ONE MIND AS WE MOVE INTO THIS UNCERTAIN FUTURE.
IF YOU TRUST IN MY DESIRE TO SERVE LORD ASANO, I WILL ASK THAT YOU SIGN THIS OATH.
THIS IS AN OUTRAGE!
I WON'T SIGN SUCH A THING!
OISHI, I'VE KNOWN YOU FOR MANY YEARS, AND I KNOW YOU TO BE AN HONORABLE MAN. I HAVE ALWAYS TRUSTED YOUR JUDGMENT, AND I HAVE NO REASON TO STOP NOW.
OTHERS CAN REFUSE, BUT I WILL SIGN YOUR OATH.

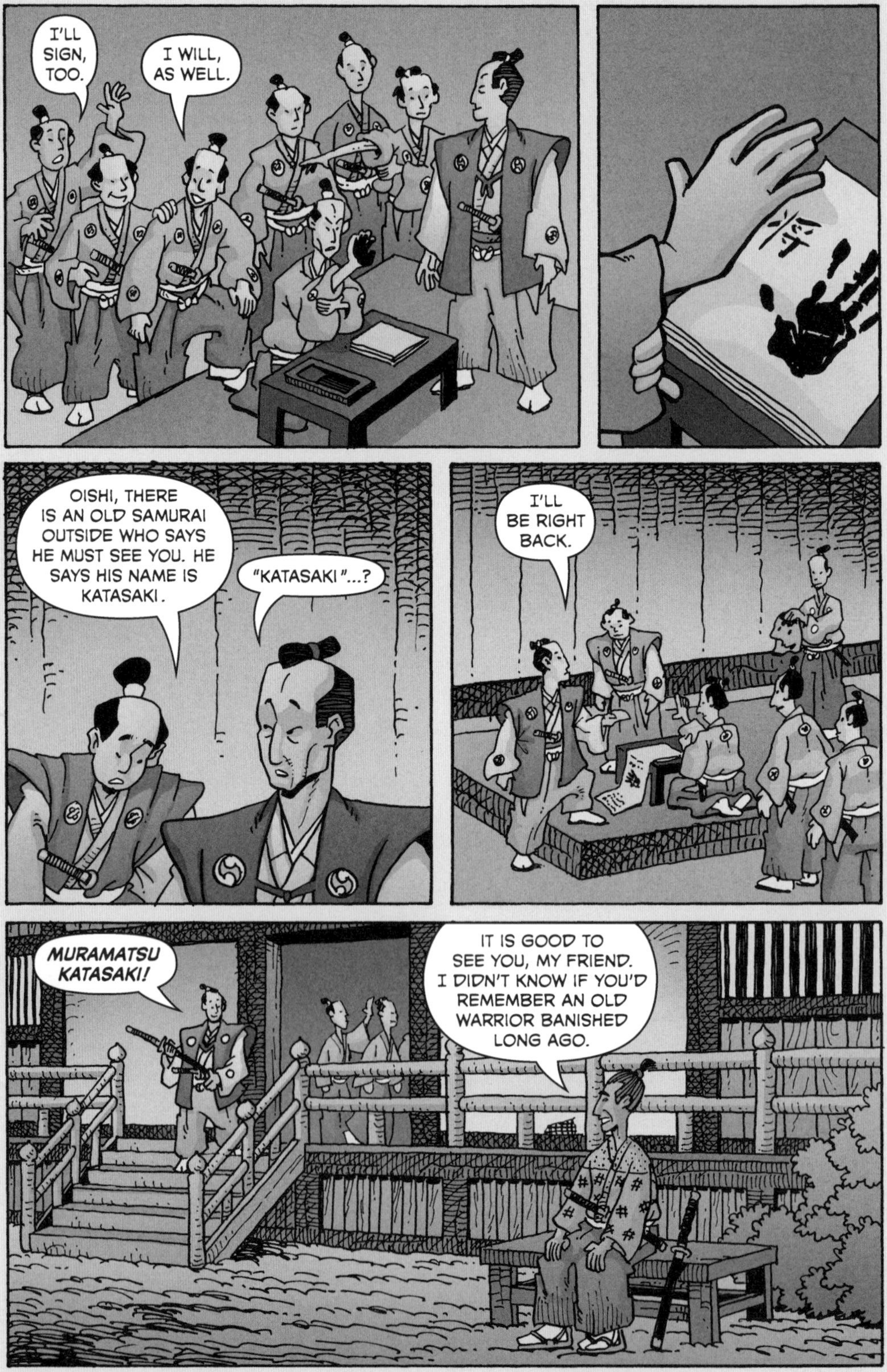
I'LL SIGN, TOO.
I WILL, AS WELL.
OISHI, THERE IS AN OLD SAMURAI OUTSIDE WHO SAYS HE MUST SEE YOU. HE SAYS HIS NAME IS KATASAKI.
"KATASAKI"...?
I'LL BE RIGHT BACK.
MURAMATSU KATASAKI!
IT IS GOOD TO SEE YOU, MY FRIEND. I DIDN'T KNOW IF YOU'D REMEMBER AN OLD WARRIOR BANISHED LONG AGO.

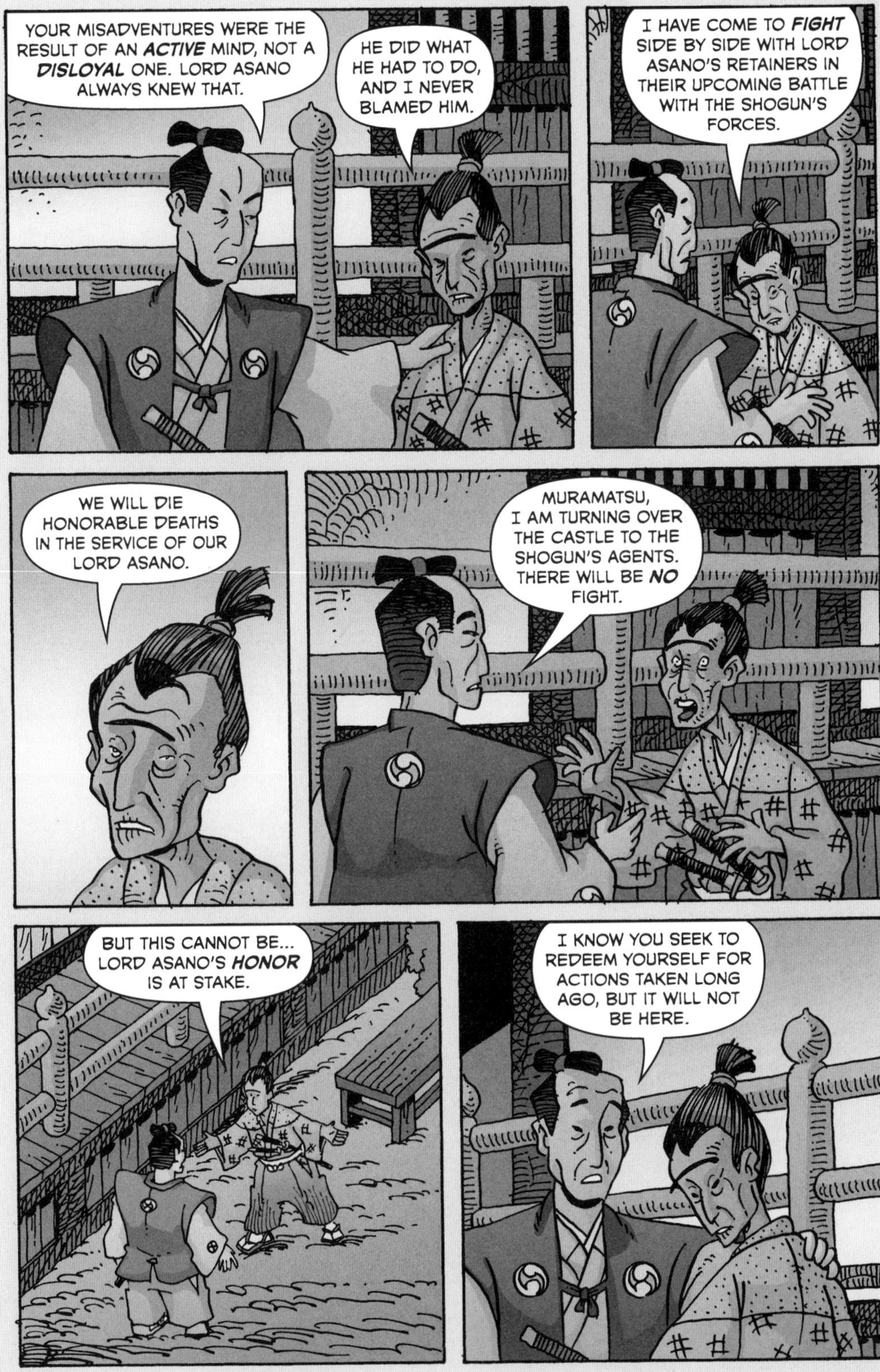
YOUR MISADVENTURES WERE THE RESULT OF AN ACTIVE MIND, NOT A DISLOYAL ONE. LORD ASANO ALWAYS KNEW THAT.
HE DID WHAT HE HAD TO DO, AND I NEVER BLAMED HIM.
I HAVE COME TO FIGHT SIDE BY SIDE WITH LORD ASANO'S RETAINERS IN THEIR UPCOMING BATTLE WITH THE SHOGUN'S FORCES.
WE WILL DIE HONORABLE DEATHS IN THE SERVICE OF OUR LORD ASANO.
MURAMATSU, I AM TURNING OVER THE CASTLE TO THE SHOGUN'S AGENTS. THERE WILL BE NO FIGHT.
BUT THIS CANNOT BE... LORD ASANO'S HONOR IS AT STAKE.
I KNOW YOU SEEK TO REDEEM YOURSELF FOR ACTIONS TAKEN LONG AGO, BUT IT WILL NOT BE HERE.

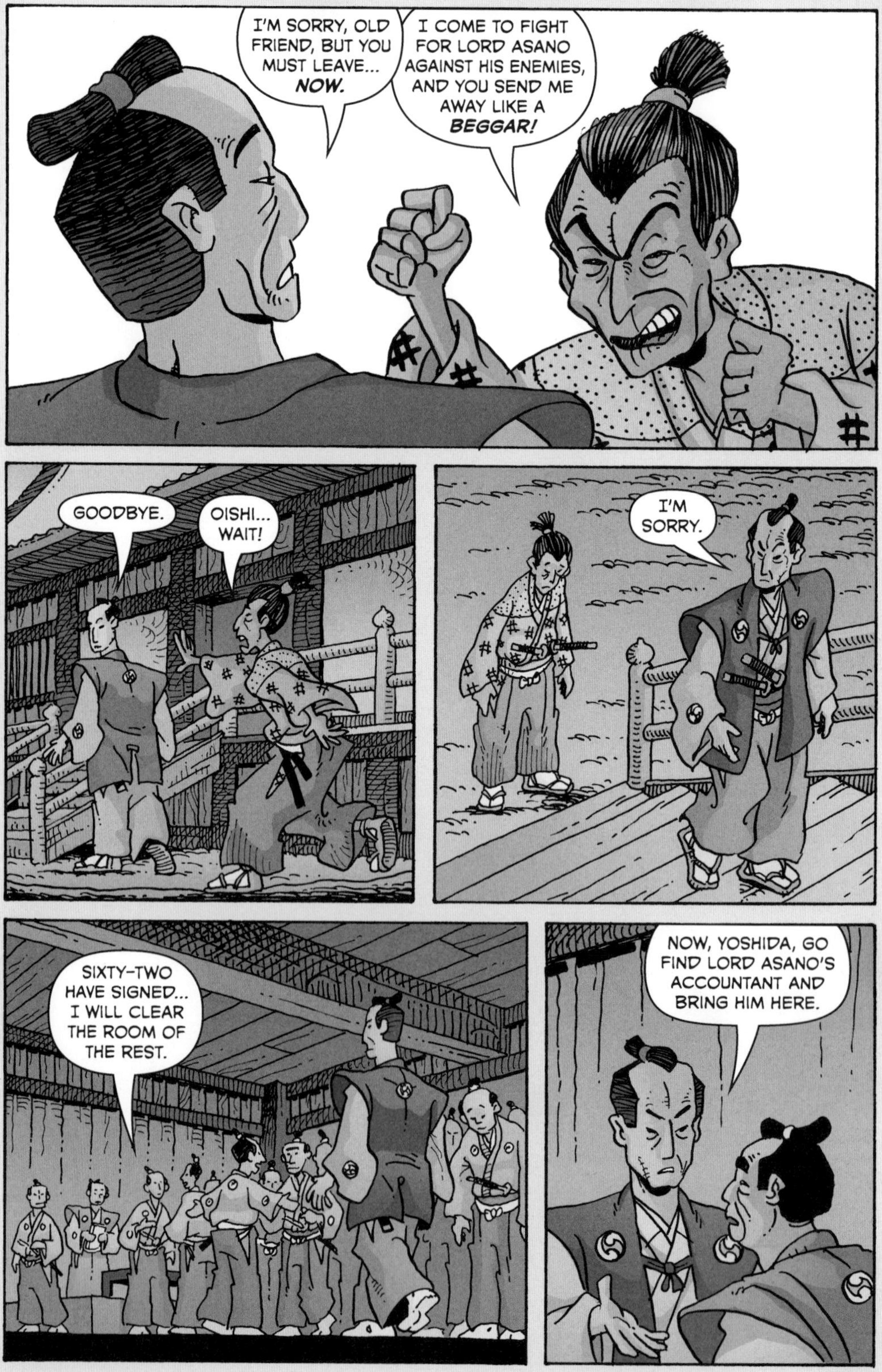
I'M SORRY, OLD FRIEND, BUT YOU MUST LEAVE... NOW.
I COME TO FIGHT FOR LORD ASANO AGAINST HIS ENEMIES, AND YOU SEND ME AWAY LIKE A BEGGAR!
GOODBYE.
OISHI... WAIT!
I'M SORRY.
SIXTY-TWO HAVE SIGNED... I WILL CLEAR THE ROOM OF THE REST.
NOW, YOSHIDA, GO FIND LORD ASANO'S ACCOUNTANT AND BRING HIM HERE.

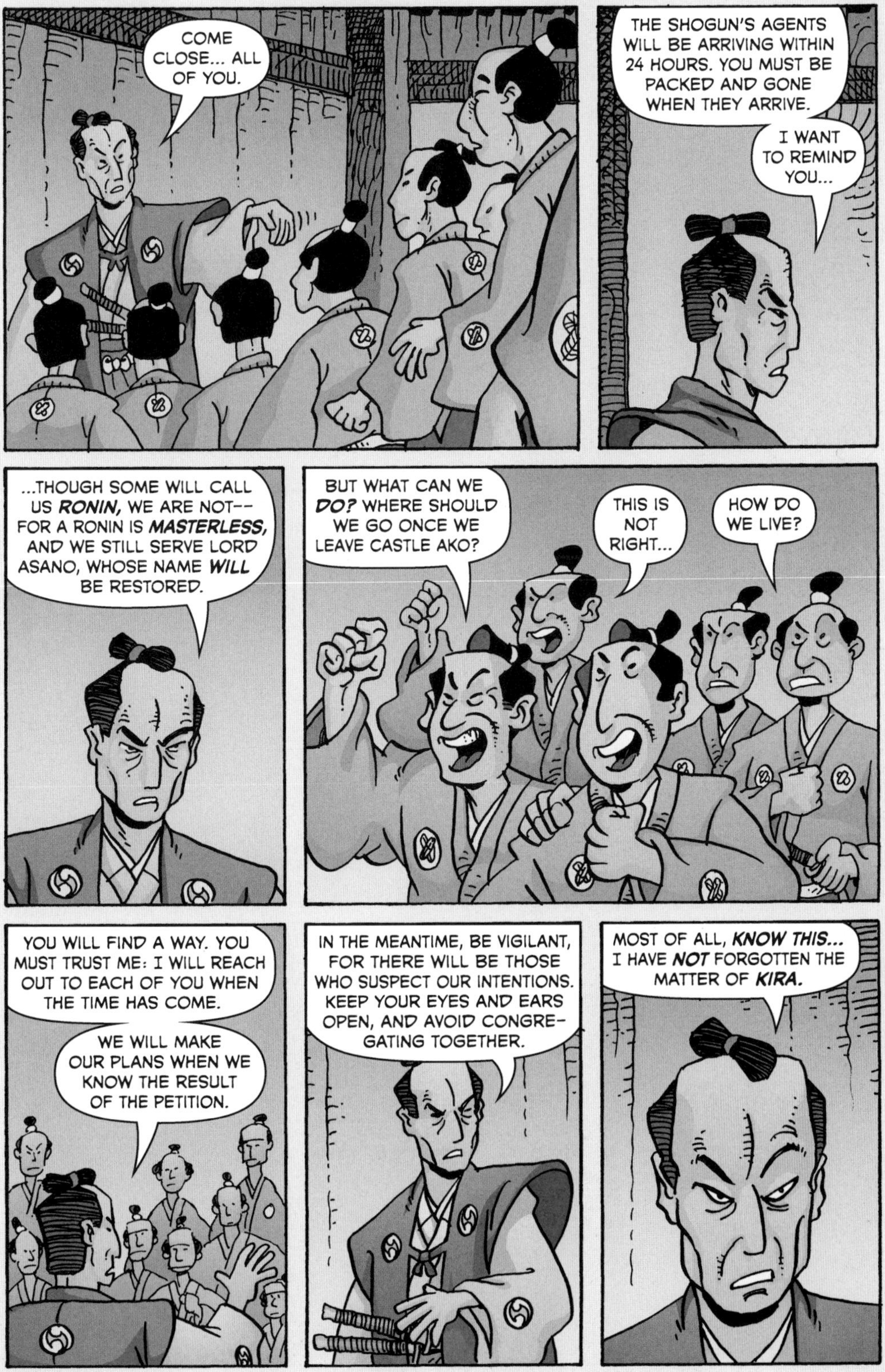
COME CLOSE... ALL OF YOU.
THE SHOGUN'S AGENTS WILL BE ARRIVING WITHIN 24 HOURS. YOU MUST BE PACKED AND GONE WHEN THEY ARRIVE.
I WANT TO REMIND YOU...
...THOUGH SOME WILL CALL US *RONIN,* WE ARE NOT-- FOR A RONIN IS *MASTERLESS,* AND WE STILL SERVE LORD ASANO, WHOSE NAME *WILL* BE RESTORED.
BUT WHAT CAN WE *DO?* WHERE SHOULD WE GO ONCE WE LEAVE CASTLE AKO?
THIS IS NOT RIGHT...
HOW DO WE LIVE?
YOU WILL FIND A WAY. YOU MUST TRUST ME: I WILL REACH OUT TO EACH OF YOU WHEN THE TIME HAS COME.
WE WILL MAKE OUR PLANS WHEN WE KNOW THE RESULT OF THE PETITION.
IN THE MEANTIME, BE VIGILANT, FOR THERE WILL BE THOSE WHO SUSPECT OUR INTENTIONS. KEEP YOUR EYES AND EARS OPEN, AND AVOID CONGREGATING TOGETHER.
MOST OF ALL, *KNOW THIS...* I HAVE *NOT* FORGOTTEN THE MATTER OF *KIRA.*

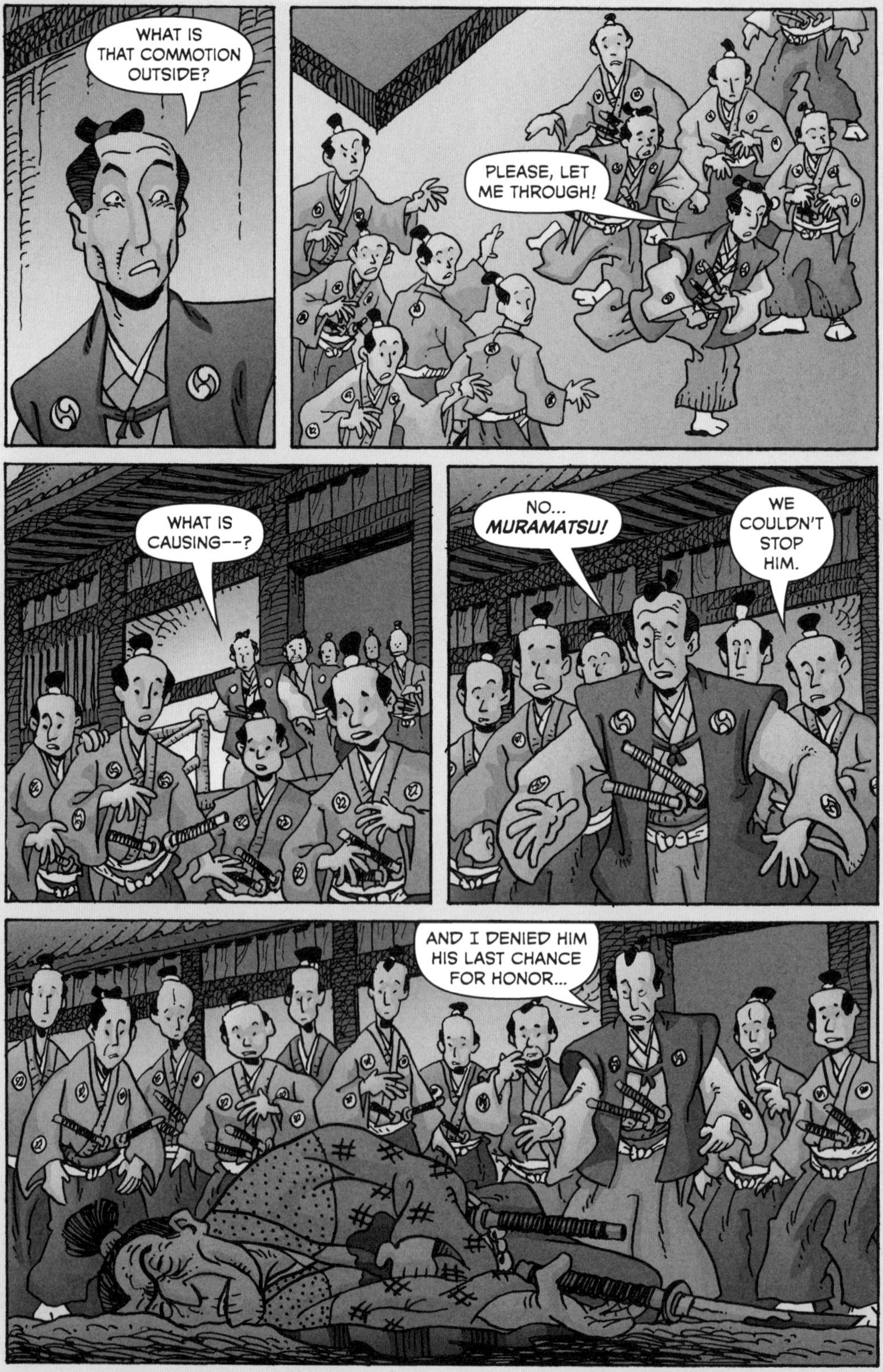
WHAT IS THAT COMMOTION OUTSIDE?
PLEASE, LET ME THROUGH!
WHAT IS CAUSING--?
NO... *MURAMATSU!*
WE COULDN'T STOP HIM.
AND I DENIED HIM HIS LAST CHANCE FOR HONOR...

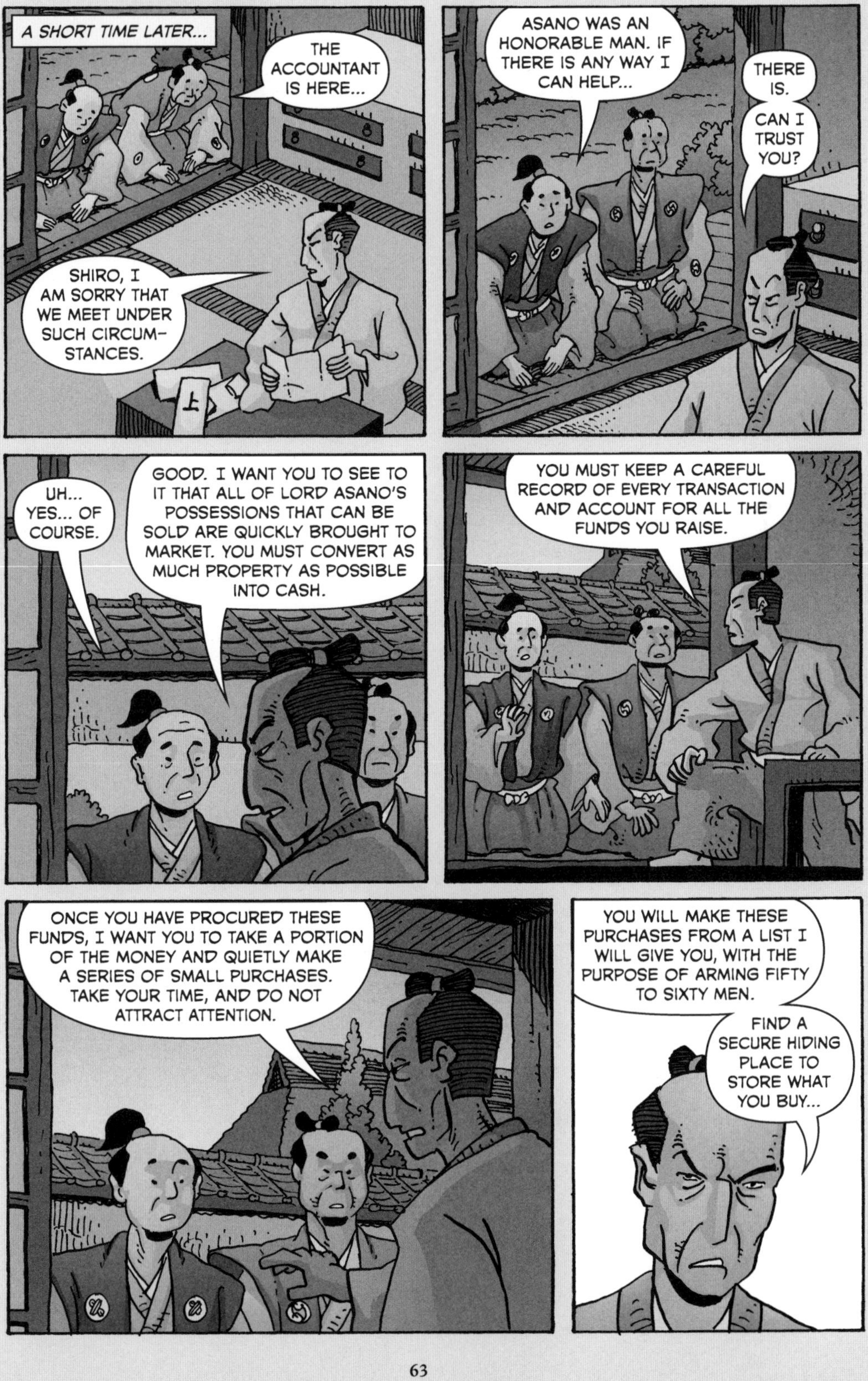
A SHORT TIME LATER...
THE ACCOUNTANT IS HERE...
SHIRO, I AM SORRY THAT WE MEET UNDER SUCH CIRCUM-STANCES.
ASANO WAS AN HONORABLE MAN. IF THERE IS ANY WAY I CAN HELP...
THERE IS.
CAN I TRUST YOU?
UH... YES... OF COURSE.
GOOD. I WANT YOU TO SEE TO IT THAT ALL OF LORD ASANO'S POSSESSIONS THAT CAN BE SOLD ARE QUICKLY BROUGHT TO MARKET. YOU MUST CONVERT AS MUCH PROPERTY AS POSSIBLE INTO CASH.
YOU MUST KEEP A CAREFUL RECORD OF EVERY TRANSACTION AND ACCOUNT FOR ALL THE FUNDS YOU RAISE.
ONCE YOU HAVE PROCURED THESE FUNDS, I WANT YOU TO TAKE A PORTION OF THE MONEY AND QUIETLY MAKE A SERIES OF SMALL PURCHASES. TAKE YOUR TIME, AND DO NOT ATTRACT ATTENTION.
YOU WILL MAKE THESE PURCHASES FROM A LIST I WILL GIVE YOU, WITH THE PURPOSE OF ARMING FIFTY TO SIXTY MEN.
FIND A SECURE HIDING PLACE TO STORE WHAT YOU BUY...

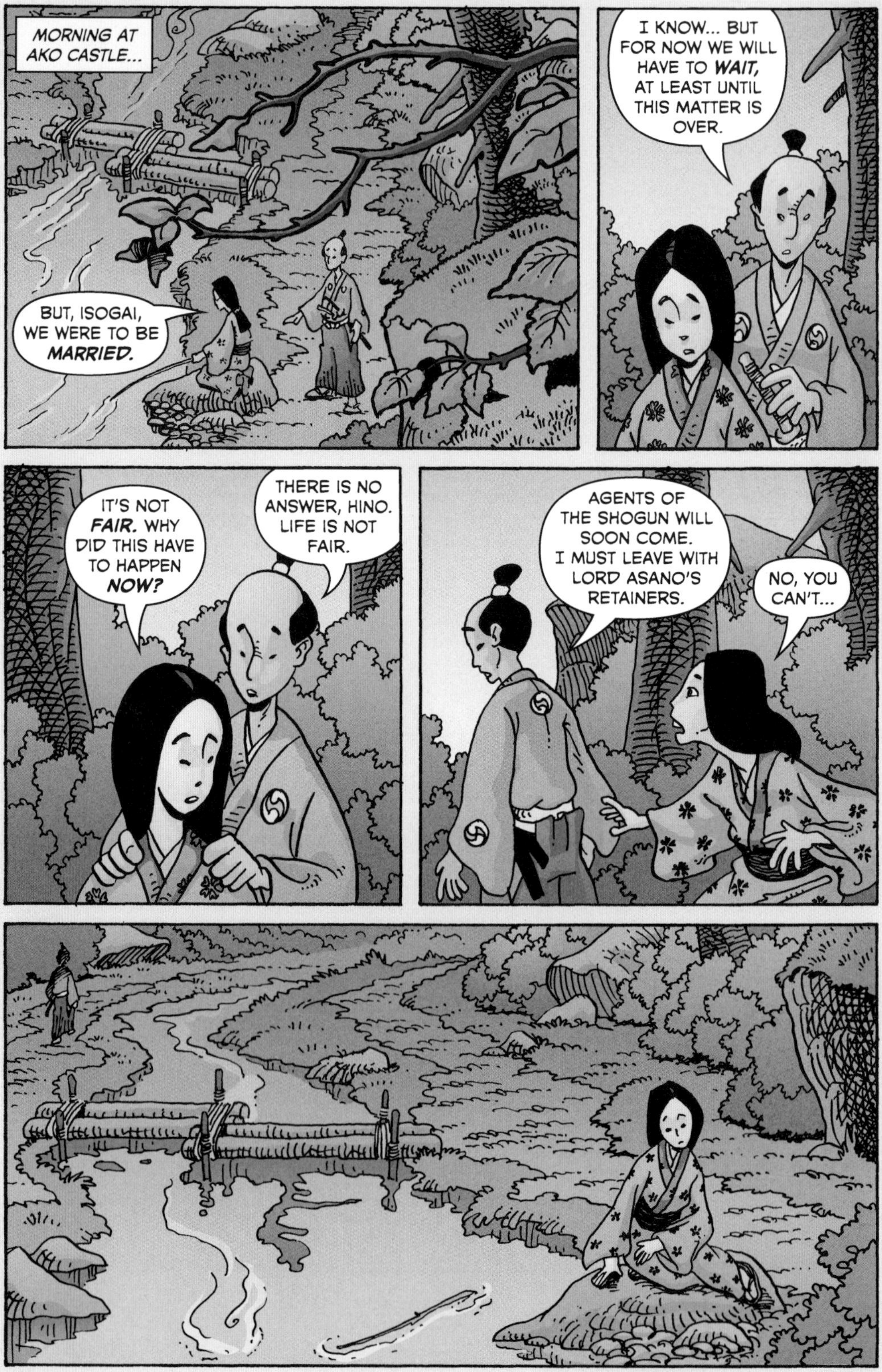

MORNING AT AKO CASTLE...
BUT, ISOGAI, WE WERE TO BE *MARRIED.*
I KNOW... BUT FOR NOW WE WILL HAVE TO *WAIT,* AT LEAST UNTIL THIS MATTER IS OVER.
IT'S NOT *FAIR.* WHY DID THIS HAVE TO HAPPEN *NOW?*
THERE IS NO ANSWER, HINO. LIFE IS NOT FAIR.
AGENTS OF THE SHOGUN WILL SOON COME. I MUST LEAVE WITH LORD ASANO'S RETAINERS.
NO, YOU CAN'T...

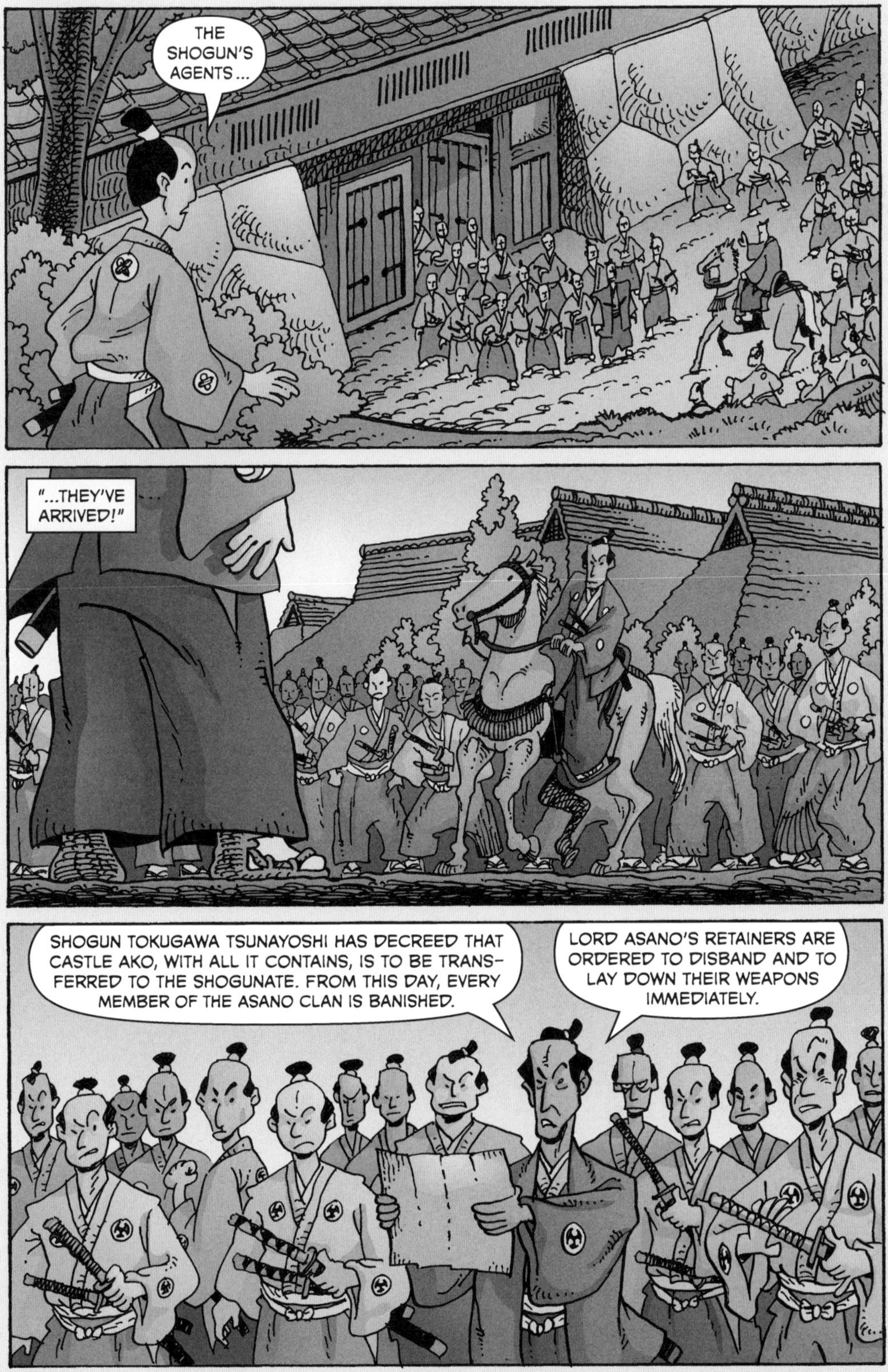
THE SHOGUN'S AGENTS...
"...THEY'VE ARRIVED!"
SHOGUN TOKUGAWA TSUNAYOSHI HAS DECREED THAT CASTLE AKO, WITH ALL IT CONTAINS, IS TO BE TRANS-FERRED TO THE SHOGUNATE. FROM THIS DAY, EVERY MEMBER OF THE ASANO CLAN IS BANISHED.
LORD ASANO'S RETAINERS ARE ORDERED TO DISBAND AND TO LAY DOWN THEIR WEAPONS IMMEDIATELY.

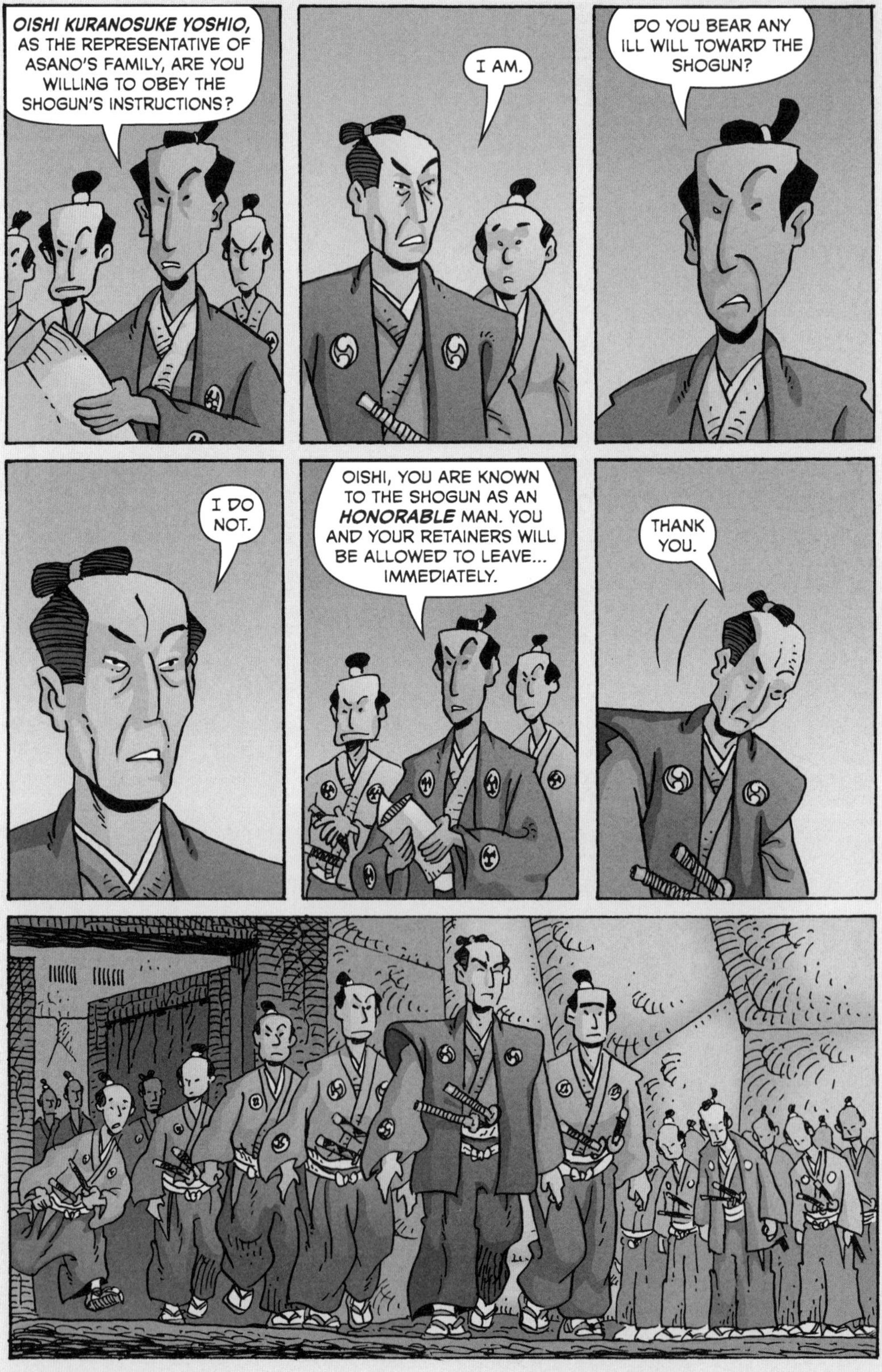
OISHI KURANOSUKE YOSHIO, AS THE REPRESENTATIVE OF ASANO'S FAMILY, ARE YOU WILLING TO OBEY THE SHOGUN'S INSTRUCTIONS?
I AM.
DO YOU BEAR ANY ILL WILL TOWARD THE SHOGUN?
I DO NOT.
OISHI, YOU ARE KNOWN TO THE SHOGUN AS AN HONORABLE MAN. YOU AND YOUR RETAINERS WILL BE ALLOWED TO LEAVE... IMMEDIATELY.
THANK YOU.

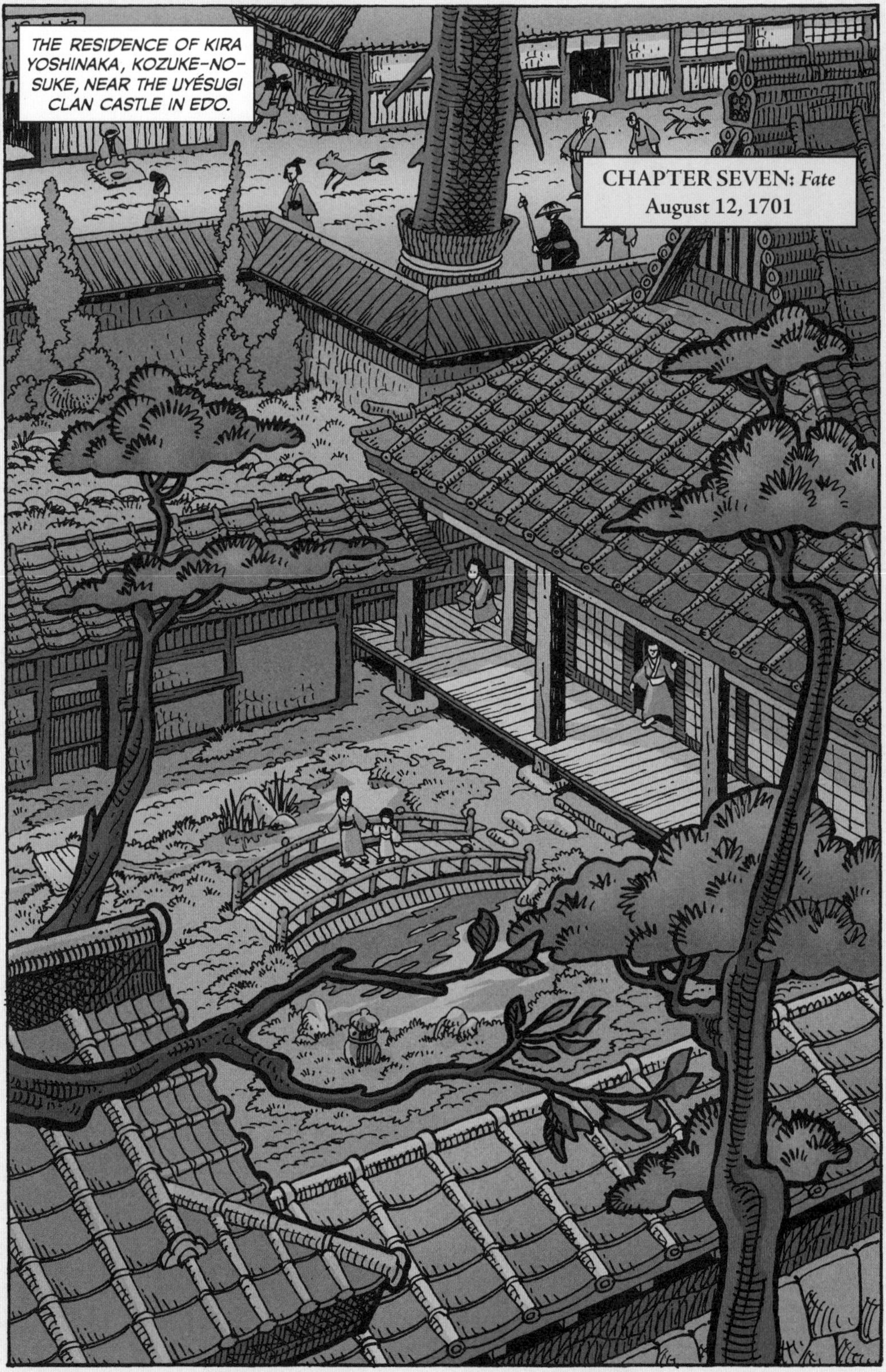
THE RESIDENCE OF KIRA YOSHINAKA, KOZUKE-NO-SUKE, NEAR THE UYÉSUGI CLAN CASTLE IN EDO.
CHAPTER SEVEN: *Fate*
August 12, 1701

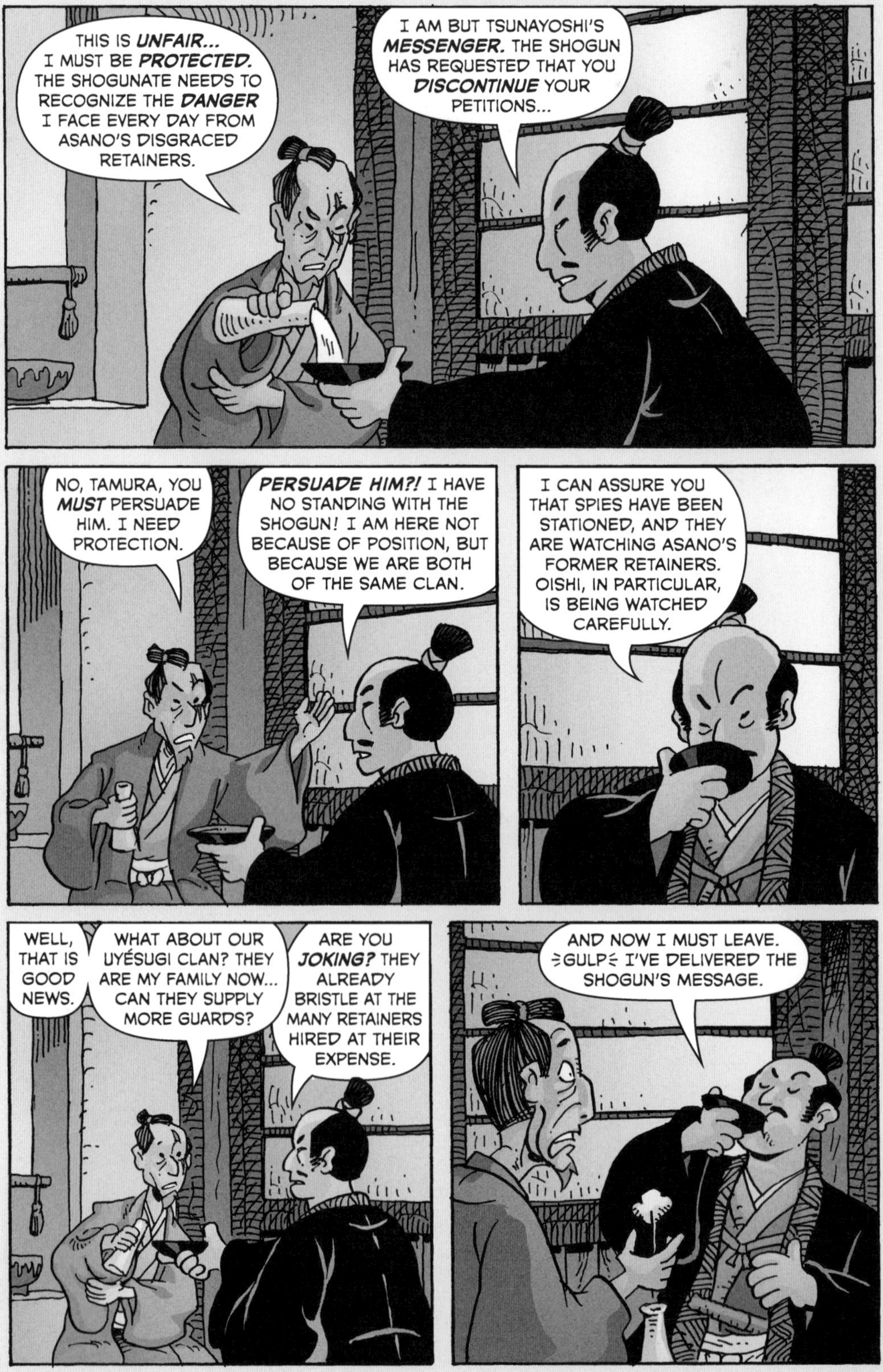
THIS IS UNFAIR... I MUST BE PROTECTED. THE SHOGUNATE NEEDS TO RECOGNIZE THE DANGER I FACE EVERY DAY FROM ASANO'S DISGRACED RETAINERS.
I AM BUT TSUNAYOSHI'S MESSENGER. THE SHOGUN HAS REQUESTED THAT YOU DISCONTINUE YOUR PETITIONS...
NO, TAMURA, YOU MUST PERSUADE HIM. I NEED PROTECTION.
PERSUADE HIM?! I HAVE NO STANDING WITH THE SHOGUN! I AM HERE NOT BECAUSE OF POSITION, BUT BECAUSE WE ARE BOTH OF THE SAME CLAN.
I CAN ASSURE YOU THAT SPIES HAVE BEEN STATIONED, AND THEY ARE WATCHING ASANO'S FORMER RETAINERS. OISHI, IN PARTICULAR, IS BEING WATCHED CAREFULLY.
WELL, THAT IS GOOD NEWS.
WHAT ABOUT OUR UYÉSUGI CLAN? THEY ARE MY FAMILY NOW... CAN THEY SUPPLY MORE GUARDS?
ARE YOU JOKING? THEY ALREADY BRISTLE AT THE MANY RETAINERS HIRED AT THEIR EXPENSE.
AND NOW I MUST LEAVE. ≑GULP≑ I'VE DELIVERED THE SHOGUN'S MESSAGE.

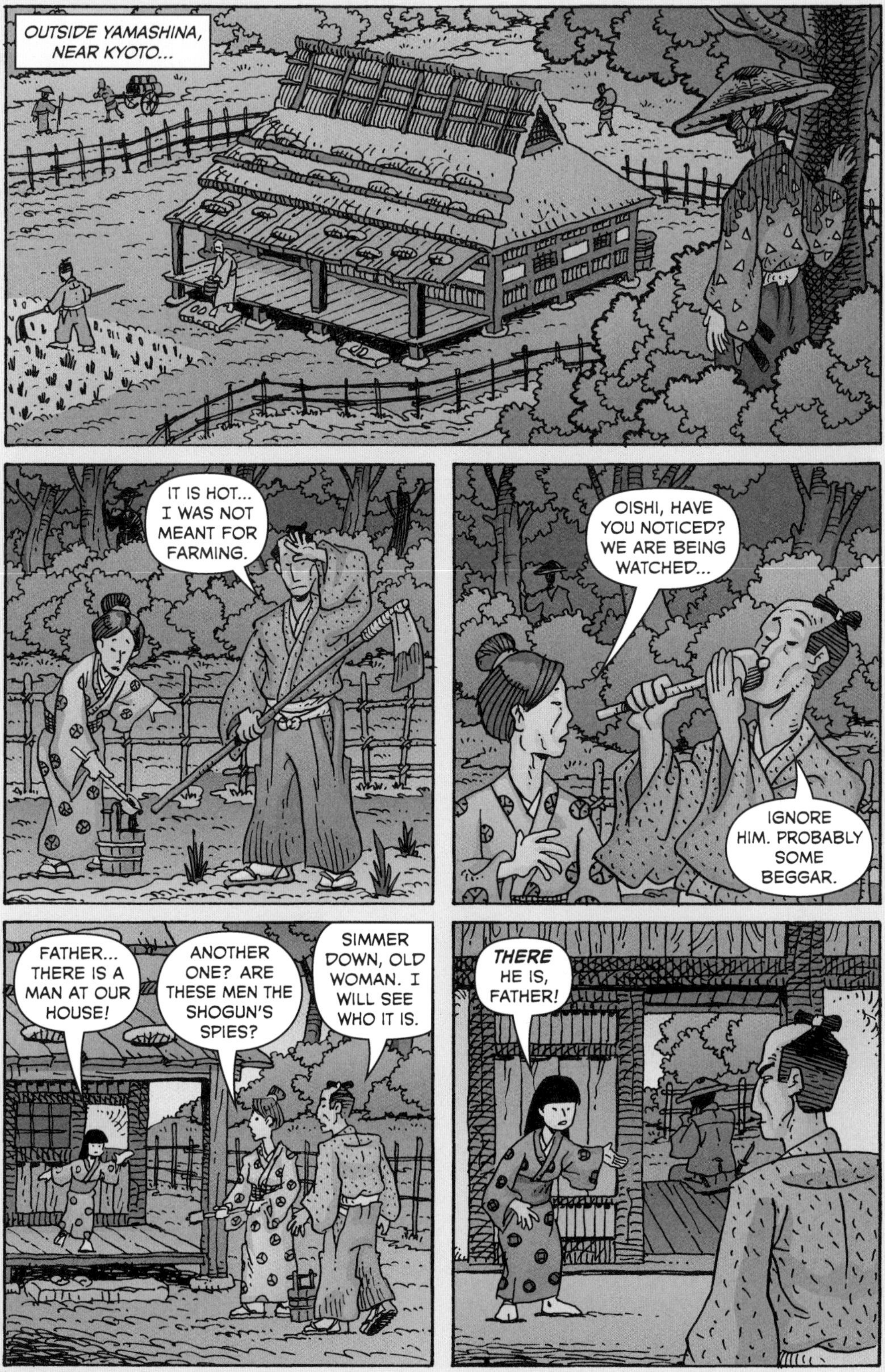
OUTSIDE YAMASHINA, NEAR KYOTO...
IT IS HOT... I WAS NOT MEANT FOR FARMING.
OISHI, HAVE YOU NOTICED? WE ARE BEING WATCHED...
IGNORE HIM. PROBABLY SOME BEGGAR.
FATHER... THERE IS A MAN AT OUR HOUSE!
ANOTHER ONE? ARE THESE MEN THE SHOGUN'S SPIES?
SIMMER DOWN, OLD WOMAN. I WILL SEE WHO IT IS.
THERE HE IS, FATHER!

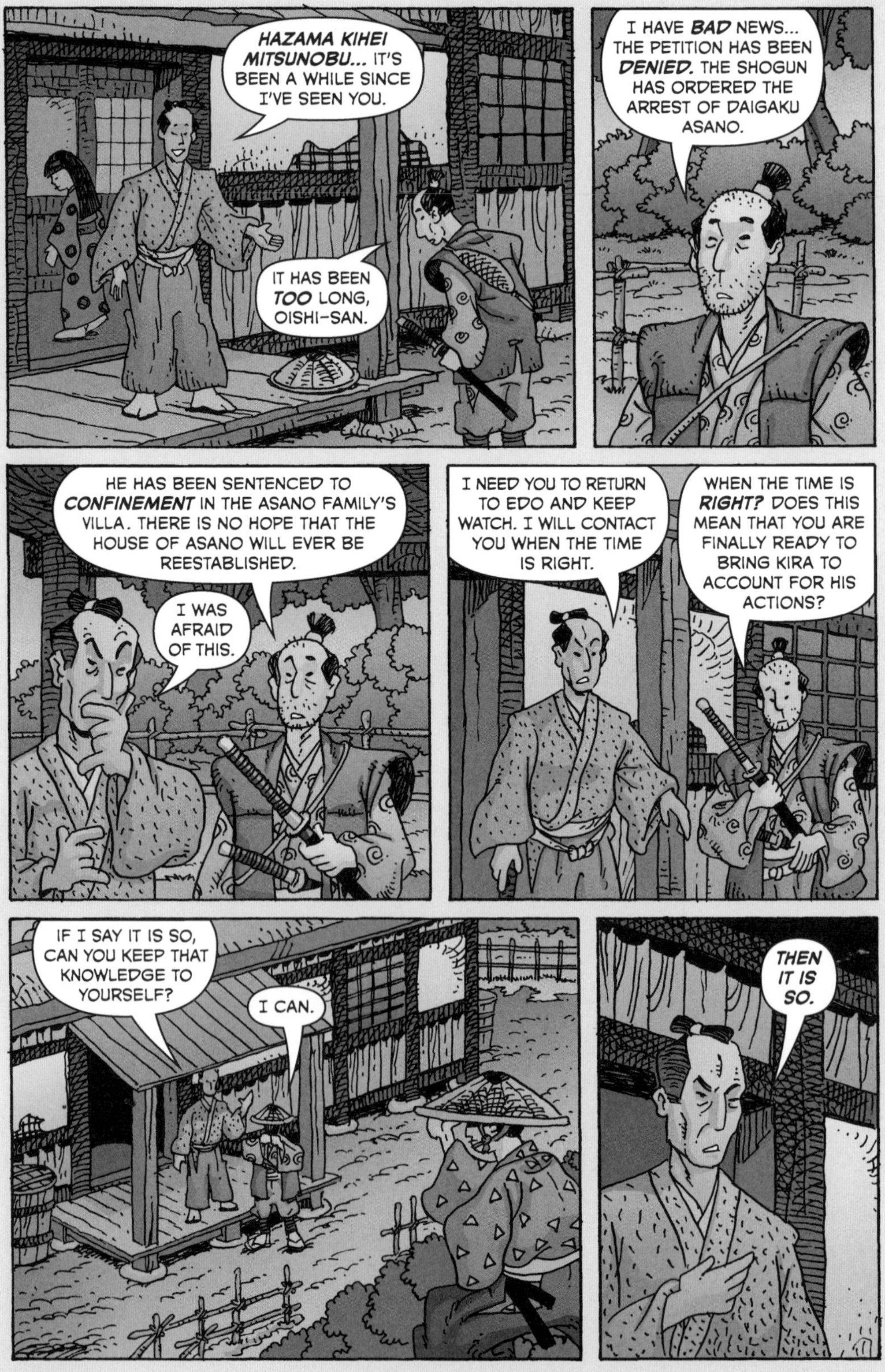
HAZAMA KIHEI MITSUNOBU... IT'S BEEN A WHILE SINCE I'VE SEEN YOU.
IT HAS BEEN TOO LONG, OISHI-SAN.
I HAVE BAD NEWS... THE PETITION HAS BEEN DENIED. THE SHOGUN HAS ORDERED THE ARREST OF DAIGAKU ASANO.
HE HAS BEEN SENTENCED TO CONFINEMENT IN THE ASANO FAMILY'S VILLA. THERE IS NO HOPE THAT THE HOUSE OF ASANO WILL EVER BE REESTABLISHED.
I WAS AFRAID OF THIS.
I NEED YOU TO RETURN TO EDO AND KEEP WATCH. I WILL CONTACT YOU WHEN THE TIME IS RIGHT.
WHEN THE TIME IS RIGHT? DOES THIS MEAN THAT YOU ARE FINALLY READY TO BRING KIRA TO ACCOUNT FOR HIS ACTIONS?
IF I SAY IT IS SO, CAN YOU KEEP THAT KNOWLEDGE TO YOURSELF?
I CAN.
THEN IT IS SO.

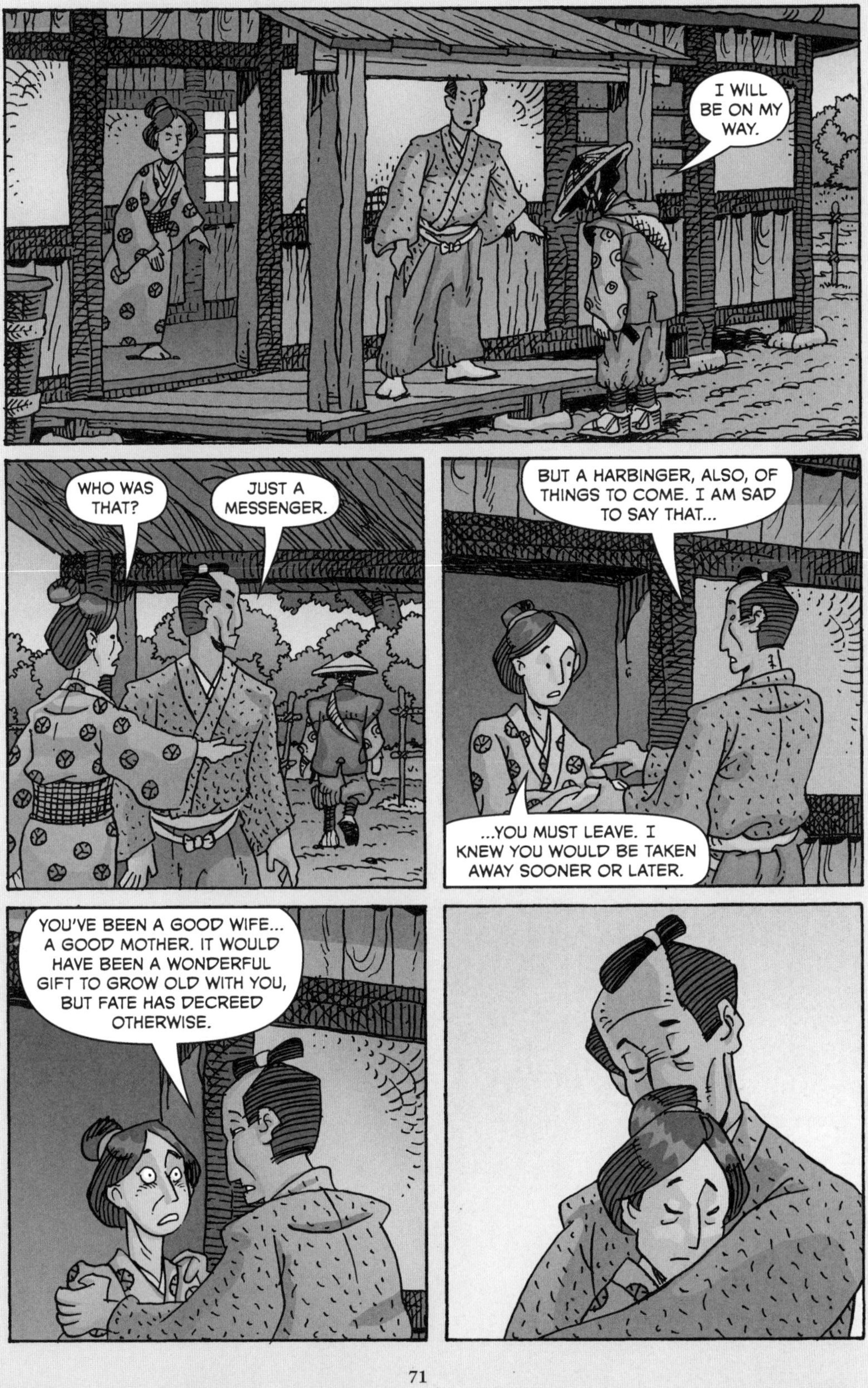
I WILL BE ON MY WAY.
WHO WAS THAT?
JUST A MESSENGER.
BUT A HARBINGER, ALSO, OF THINGS TO COME. I AM SAD TO SAY THAT...
...YOU MUST LEAVE. I KNEW YOU WOULD BE TAKEN AWAY SOONER OR LATER.
YOU'VE BEEN A GOOD WIFE... A GOOD MOTHER. IT WOULD HAVE BEEN A WONDERFUL GIFT TO GROW OLD WITH YOU, BUT FATE HAS DECREED OTHERWISE.

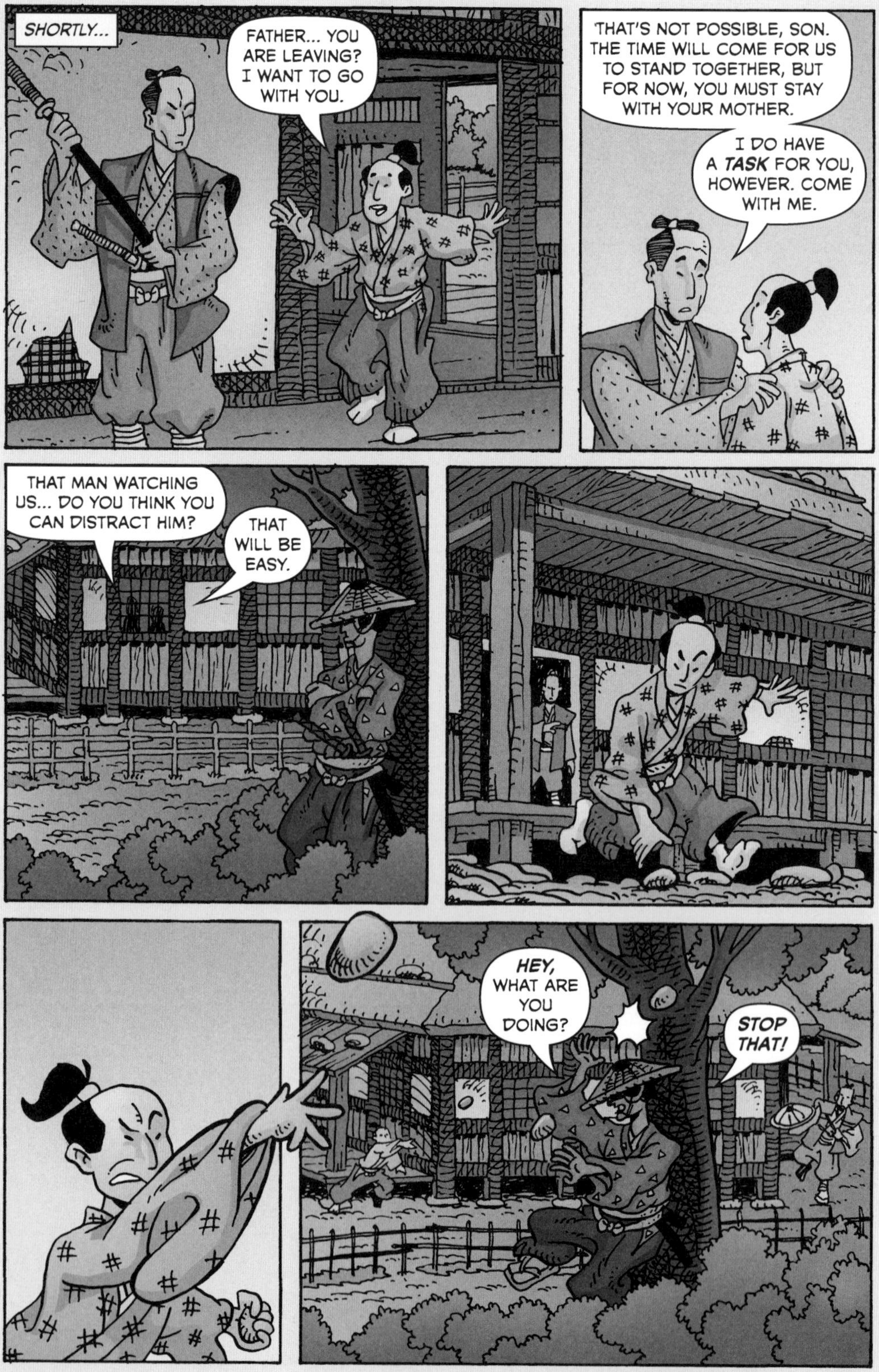
SHORTLY...
FATHER... YOU ARE LEAVING? I WANT TO GO WITH YOU.
THAT'S NOT POSSIBLE, SON. THE TIME WILL COME FOR US TO STAND TOGETHER, BUT FOR NOW, YOU MUST STAY WITH YOUR MOTHER.
I DO HAVE A TASK FOR YOU, HOWEVER. COME WITH ME.
THAT MAN WATCHING US... DO YOU THINK YOU CAN DISTRACT HIM?
THAT WILL BE EASY.
HEY, WHAT ARE YOU DOING?
STOP THAT!

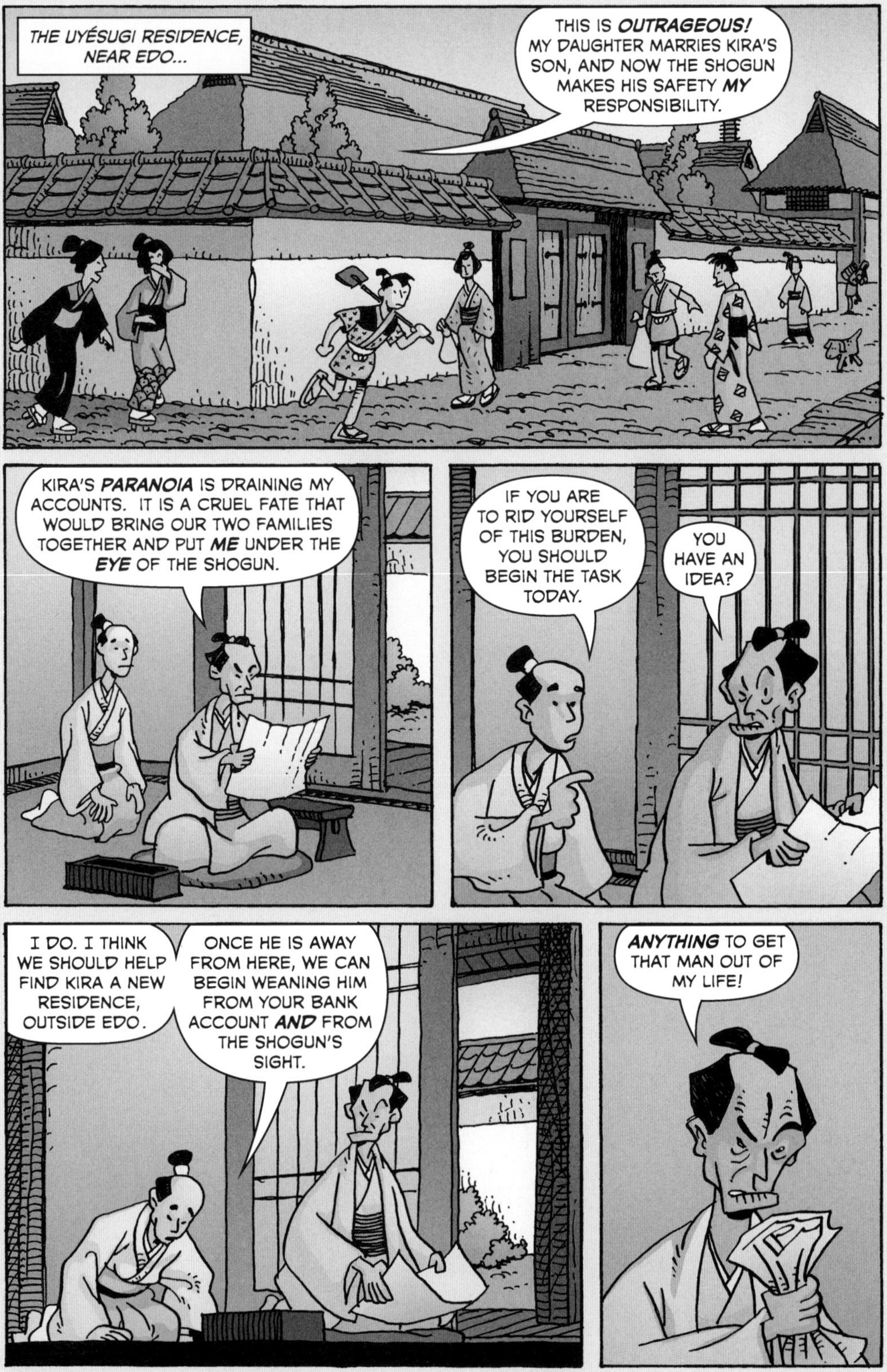
THE UYÉSUGI RESIDENCE, NEAR EDO...
THIS IS OUTRAGEOUS! MY DAUGHTER MARRIES KIRA'S SON, AND NOW THE SHOGUN MAKES HIS SAFETY MY RESPONSIBILITY.
KIRA'S PARANOIA IS DRAINING MY ACCOUNTS. IT IS A CRUEL FATE THAT WOULD BRING OUR TWO FAMILIES TOGETHER AND PUT ME UNDER THE EYE OF THE SHOGUN.
IF YOU ARE TO RID YOURSELF OF THIS BURDEN, YOU SHOULD BEGIN THE TASK TODAY.
YOU HAVE AN IDEA?
I DO. I THINK WE SHOULD HELP FIND KIRA A NEW RESIDENCE, OUTSIDE EDO.
ONCE HE IS AWAY FROM HERE, WE CAN BEGIN WEANING HIM FROM YOUR BANK ACCOUNT AND FROM THE SHOGUN'S SIGHT.
ANYTHING TO GET THAT MAN OUT OF MY LIFE!

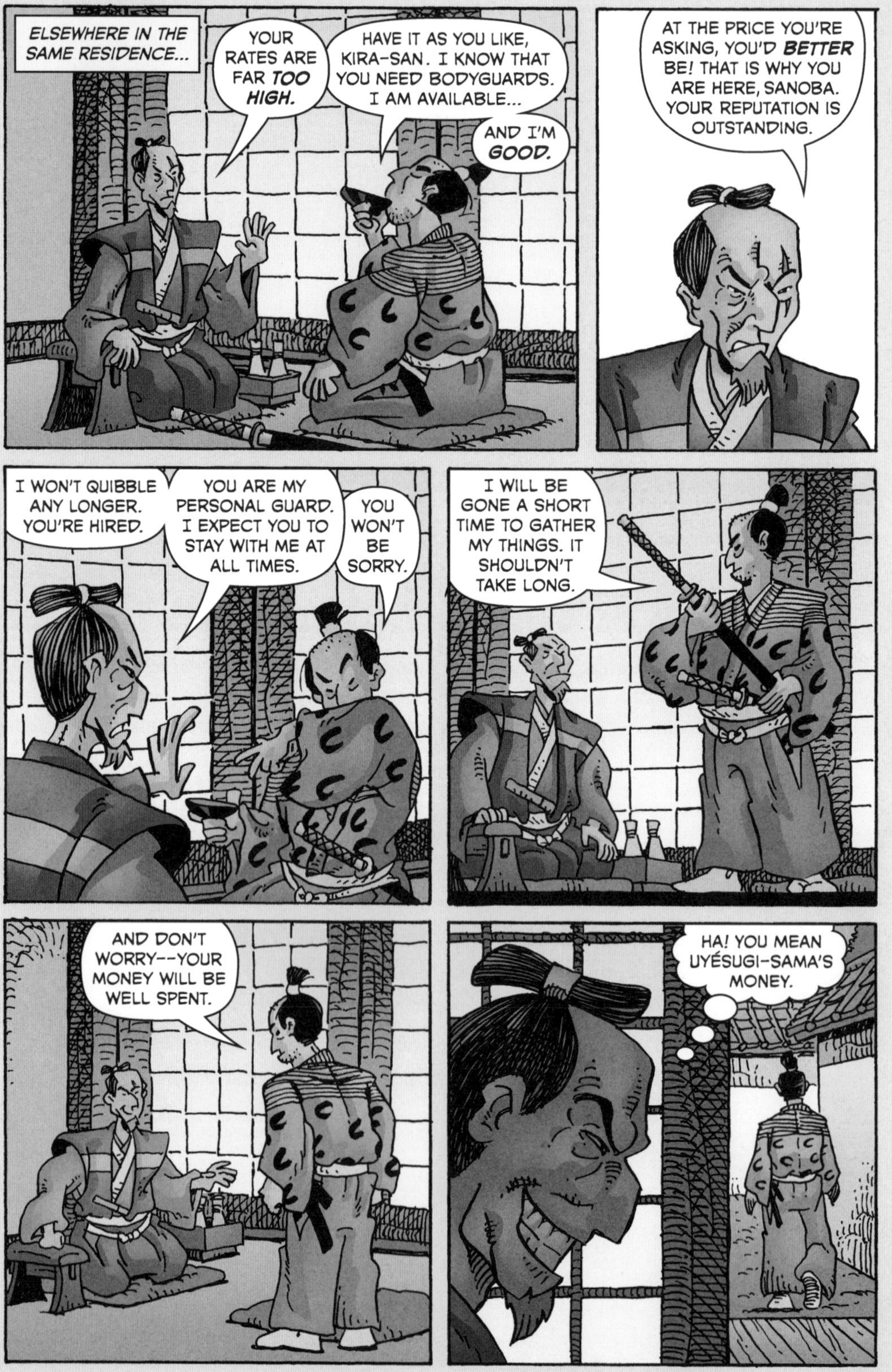
ELSEWHERE IN THE SAME RESIDENCE...
YOUR RATES ARE FAR TOO HIGH.
HAVE IT AS YOU LIKE, KIRA-SAN. I KNOW THAT YOU NEED BODYGUARDS. I AM AVAILABLE...
AND I'M GOOD.
AT THE PRICE YOU'RE ASKING, YOU'D BETTER BE! THAT IS WHY YOU ARE HERE, SANOBA. YOUR REPUTATION IS OUTSTANDING.
I WON'T QUIBBLE ANY LONGER. YOU'RE HIRED.
YOU ARE MY PERSONAL GUARD. I EXPECT YOU TO STAY WITH ME AT ALL TIMES.
YOU WON'T BE SORRY.
I WILL BE GONE A SHORT TIME TO GATHER MY THINGS. IT SHOULDN'T TAKE LONG.
AND DON'T WORRY--YOUR MONEY WILL BE WELL SPENT.
HA! YOU MEAN UYÉSUGI-SAMA'S MONEY.

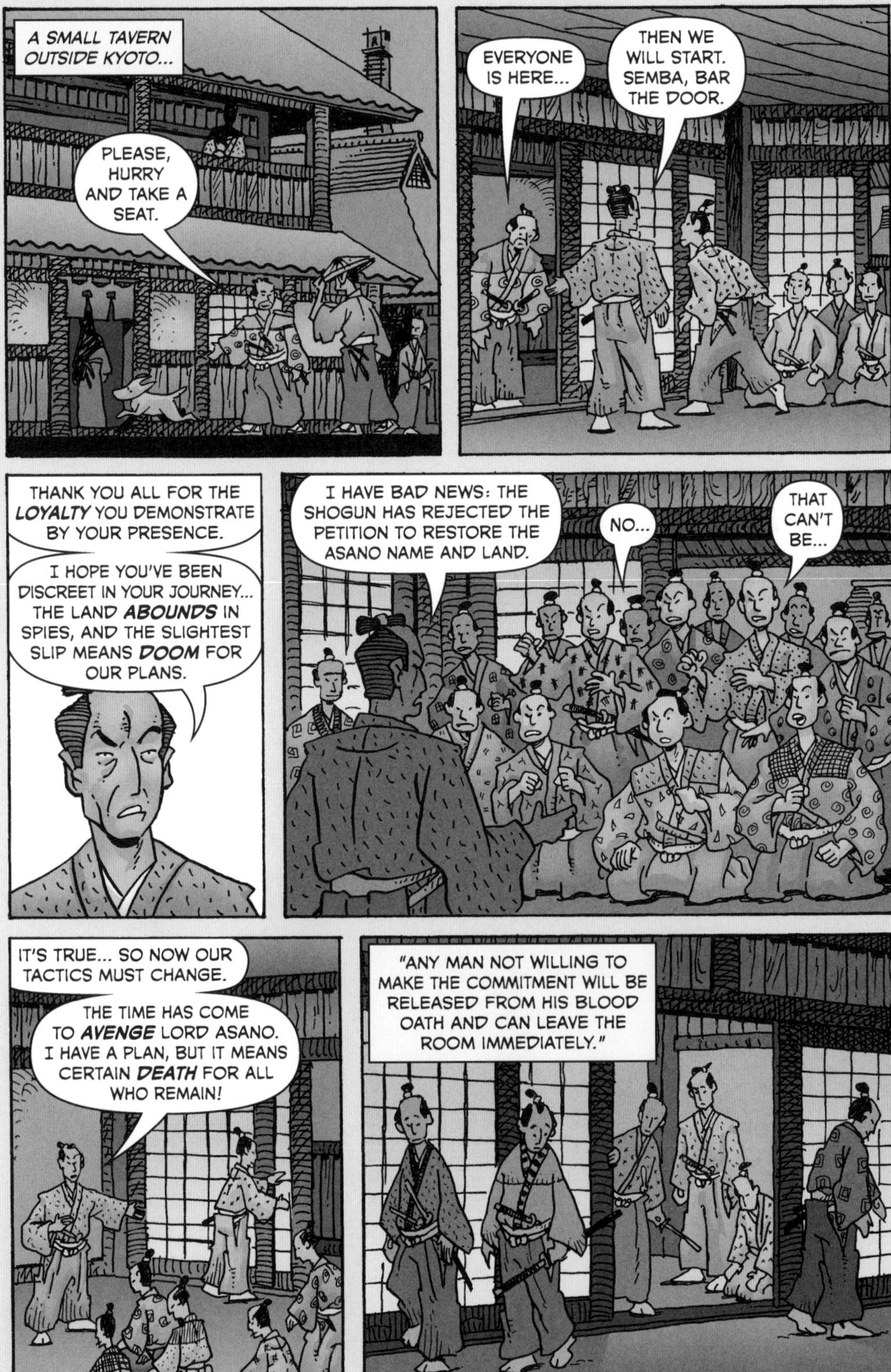
A SMALL TAVERN OUTSIDE KYOTO...
PLEASE, HURRY AND TAKE A SEAT.
EVERYONE IS HERE...
THEN WE WILL START. SEMBA, BAR THE DOOR.
THANK YOU ALL FOR THE LOYALTY YOU DEMONSTRATE BY YOUR PRESENCE.
I HOPE YOU'VE BEEN DISCREET IN YOUR JOURNEY... THE LAND ABOUNDS IN SPIES, AND THE SLIGHTEST SLIP MEANS DOOM FOR OUR PLANS.
I HAVE BAD NEWS: THE SHOGUN HAS REJECTED THE PETITION TO RESTORE THE ASANO NAME AND LAND.
NO...
THAT CAN'T BE...
IT'S TRUE... SO NOW OUR TACTICS MUST CHANGE.
THE TIME HAS COME TO AVENGE LORD ASANO. I HAVE A PLAN, BUT IT MEANS CERTAIN DEATH FOR ALL WHO REMAIN!
"ANY MAN NOT WILLING TO MAKE THE COMMITMENT WILL BE RELEASED FROM HIS BLOOD OATH AND CAN LEAVE THE ROOM IMMEDIATELY."

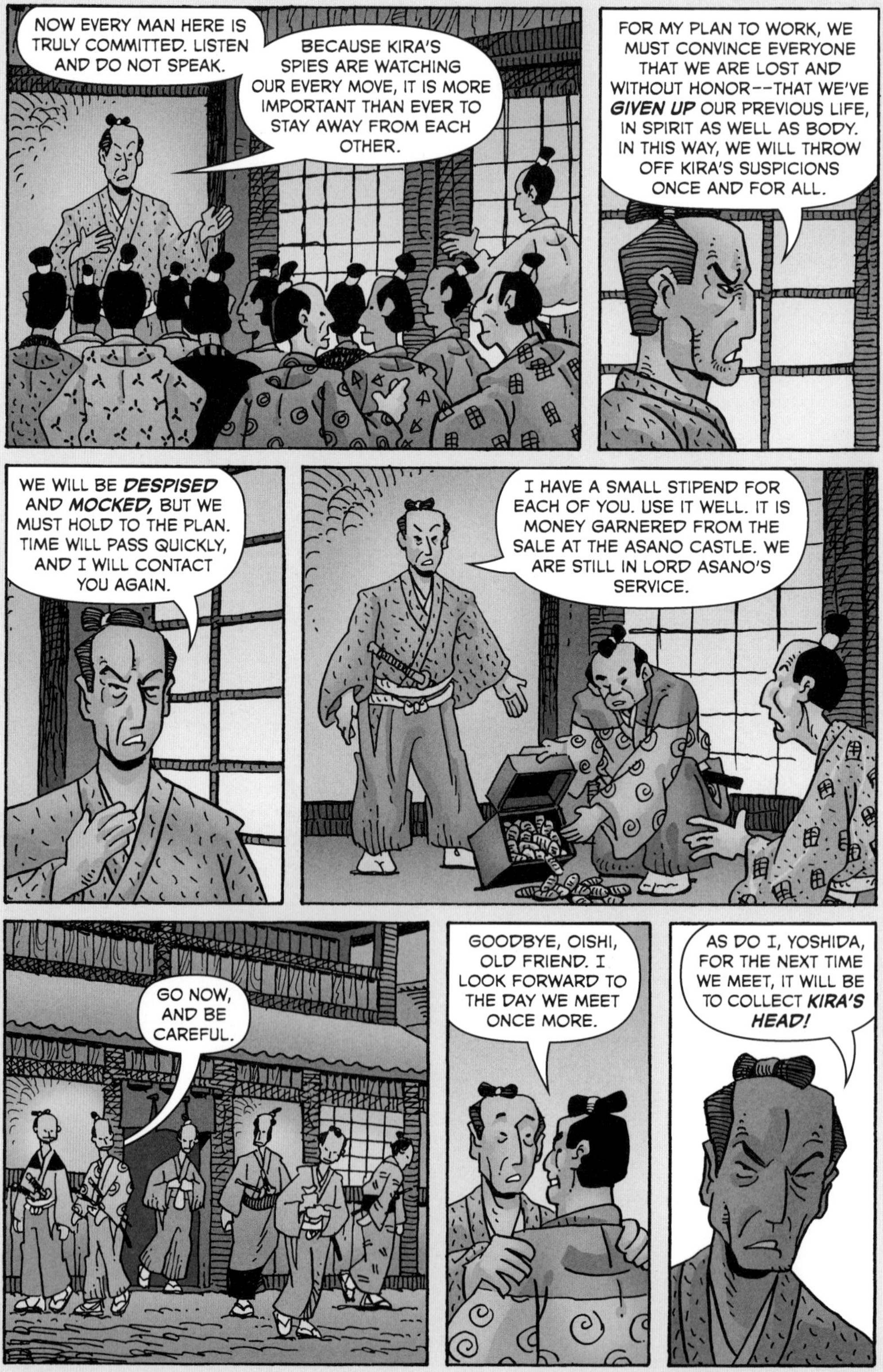
NOW EVERY MAN HERE IS TRULY COMMITTED. LISTEN AND DO NOT SPEAK.
BECAUSE KIRA'S SPIES ARE WATCHING OUR EVERY MOVE, IT IS MORE IMPORTANT THAN EVER TO STAY AWAY FROM EACH OTHER.
FOR MY PLAN TO WORK, WE MUST CONVINCE EVERYONE THAT WE ARE LOST AND WITHOUT HONOR--THAT WE'VE GIVEN UP OUR PREVIOUS LIFE, IN SPIRIT AS WELL AS BODY. IN THIS WAY, WE WILL THROW OFF KIRA'S SUSPICIONS ONCE AND FOR ALL.
WE WILL BE DESPISED AND MOCKED, BUT WE MUST HOLD TO THE PLAN. TIME WILL PASS QUICKLY, AND I WILL CONTACT YOU AGAIN.
I HAVE A SMALL STIPEND FOR EACH OF YOU. USE IT WELL. IT IS MONEY GARNERED FROM THE SALE AT THE ASANO CASTLE. WE ARE STILL IN LORD ASANO'S SERVICE.
GO NOW, AND BE CAREFUL.
GOODBYE, OISHI, OLD FRIEND. I LOOK FORWARD TO THE DAY WE MEET ONCE MORE.
AS DO I, YOSHIDA, FOR THE NEXT TIME WE MEET, IT WILL BE TO COLLECT KIRA'S HEAD!

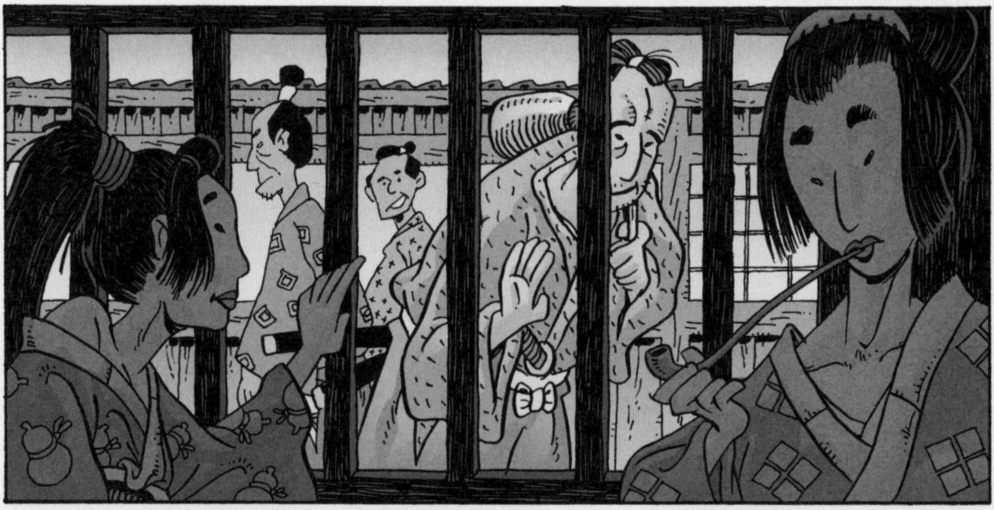

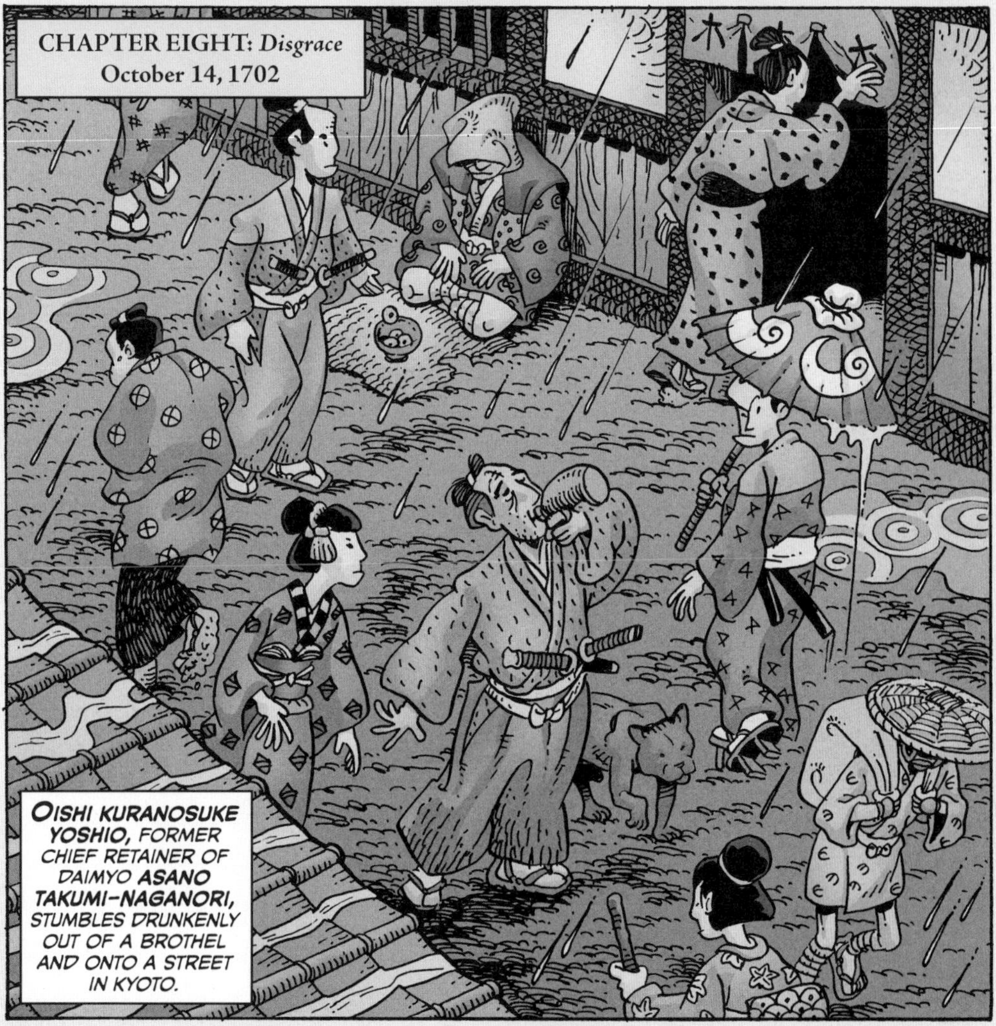
CHAPTER EIGHT: *Disgrace*
October 14, 1702
OISHI KURANOSUKE YOSHIO, FORMER CHIEF RETAINER OF DAIMYO ASANO TAKUMI-NAGANORI, STUMBLES DRUNKENLY OUT OF A BROTHEL AND ONTO A STREET IN KYOTO.

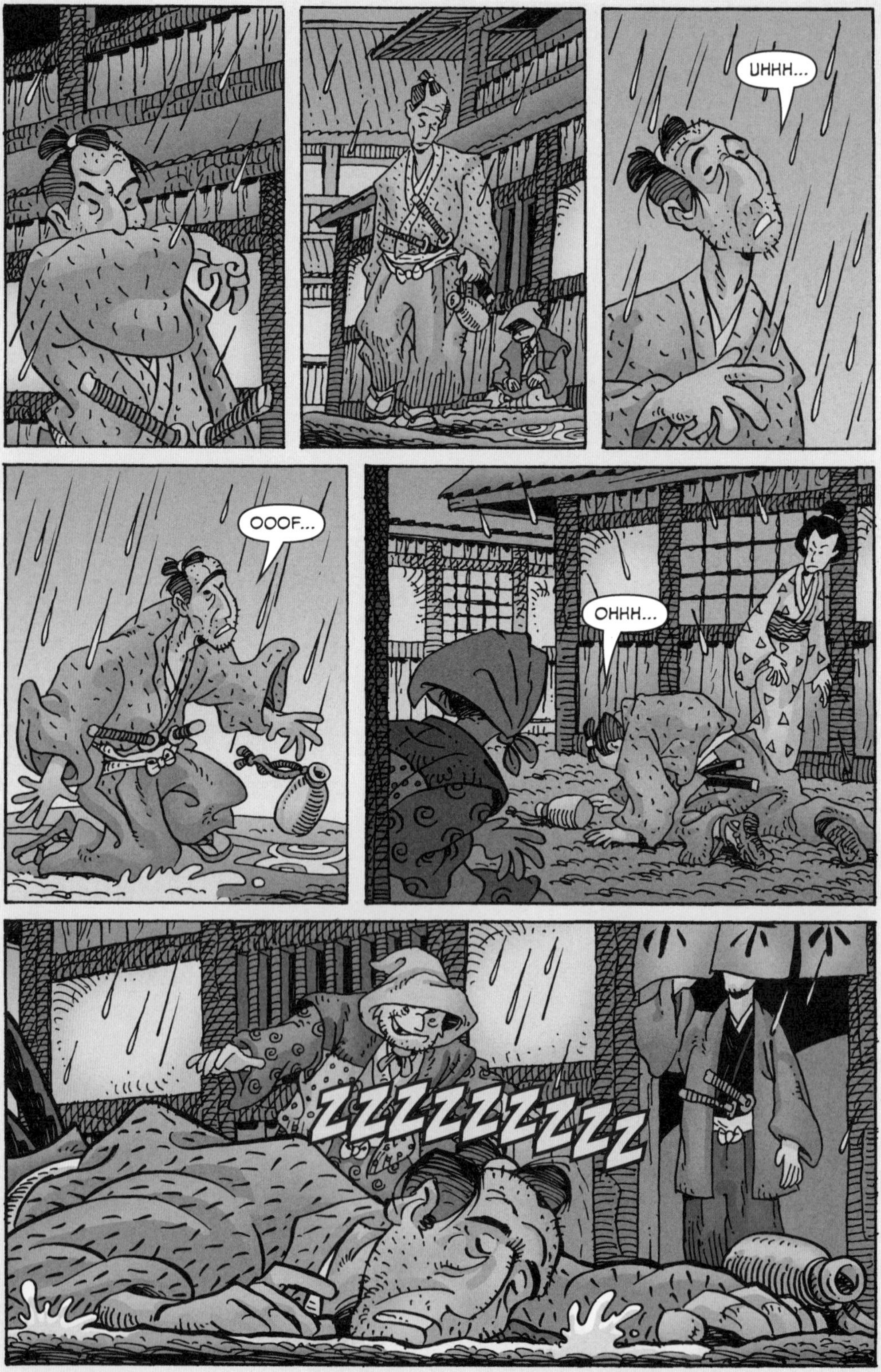
UHHH...
OOOF...
OHHH...
ZZZZZZZZZZ

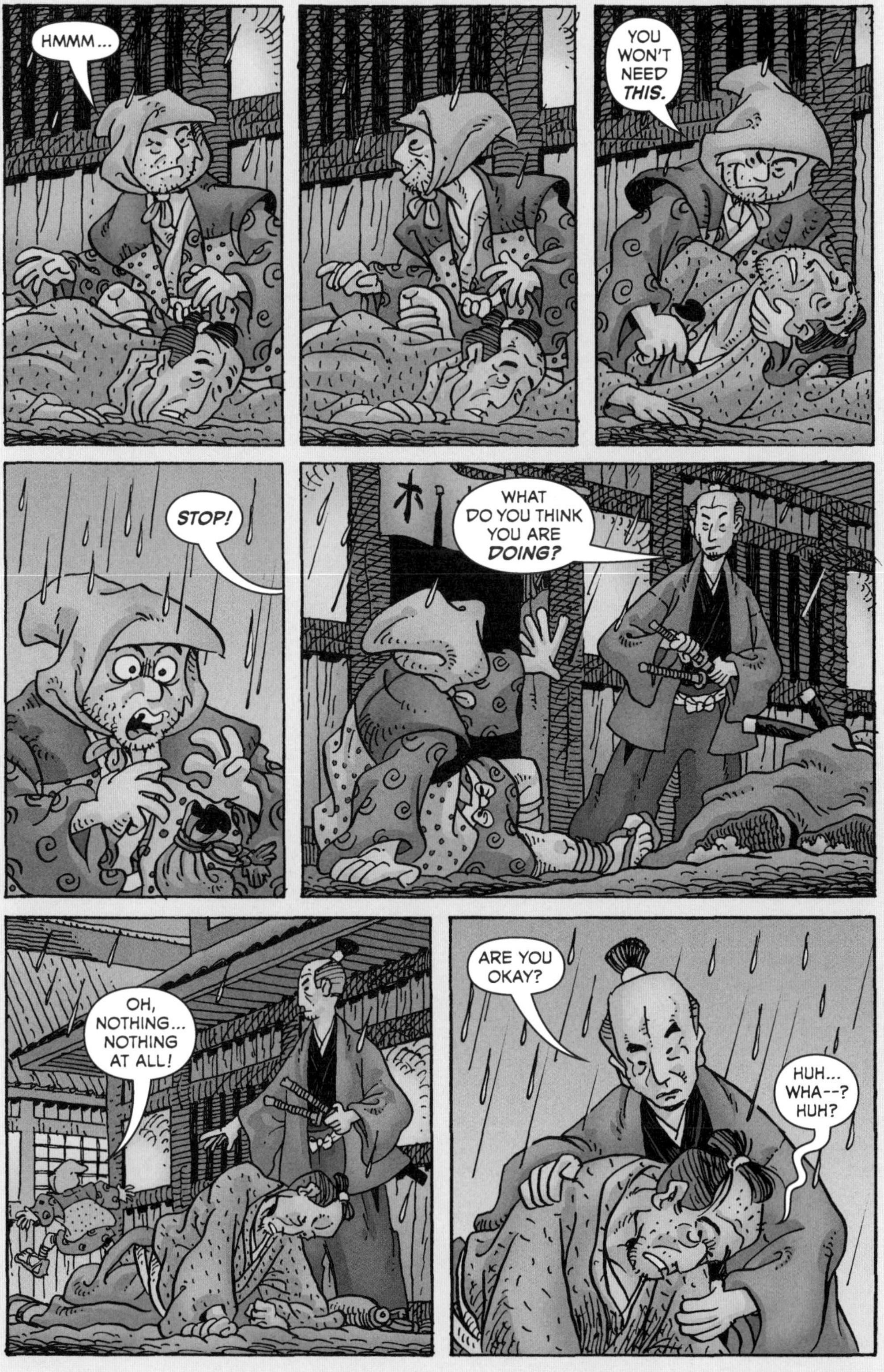
HMMM...
YOU WON'T NEED THIS.
STOP!
WHAT DO YOU THINK YOU ARE DOING?
OH, NOTHING... NOTHING AT ALL!
ARE YOU OKAY?
HUH... WHA--? HUH?

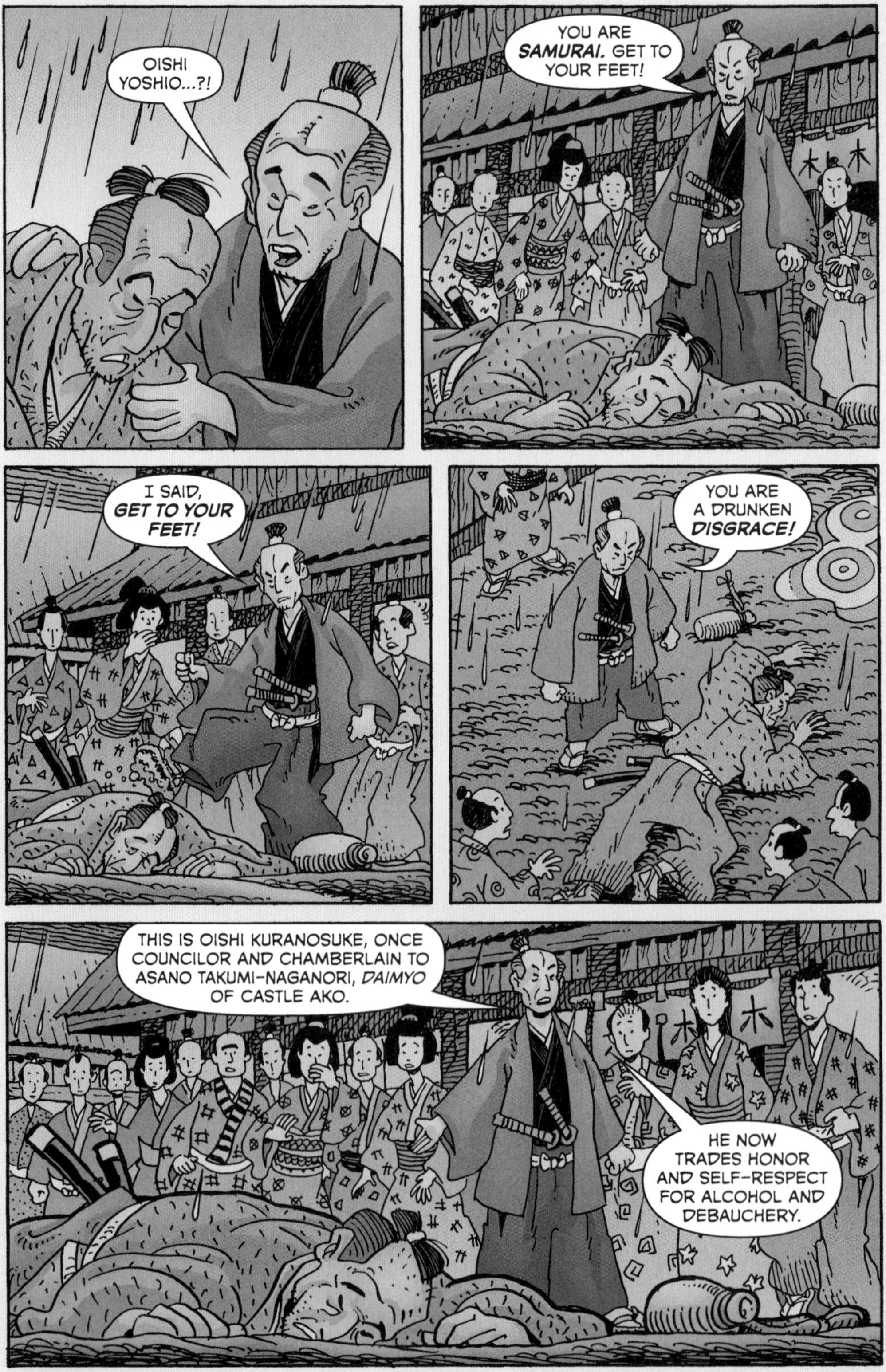
OISHI YOSHIO...?!
YOU ARE *SAMURAI.* GET TO YOUR FEET!
I SAID, *GET TO YOUR FEET!*
YOU ARE A DRUNKEN *DISGRACE!*
THIS IS OISHI KURANOSUKE, ONCE COUNCILOR AND CHAMBERLAIN TO ASANO TAKUMI-NAGANORI, *DAIMYO* OF CASTLE AKO.
HE NOW TRADES HONOR AND SELF-RESPECT FOR ALCOHOL AND DEBAUCHERY.

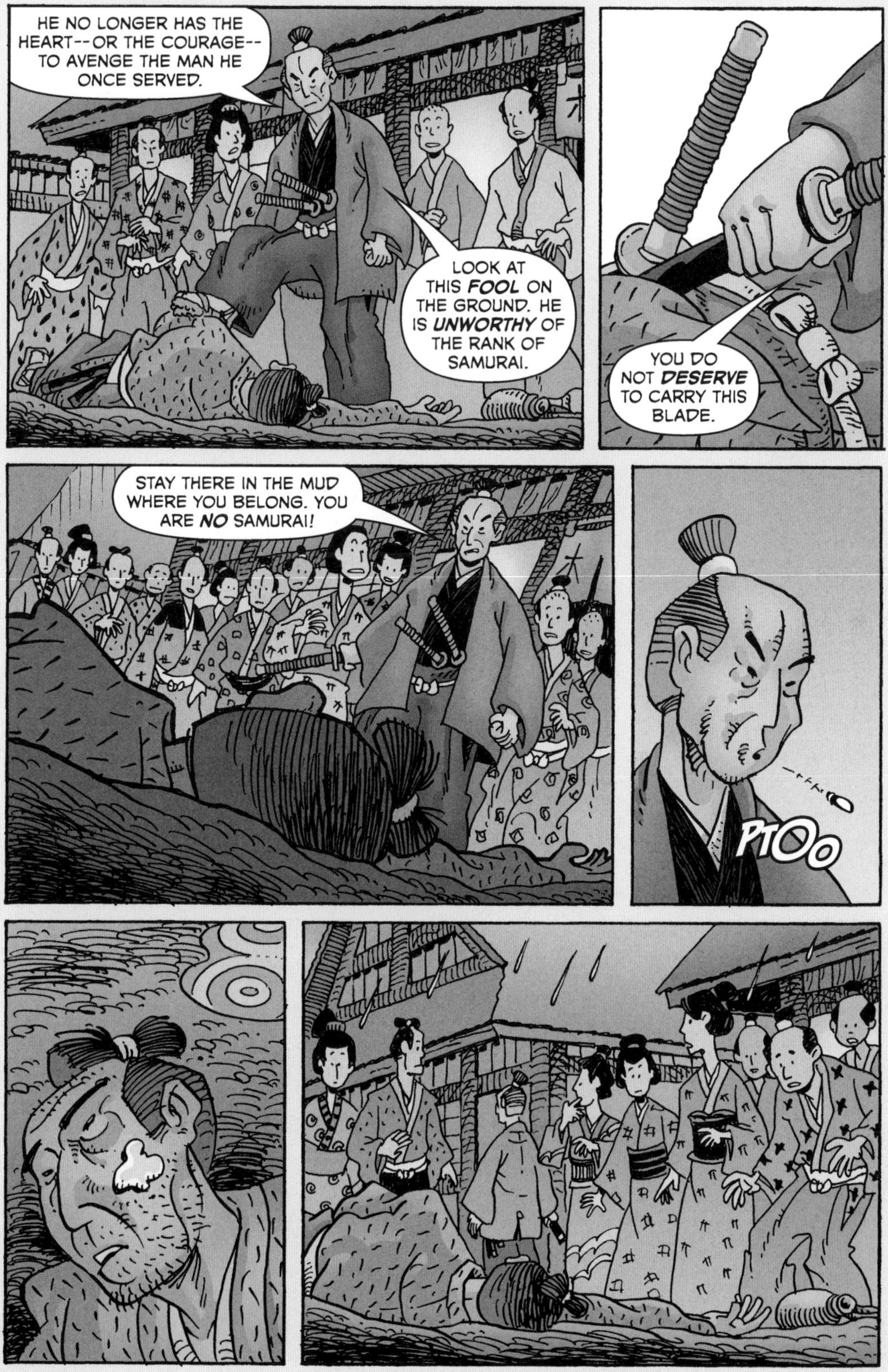
HE NO LONGER HAS THE HEART--OR THE COURAGE--TO AVENGE THE MAN HE ONCE SERVED.
LOOK AT THIS FOOL ON THE GROUND. HE IS UNWORTHY OF THE RANK OF SAMURAI.
YOU DO NOT DESERVE TO CARRY THIS BLADE.
STAY THERE IN THE MUD WHERE YOU BELONG. YOU ARE NO SAMURAI!
PTOO

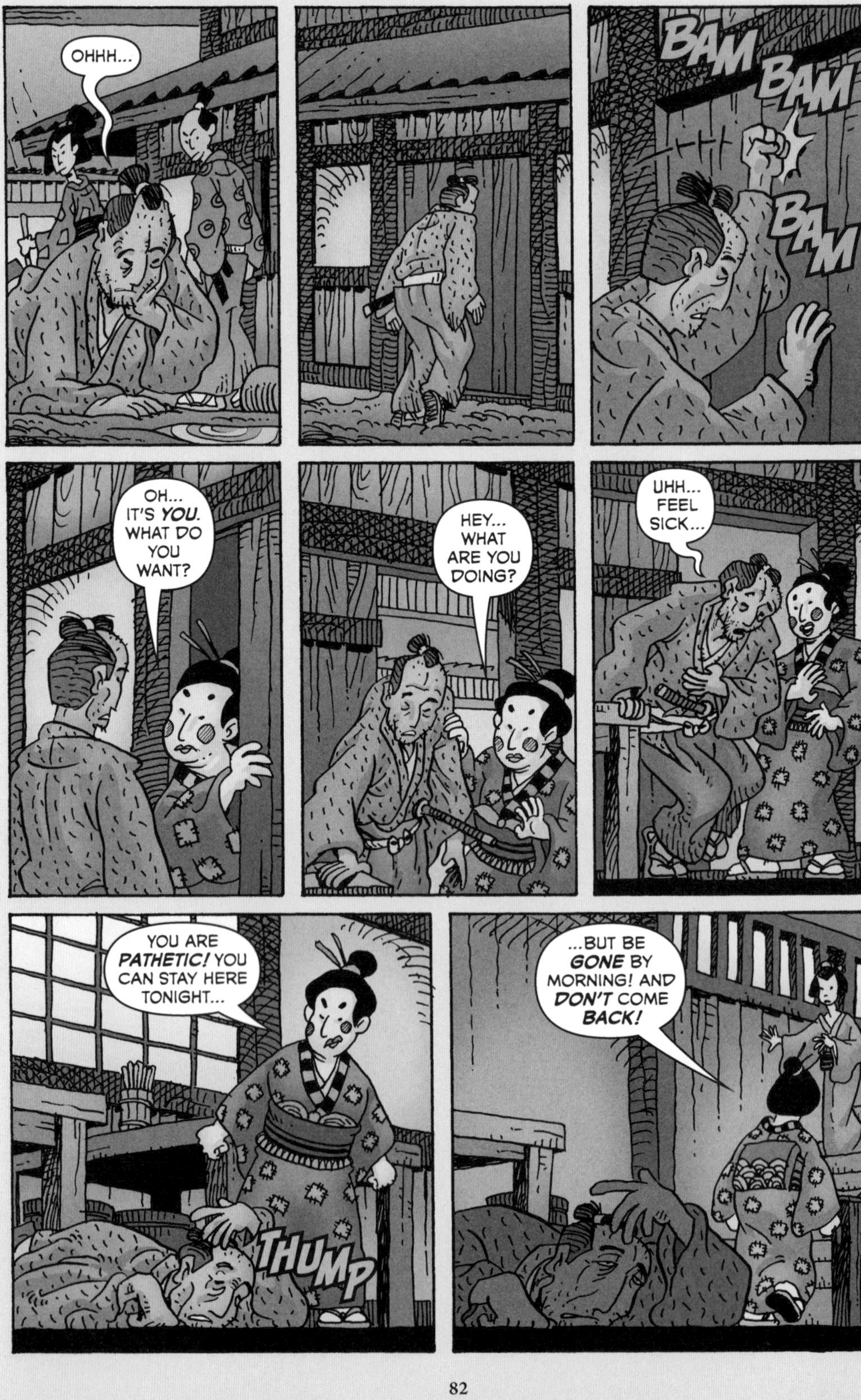
OHHH...
BAM
BAM
BAM
OH... IT'S YOU. WHAT DO YOU WANT?
HEY... WHAT ARE YOU DOING?
UHH... FEEL SICK...
YOU ARE PATHETIC! YOU CAN STAY HERE TONIGHT...
THUMP
...BUT BE GONE BY MORNING! AND DON'T COME BACK!

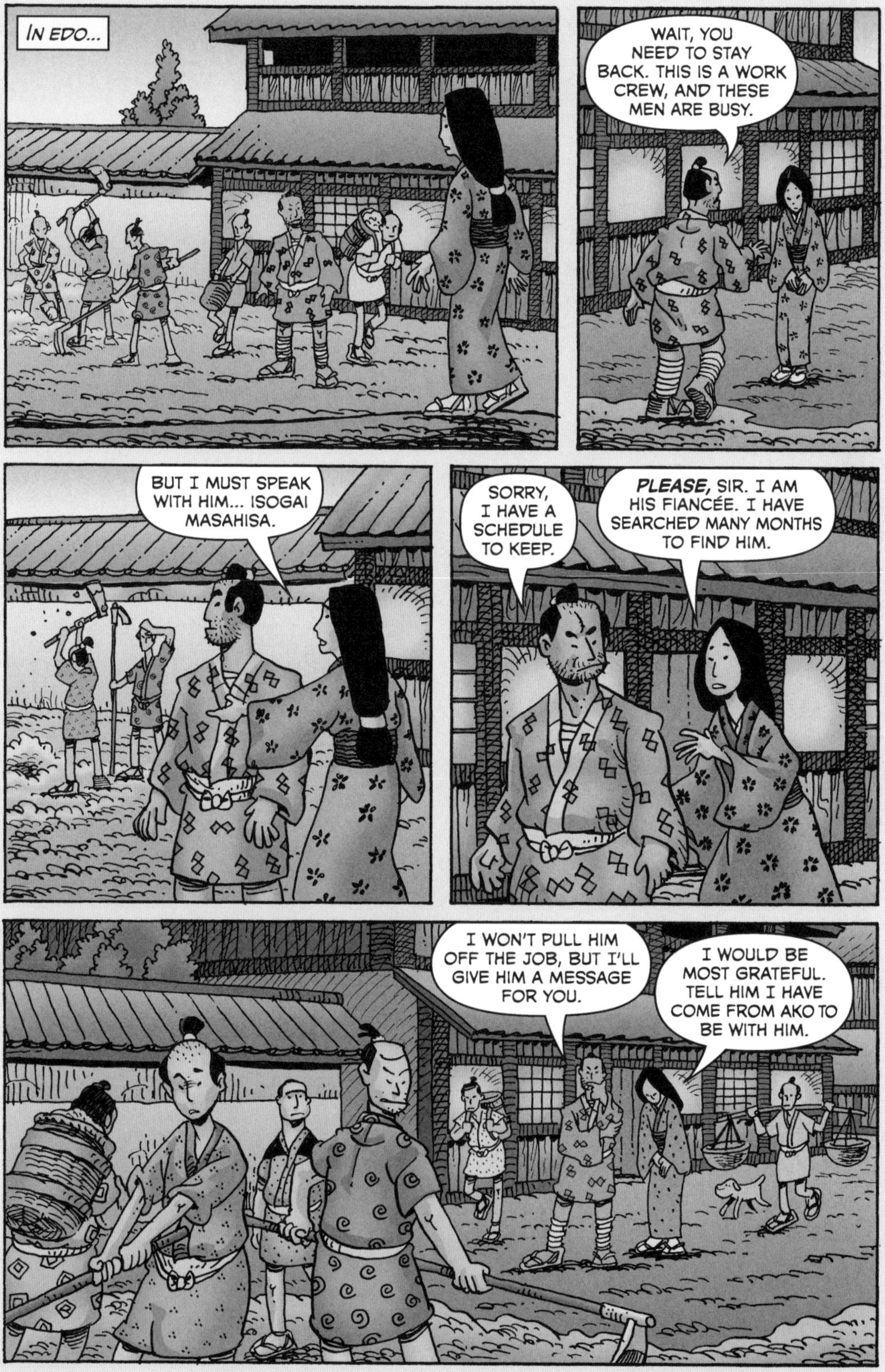
IN EDO...
WAIT, YOU NEED TO STAY BACK. THIS IS A WORK CREW, AND THESE MEN ARE BUSY.
BUT I MUST SPEAK WITH HIM... ISOGAI MASAHISA.
SORRY, I HAVE A SCHEDULE TO KEEP.
PLEASE, SIR. I AM HIS FIANCÉE. I HAVE SEARCHED MANY MONTHS TO FIND HIM.
I WON'T PULL HIM OFF THE JOB, BUT I'LL GIVE HIM A MESSAGE FOR YOU.
I WOULD BE MOST GRATEFUL. TELL HIM I HAVE COME FROM AKO TO BE WITH HIM.

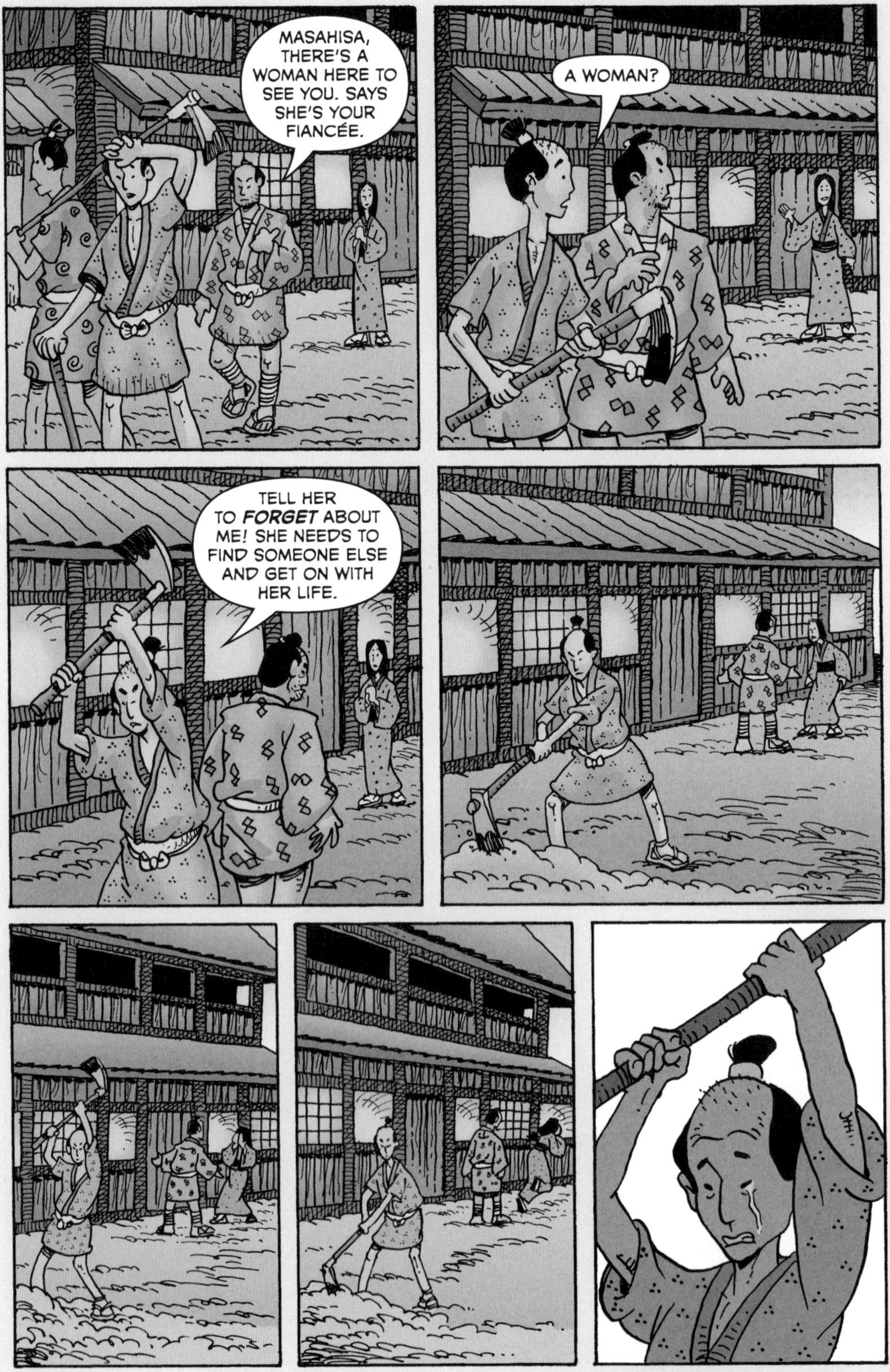
MASAHISA, THERE'S A WOMAN HERE TO SEE YOU. SAYS SHE'S YOUR FIANCÉE.
A WOMAN?
TELL HER TO **FORGET** ABOUT ME! SHE NEEDS TO FIND SOMEONE ELSE AND GET ON WITH HER LIFE.

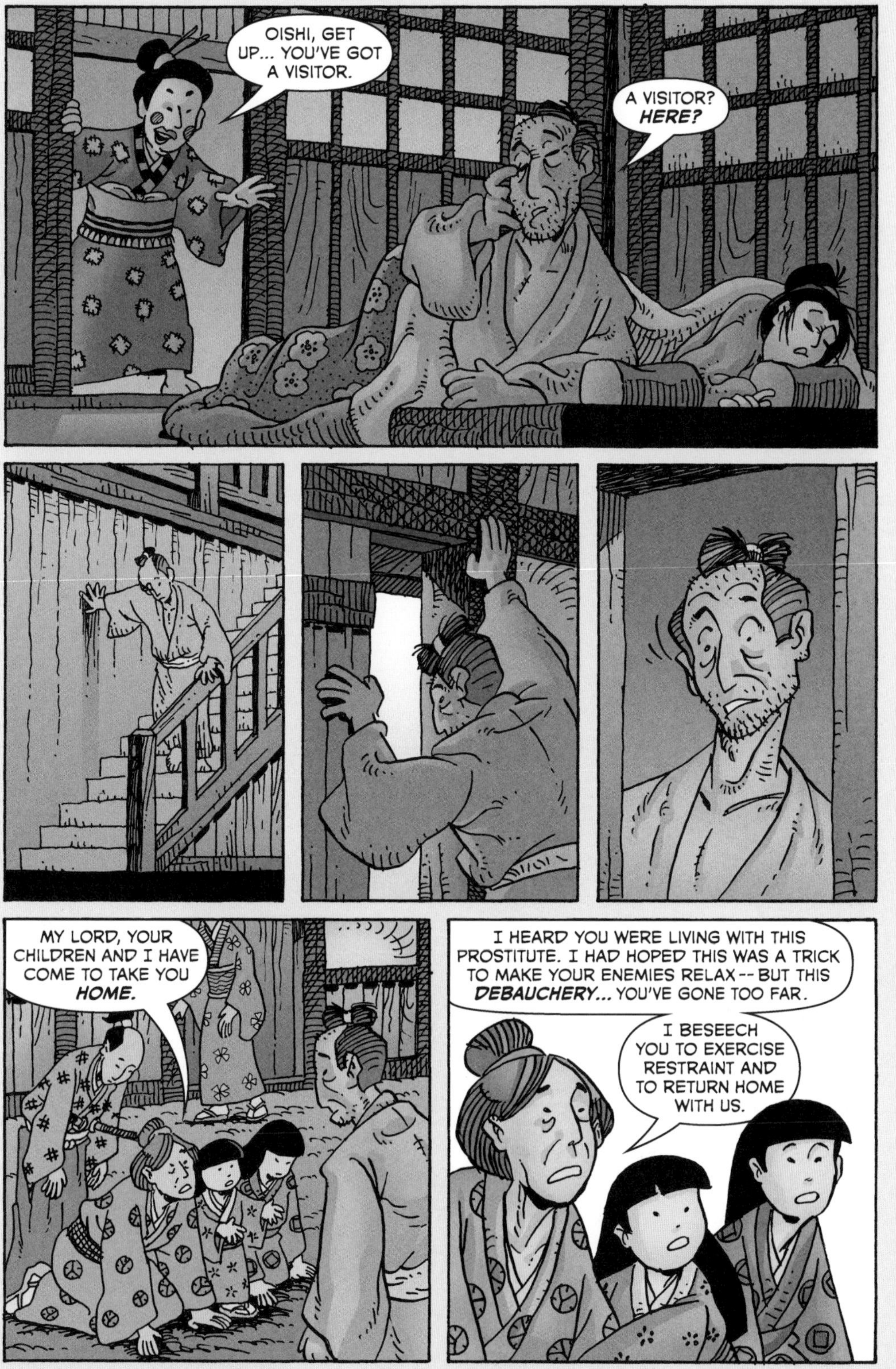
OISHI, GET UP... YOU'VE GOT A VISITOR.
A VISITOR? HERE?
MY LORD, YOUR CHILDREN AND I HAVE COME TO TAKE YOU HOME.
I HEARD YOU WERE LIVING WITH THIS PROSTITUTE. I HAD HOPED THIS WAS A TRICK TO MAKE YOUR ENEMIES RELAX -- BUT THIS DEBAUCHERY... YOU'VE GONE TOO FAR.
I BESEECH YOU TO EXERCISE RESTRAINT AND TO RETURN HOME WITH US.

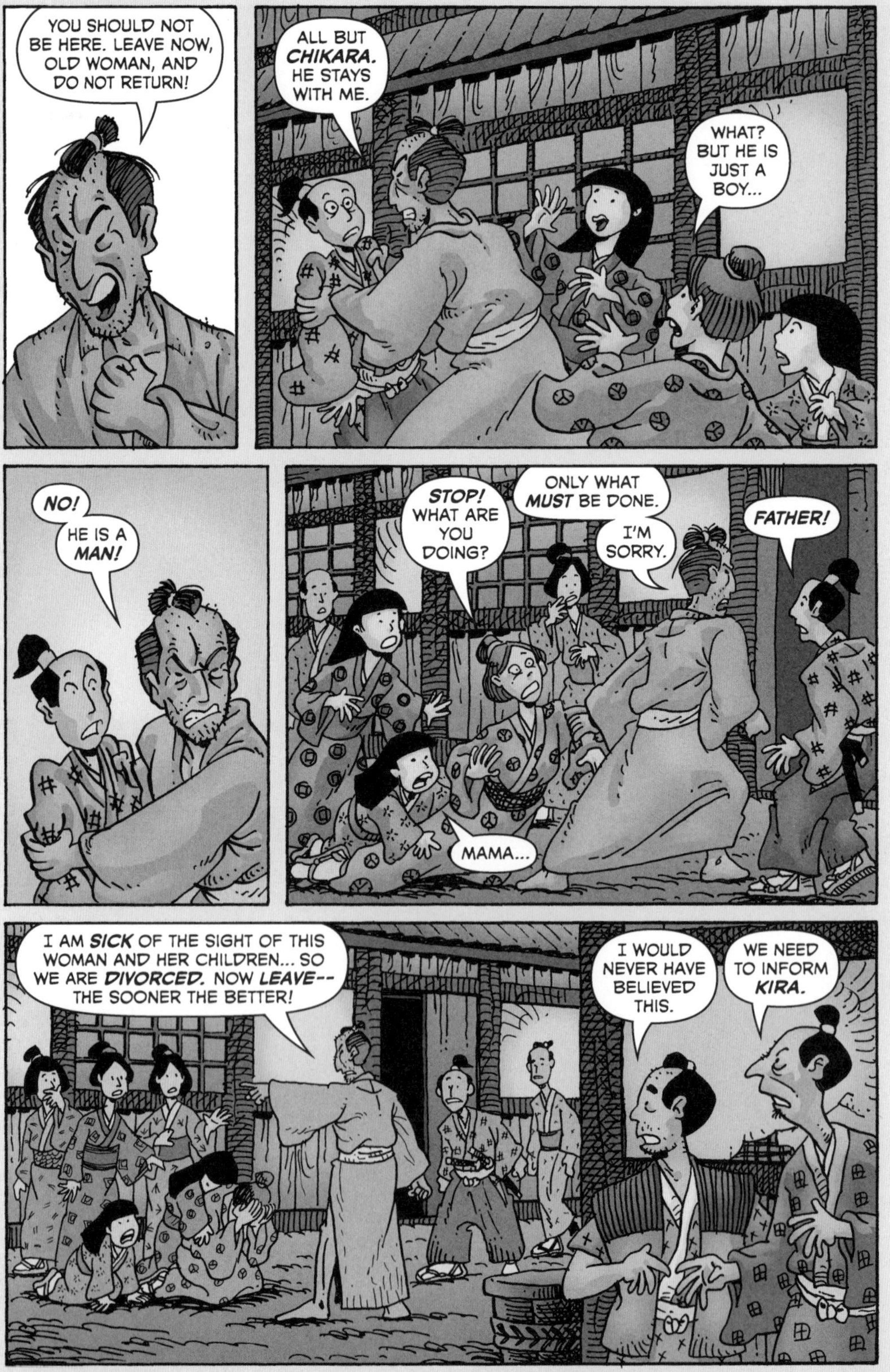
YOU SHOULD NOT BE HERE. LEAVE NOW, OLD WOMAN, AND DO NOT RETURN!
ALL BUT CHIKARA. HE STAYS WITH ME.
WHAT? BUT HE IS JUST A BOY...
NO!
HE IS A MAN!
STOP! WHAT ARE YOU DOING?
ONLY WHAT MUST BE DONE.
I'M SORRY.
FATHER!
MAMA...
I AM SICK OF THE SIGHT OF THIS WOMAN AND HER CHILDREN... SO WE ARE DIVORCED. NOW LEAVE-- THE SOONER THE BETTER!
I WOULD NEVER HAVE BELIEVED THIS.
WE NEED TO INFORM KIRA.

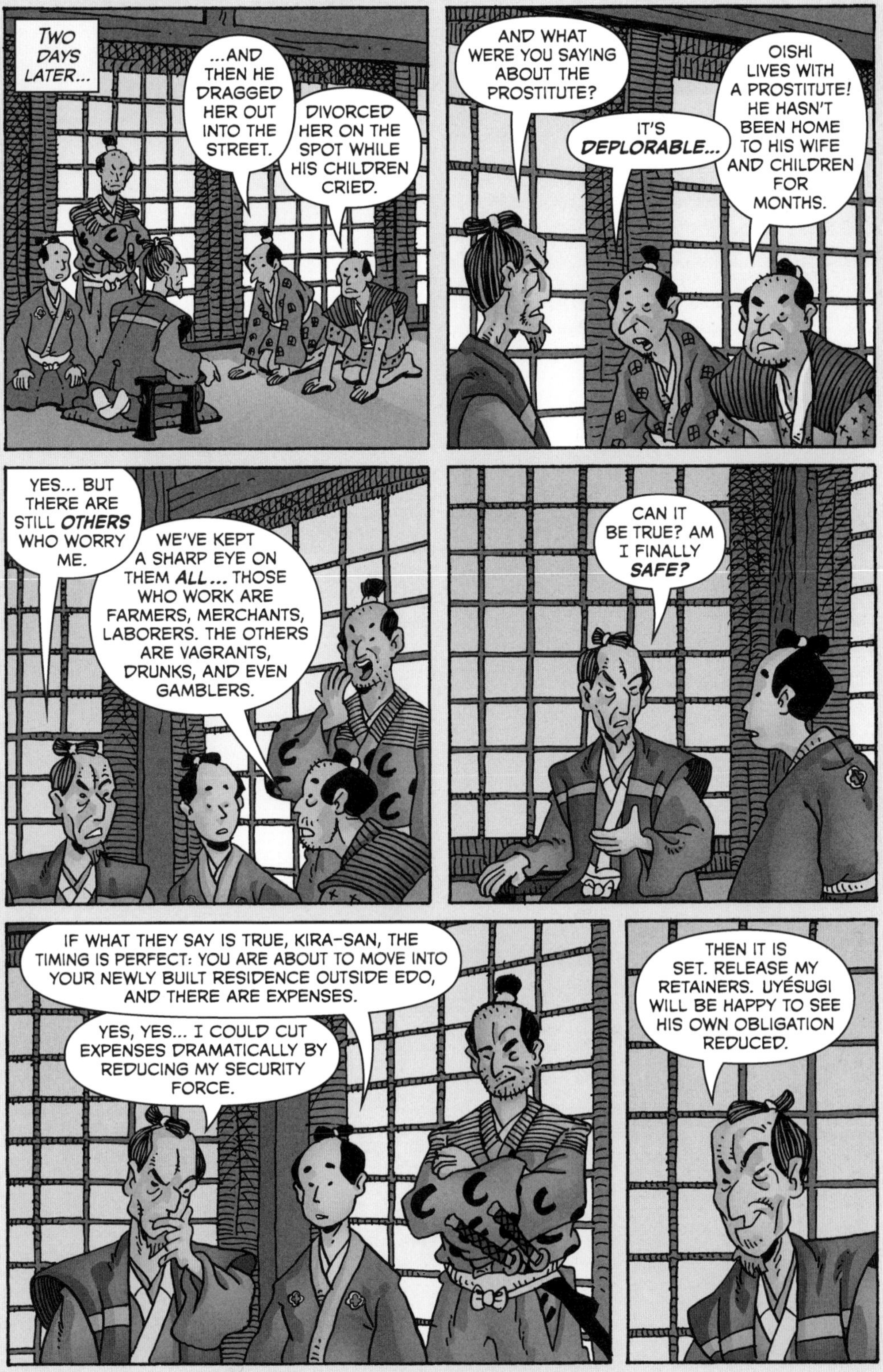
TWO DAYS LATER...
...AND THEN HE DRAGGED HER OUT INTO THE STREET.
DIVORCED HER ON THE SPOT WHILE HIS CHILDREN CRIED.
AND WHAT WERE YOU SAYING ABOUT THE PROSTITUTE?
IT'S *DEPLORABLE...*
OISHI LIVES WITH A PROSTITUTE! HE HASN'T BEEN HOME TO HIS WIFE AND CHILDREN FOR MONTHS.
YES... BUT THERE ARE STILL *OTHERS* WHO WORRY ME.
WE'VE KEPT A SHARP EYE ON THEM *ALL...* THOSE WHO WORK ARE FARMERS, MERCHANTS, LABORERS. THE OTHERS ARE VAGRANTS, DRUNKS, AND EVEN GAMBLERS.
CAN IT BE TRUE? AM I FINALLY *SAFE?*
IF WHAT THEY SAY IS TRUE, KIRA-SAN, THE TIMING IS PERFECT: YOU ARE ABOUT TO MOVE INTO YOUR NEWLY BUILT RESIDENCE OUTSIDE EDO, AND THERE ARE EXPENSES.
YES, YES... I COULD CUT EXPENSES DRAMATICALLY BY REDUCING MY SECURITY FORCE.
THEN IT IS SET. RELEASE MY RETAINERS. UYÉSUGI WILL BE HAPPY TO SEE HIS OWN OBLIGATION REDUCED.

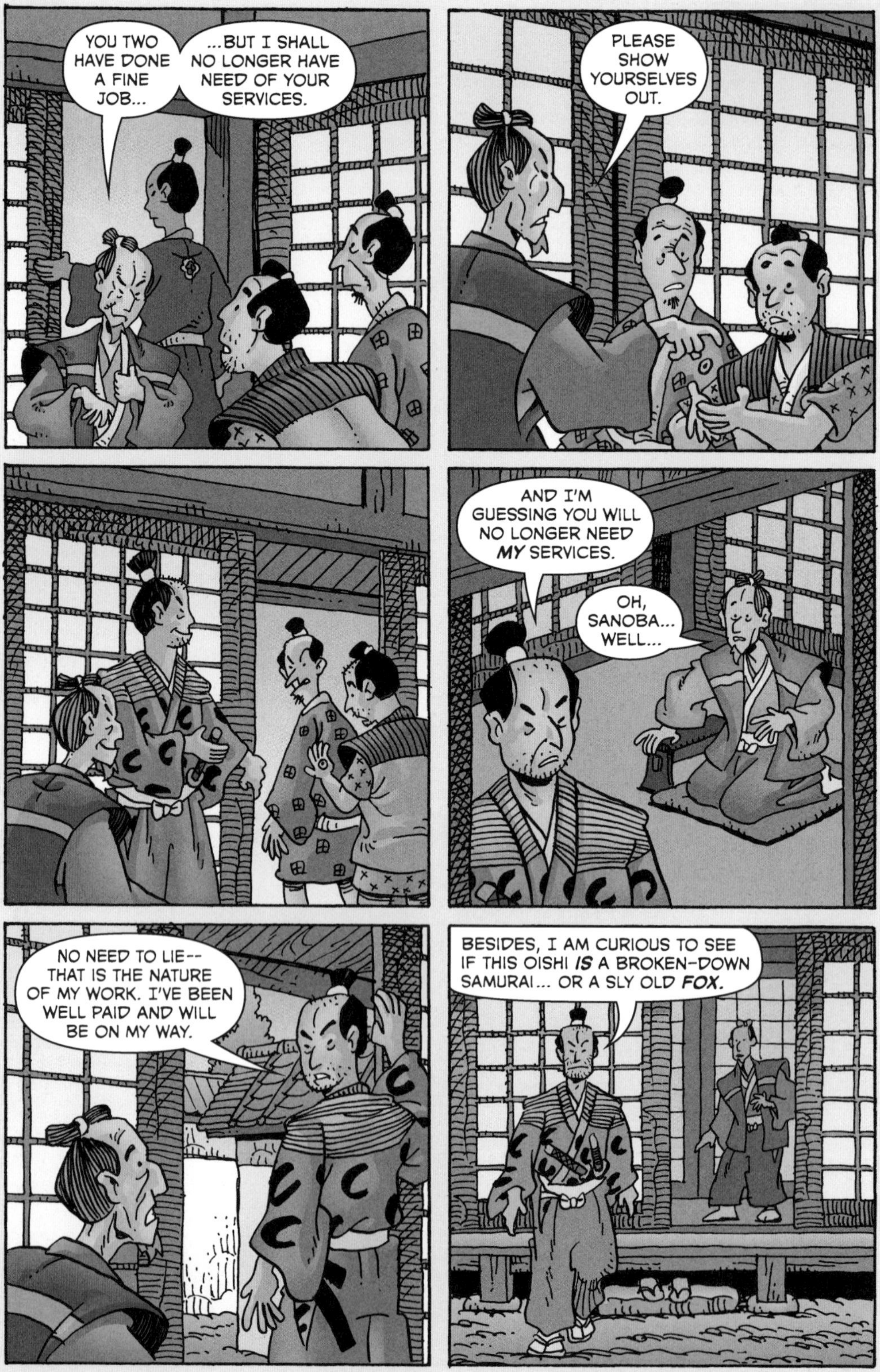

YOU TWO HAVE DONE A FINE JOB...
...BUT I SHALL NO LONGER HAVE NEED OF YOUR SERVICES.
PLEASE SHOW YOURSELVES OUT.
AND I'M GUESSING YOU WILL NO LONGER NEED MY SERVICES.
OH, SANOBA... WELL...
NO NEED TO LIE-- THAT IS THE NATURE OF MY WORK. I'VE BEEN WELL PAID AND WILL BE ON MY WAY.
BESIDES, I AM CURIOUS TO SEE IF THIS OISHI IS A BROKEN-DOWN SAMURAI... OR A SLY OLD FOX.

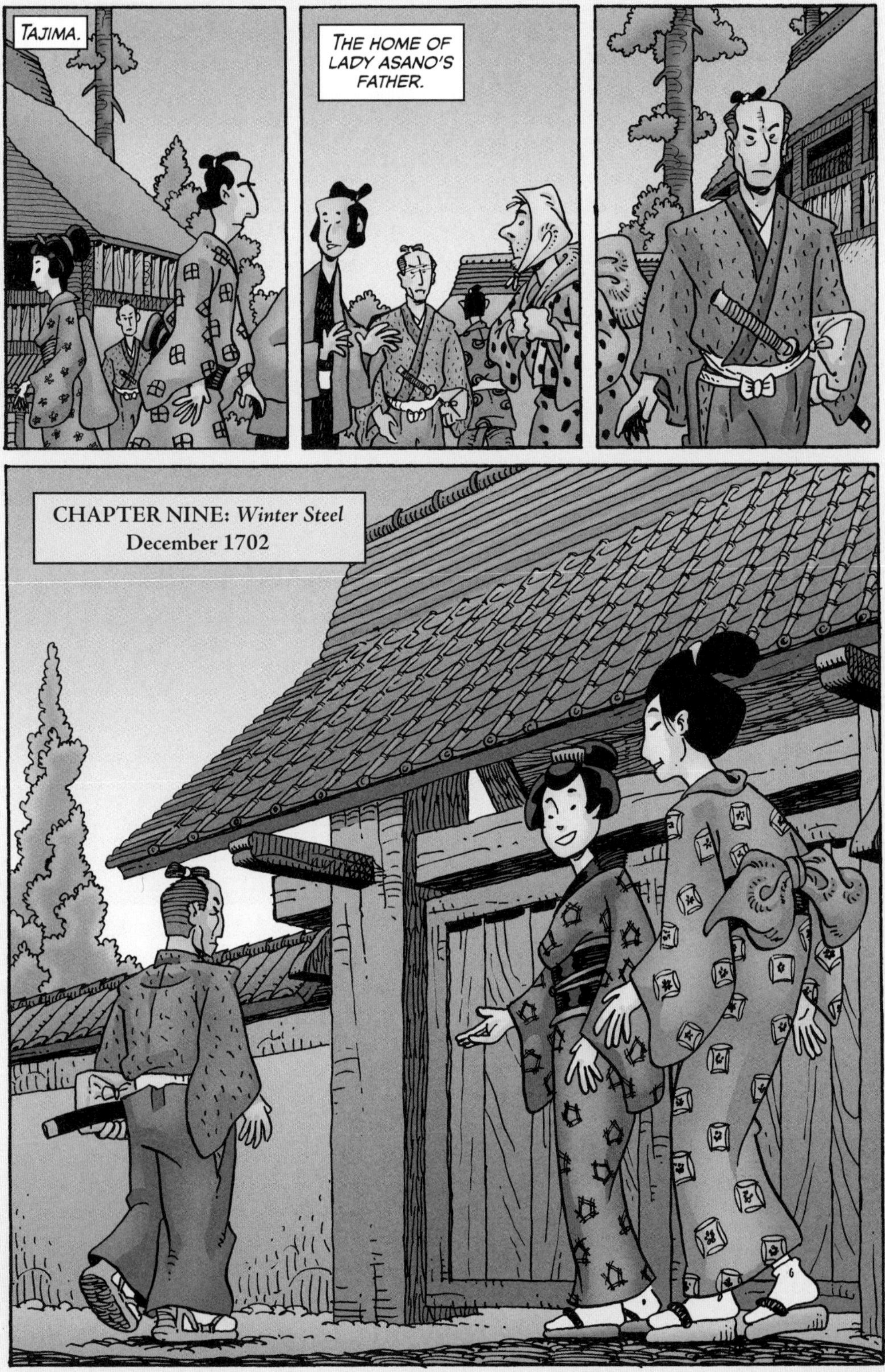
TAJIMA.
THE HOME OF LADY ASANO'S FATHER.
CHAPTER NINE: *Winter Steel*
December 1702

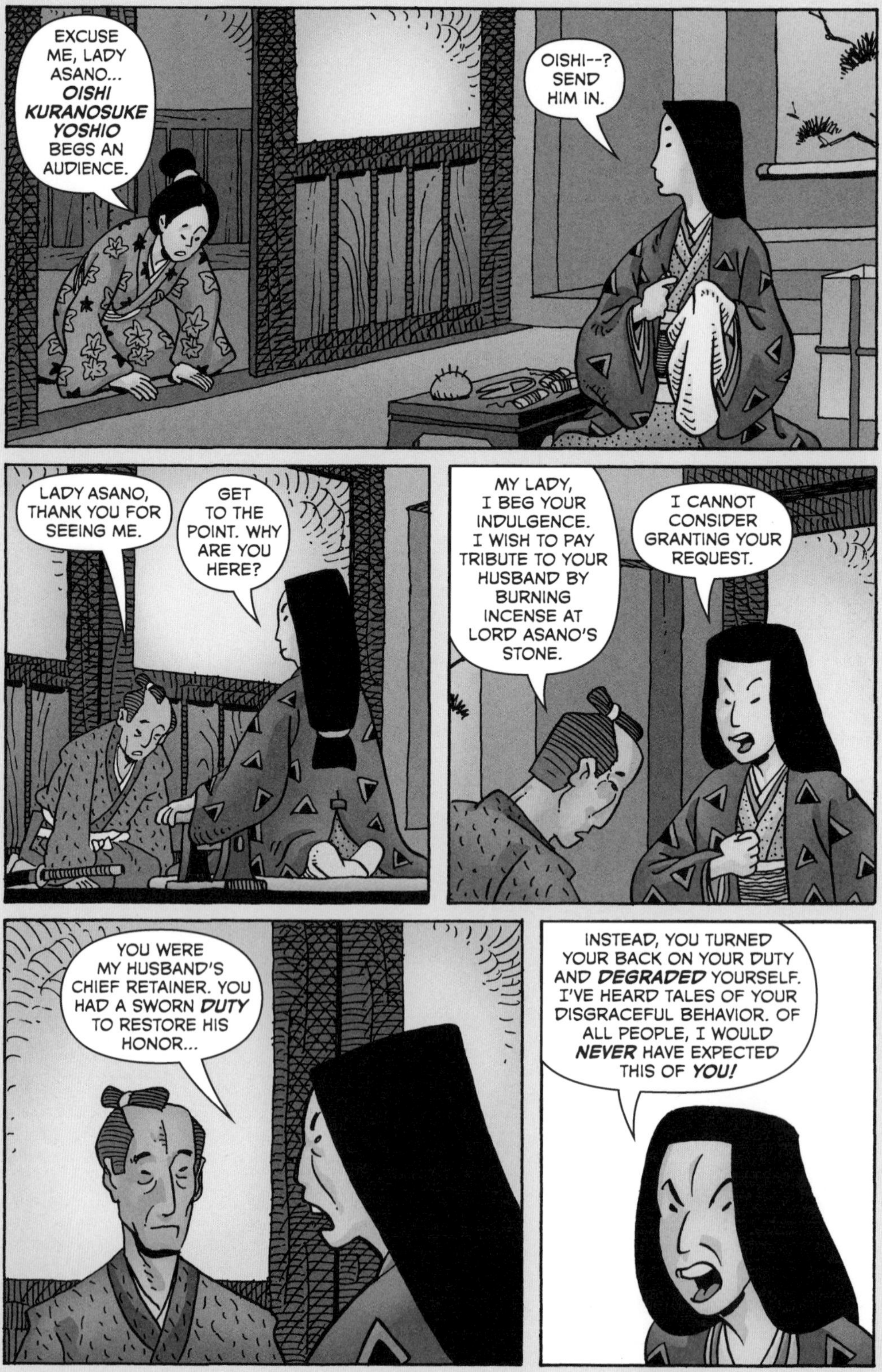
EXCUSE ME, LADY ASANO... OISHI KURANOSUKE YOSHIO BEGS AN AUDIENCE.
OISHI--? SEND HIM IN.
LADY ASANO, THANK YOU FOR SEEING ME.
GET TO THE POINT. WHY ARE YOU HERE?
MY LADY, I BEG YOUR INDULGENCE. I WISH TO PAY TRIBUTE TO YOUR HUSBAND BY BURNING INCENSE AT LORD ASANO'S STONE.
I CANNOT CONSIDER GRANTING YOUR REQUEST.
YOU WERE MY HUSBAND'S CHIEF RETAINER. YOU HAD A SWORN DUTY TO RESTORE HIS HONOR...
INSTEAD, YOU TURNED YOUR BACK ON YOUR DUTY AND DEGRADED YOURSELF. I'VE HEARD TALES OF YOUR DISGRACEFUL BEHAVIOR. OF ALL PEOPLE, I WOULD NEVER HAVE EXPECTED THIS OF YOU!

YOU ARE A *COWARD* AND A FAITHLESS MAN, OISHI KURANOSUKE YOSHIO... I WILL NEVER ALLOW YOU TO DISHONOR MY HUSBAND'S *STONE* THROUGH A WORTHLESS, INSINCERE SHOW OF "RESPECT."

MOST DISAPPOINTING OF ALL... ...YOU WERE HIS *FRIEND.*

NOW *LEAVE* MY SIGHT!

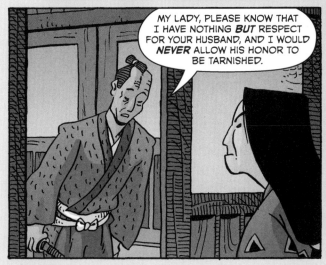

MY LADY, PLEASE KNOW THAT I HAVE NOTHING *BUT* RESPECT FOR YOUR HUSBAND, AND I WOULD *NEVER* ALLOW HIS HONOR TO BE TARNISHED.

91

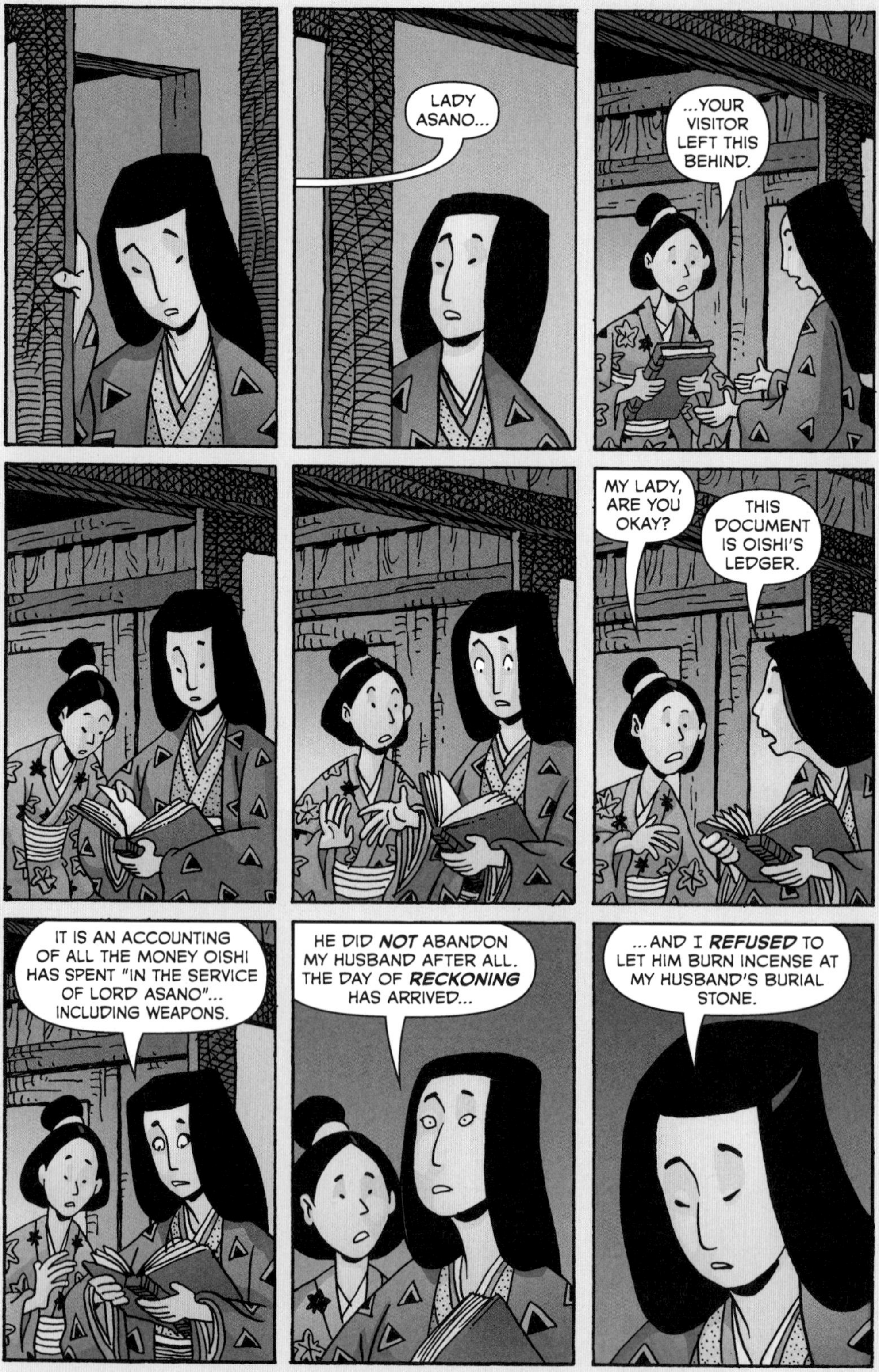
LADY ASANO...
...YOUR VISITOR LEFT THIS BEHIND.
MY LADY, ARE YOU OKAY?
THIS DOCUMENT IS OISHI'S LEDGER.
IT IS AN ACCOUNTING OF ALL THE MONEY OISHI HAS SPENT "IN THE SERVICE OF LORD ASANO"... INCLUDING WEAPONS.
HE DID NOT ABANDON MY HUSBAND AFTER ALL. THE DAY OF RECKONING HAS ARRIVED...
...AND I REFUSED TO LET HIM BURN INCENSE AT MY HUSBAND'S BURIAL STONE.

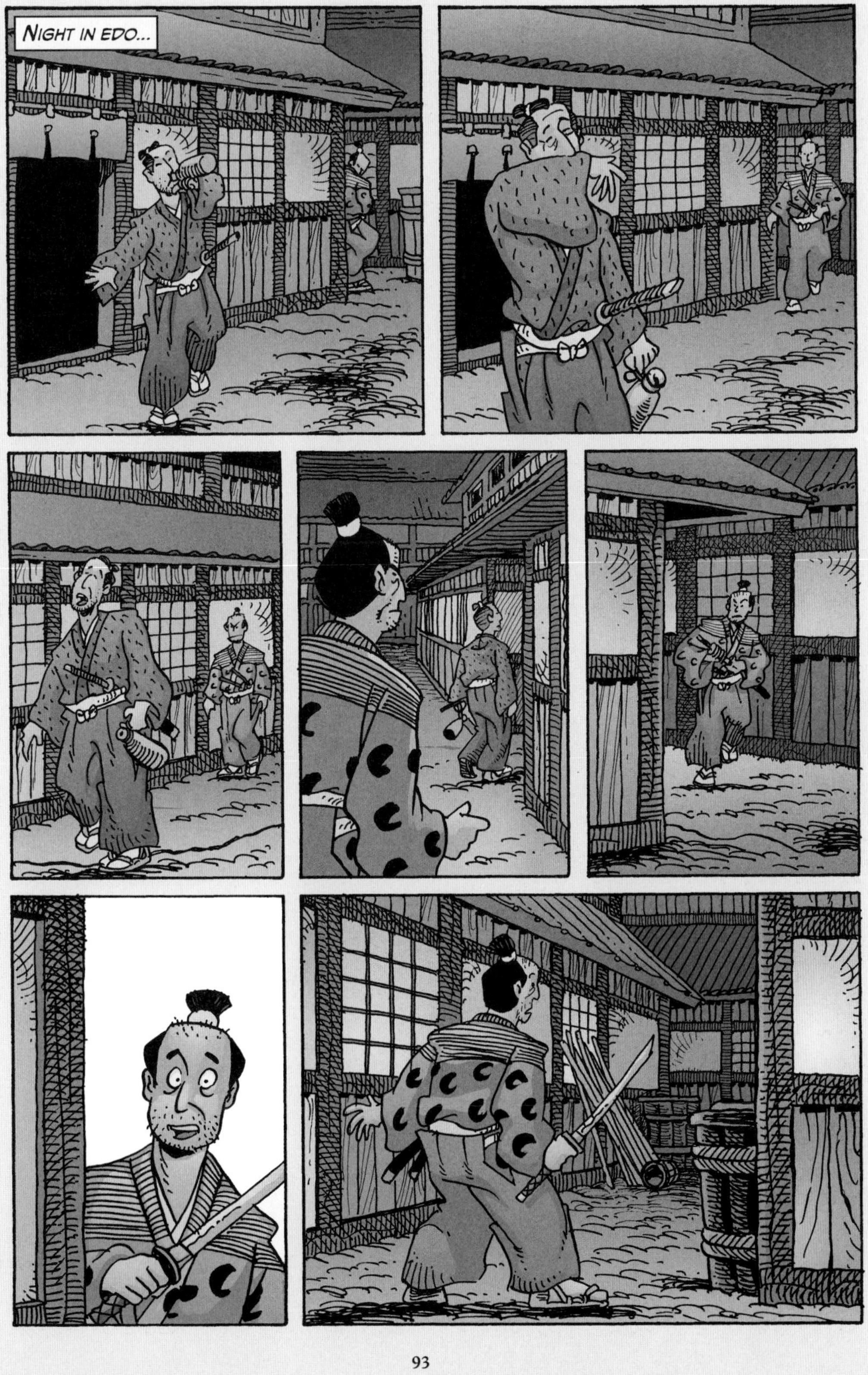
NIGHT IN EDO...

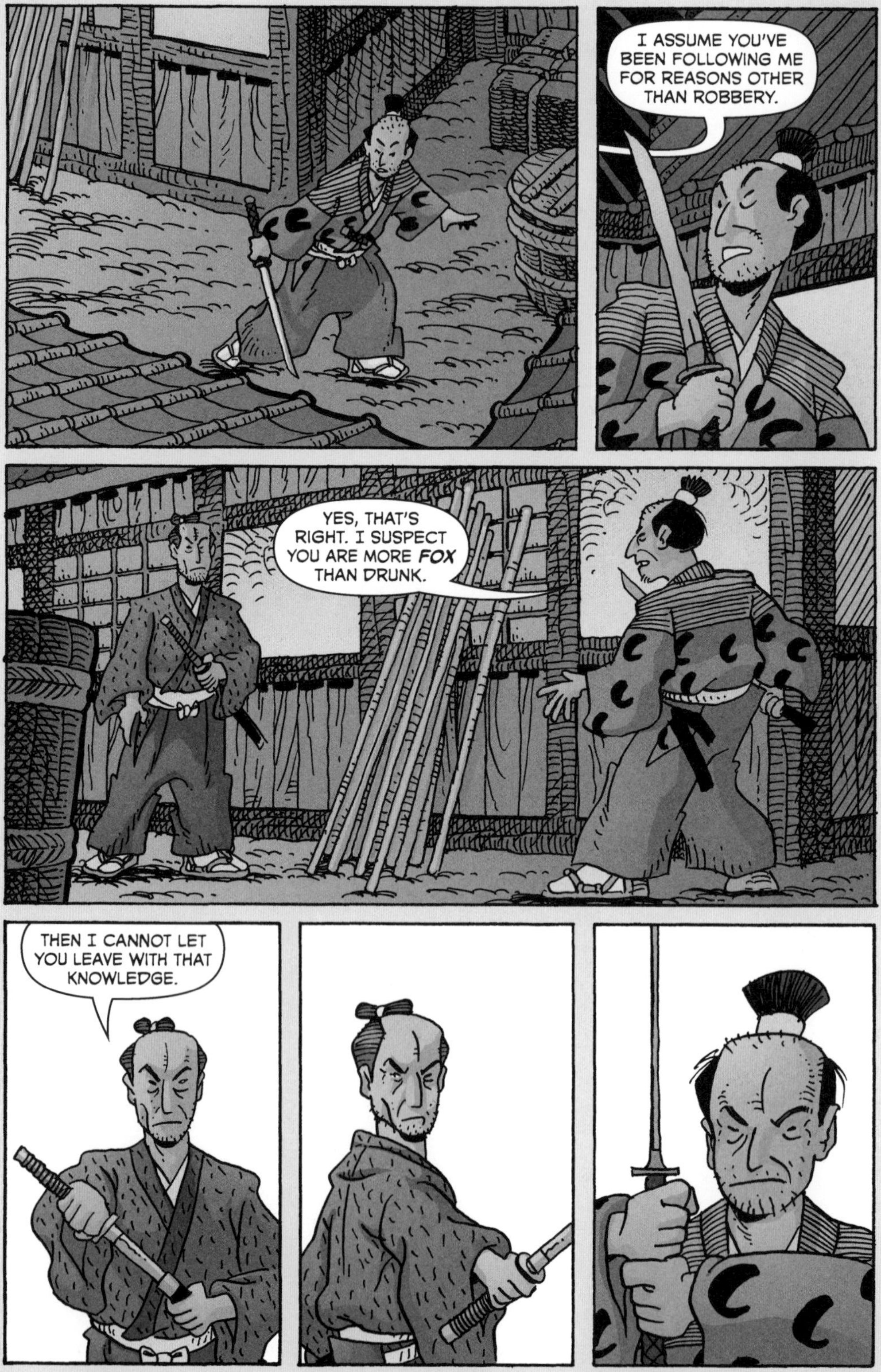
I ASSUME YOU'VE BEEN FOLLOWING ME FOR REASONS OTHER THAN ROBBERY.
YES, THAT'S RIGHT. I SUSPECT YOU ARE MORE *FOX* THAN DRUNK.
THEN I CANNOT LET YOU LEAVE WITH THAT KNOWLEDGE.

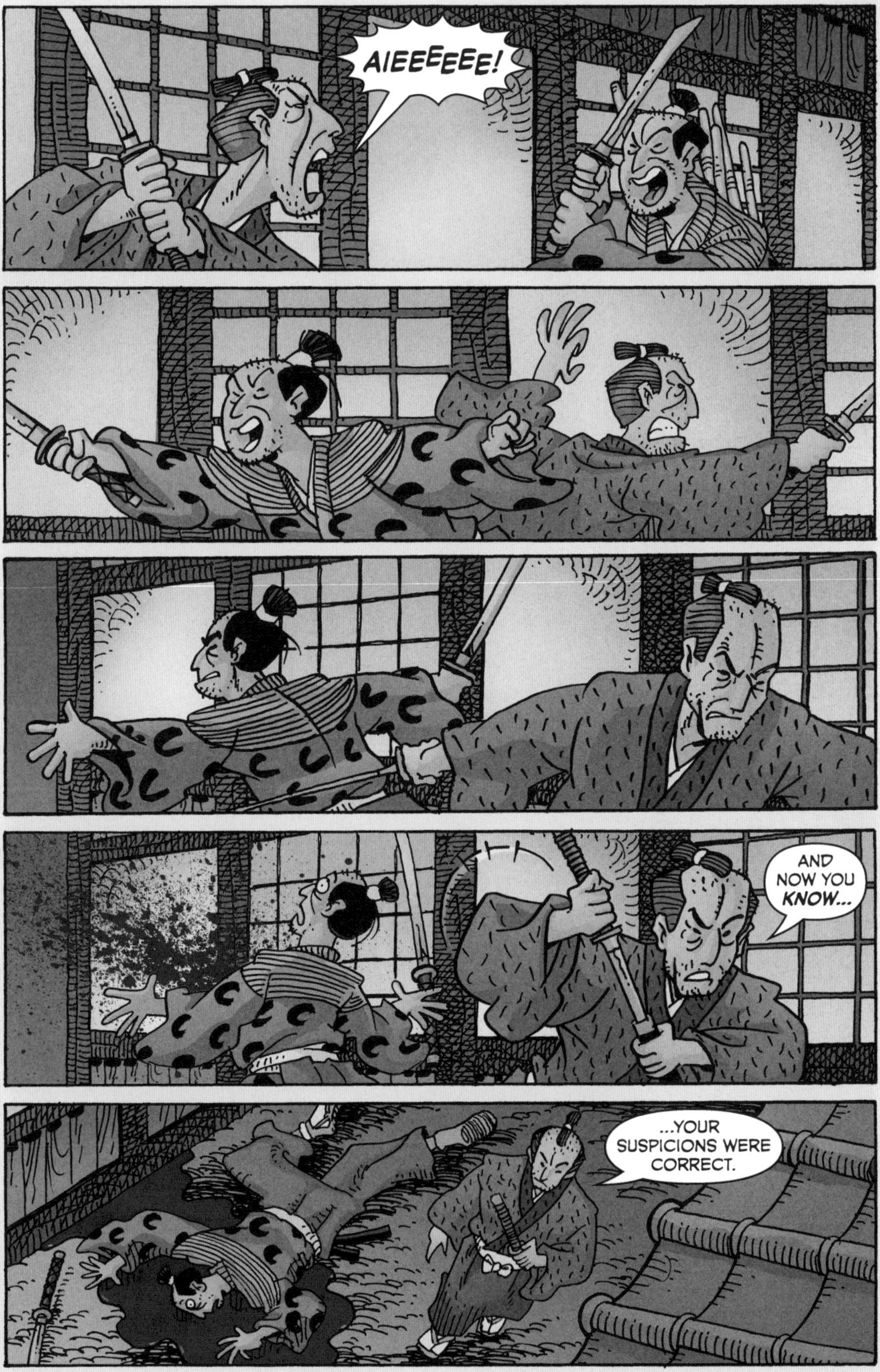
AIEEEEEE!
AND NOW YOU KNOW...
...YOUR SUSPICIONS WERE CORRECT.

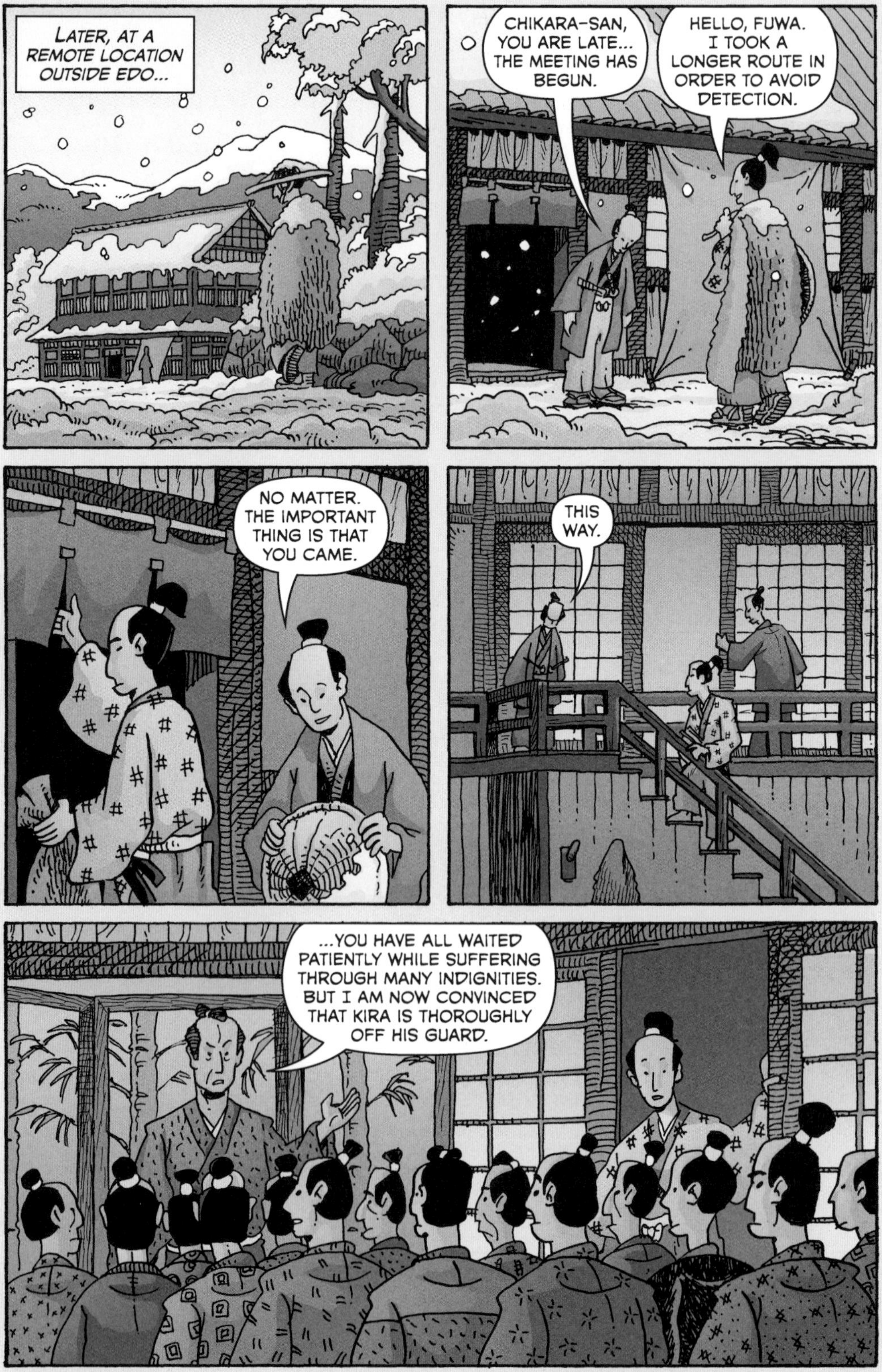
LATER, AT A REMOTE LOCATION OUTSIDE EDO...
CHIKARA-SAN, YOU ARE LATE... THE MEETING HAS BEGUN.
HELLO, FUWA. I TOOK A LONGER ROUTE IN ORDER TO AVOID DETECTION.
NO MATTER. THE IMPORTANT THING IS THAT YOU CAME.
THIS WAY.
...YOU HAVE ALL WAITED PATIENTLY WHILE SUFFERING THROUGH MANY INDIGNITIES. BUT I AM NOW CONVINCED THAT KIRA IS THOROUGHLY OFF HIS GUARD.

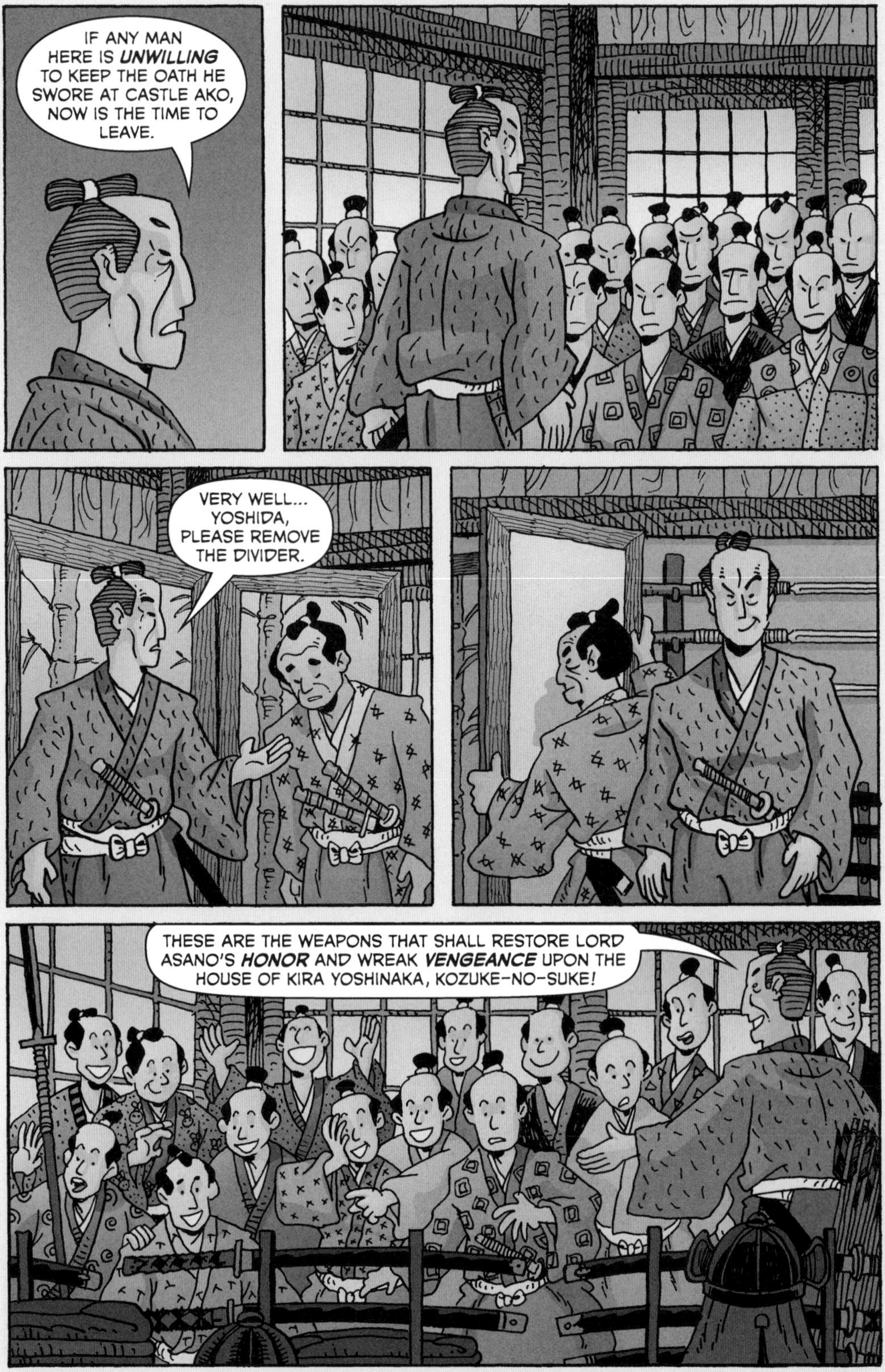
IF ANY MAN HERE IS ***UNWILLING*** TO KEEP THE OATH HE SWORE AT CASTLE AKO, NOW IS THE TIME TO LEAVE.
VERY WELL... YOSHIDA, PLEASE REMOVE THE DIVIDER.
THESE ARE THE WEAPONS THAT SHALL RESTORE LORD ASANO'S ***HONOR*** AND WREAK ***VENGEANCE*** UPON THE HOUSE OF KIRA YOSHINAKA, KOZUKE-NO-SUKE!

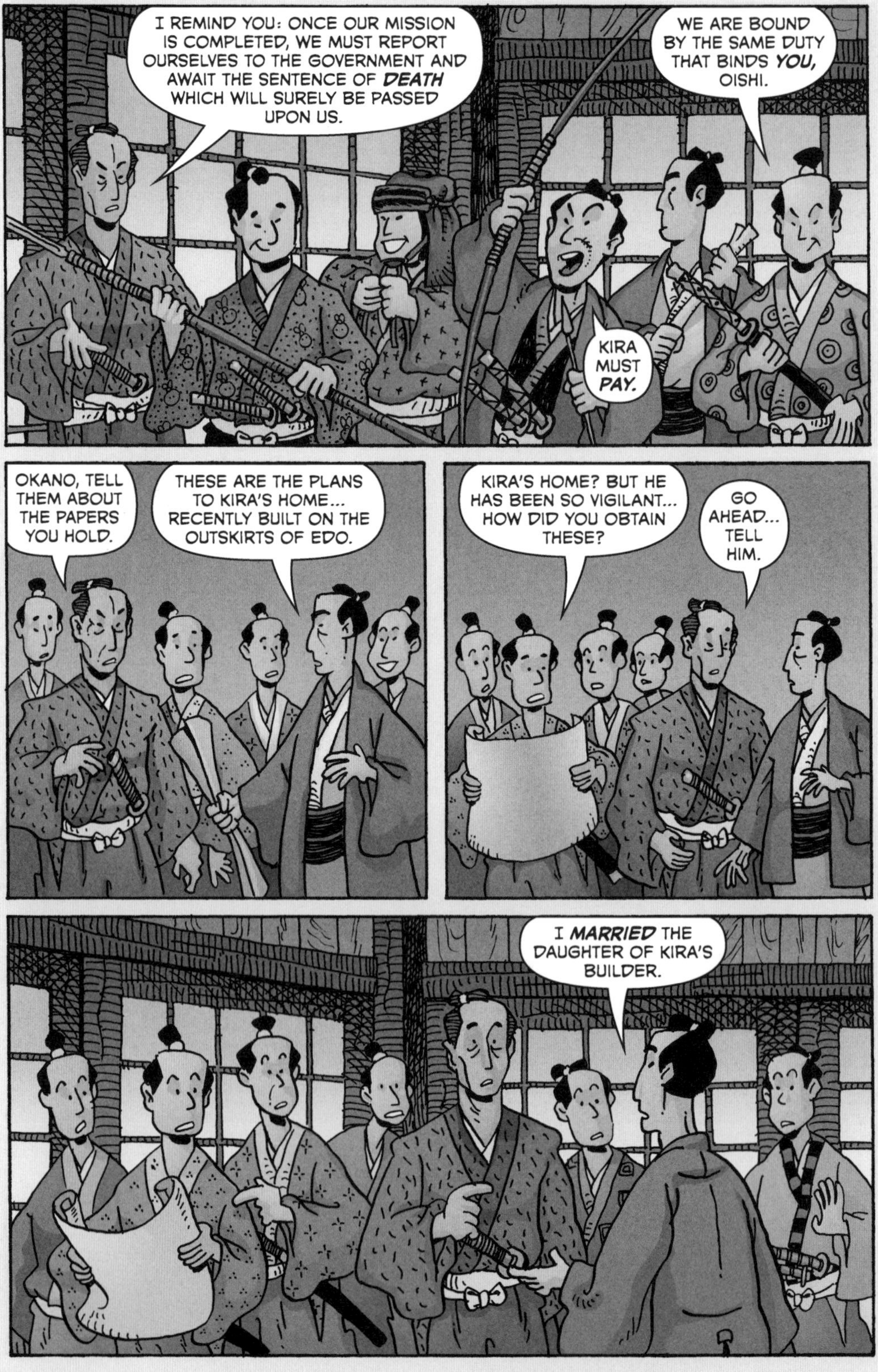

I REMIND YOU: ONCE OUR MISSION IS COMPLETED, WE MUST REPORT OURSELVES TO THE GOVERNMENT AND AWAIT THE SENTENCE OF *DEATH* WHICH WILL SURELY BE PASSED UPON US.
WE ARE BOUND BY THE SAME DUTY THAT BINDS *YOU,* OISHI.
KIRA MUST *PAY.*
OKANO, TELL THEM ABOUT THE PAPERS YOU HOLD.
THESE ARE THE PLANS TO KIRA'S HOME... RECENTLY BUILT ON THE OUTSKIRTS OF EDO.
KIRA'S HOME? BUT HE HAS BEEN SO VIGILANT... HOW DID YOU OBTAIN THESE?
GO AHEAD... TELL HIM.
I *MARRIED* THE DAUGHTER OF KIRA'S BUILDER.

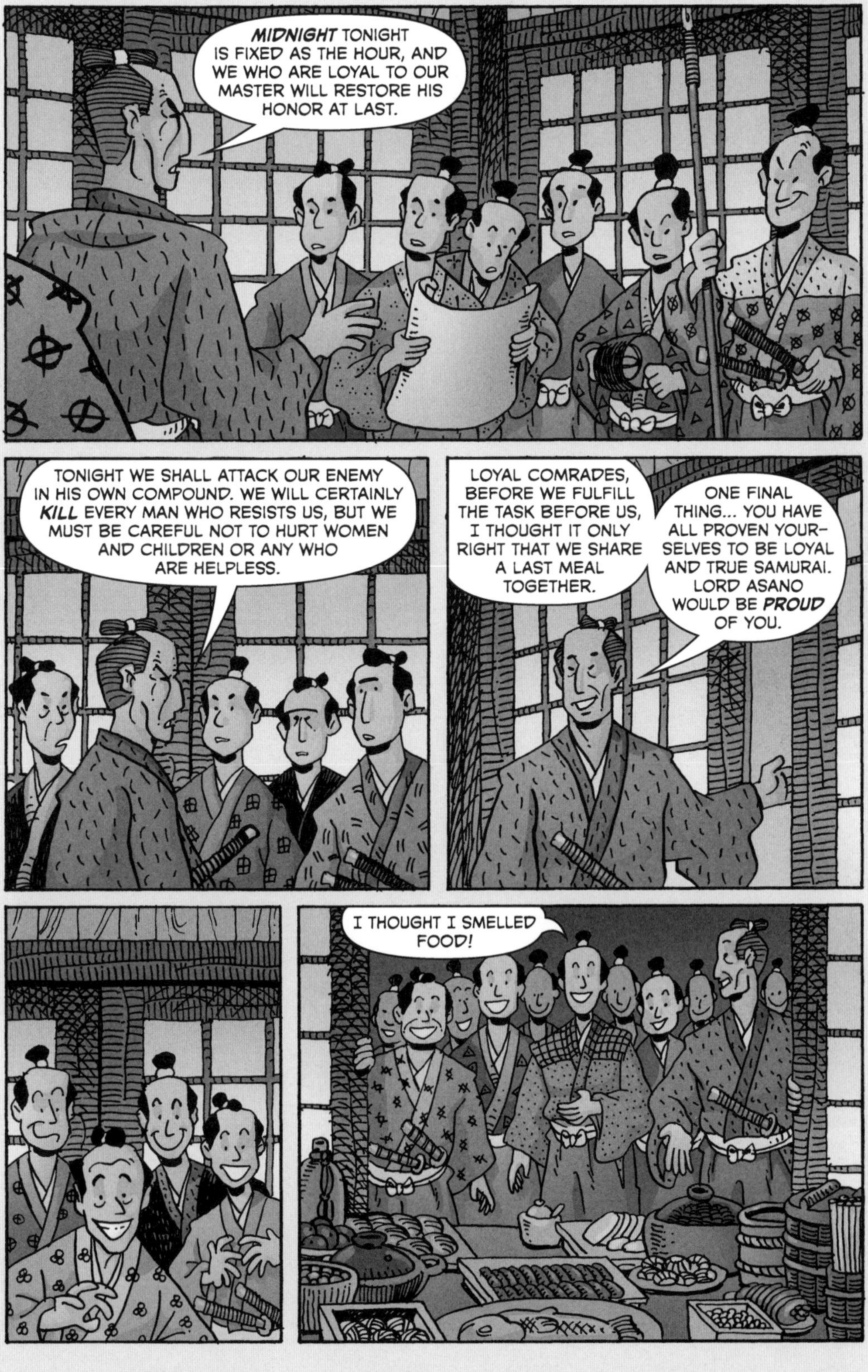
MIDNIGHT TONIGHT IS FIXED AS THE HOUR, AND WE WHO ARE LOYAL TO OUR MASTER WILL RESTORE HIS HONOR AT LAST.
TONIGHT WE SHALL ATTACK OUR ENEMY IN HIS OWN COMPOUND. WE WILL CERTAINLY KILL EVERY MAN WHO RESISTS US, BUT WE MUST BE CAREFUL NOT TO HURT WOMEN AND CHILDREN OR ANY WHO ARE HELPLESS.
LOYAL COMRADES, BEFORE WE FULFILL THE TASK BEFORE US, I THOUGHT IT ONLY RIGHT THAT WE SHARE A LAST MEAL TOGETHER.
ONE FINAL THING... YOU HAVE ALL PROVEN YOURSELVES TO BE LOYAL AND TRUE SAMURAI. LORD ASANO WOULD BE PROUD OF YOU.
I THOUGHT I SMELLED FOOD!

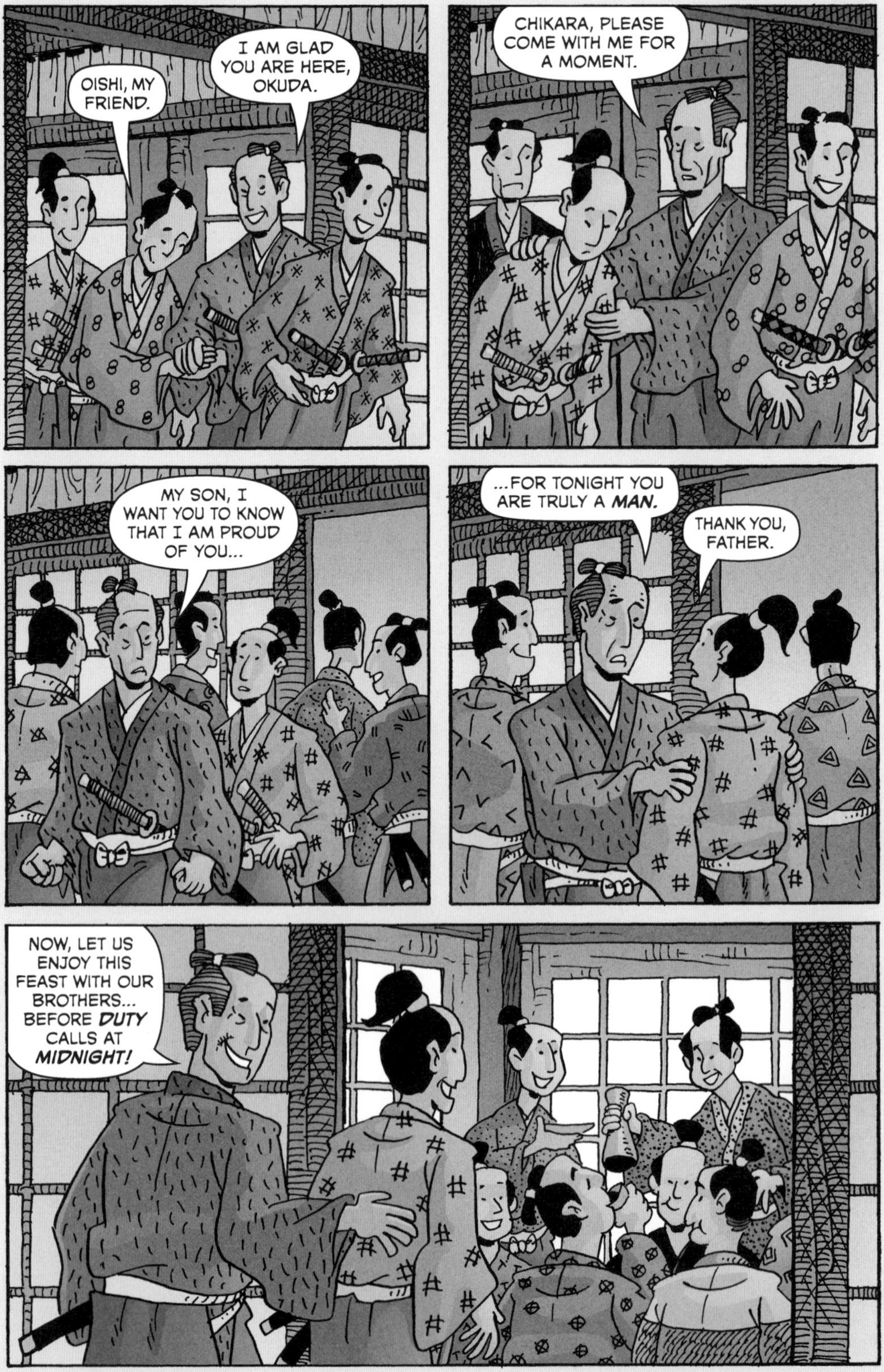
OISHI, MY FRIEND.
I AM GLAD YOU ARE HERE, OKUDA.
CHIKARA, PLEASE COME WITH ME FOR A MOMENT.
MY SON, I WANT YOU TO KNOW THAT I AM PROUD OF YOU...
...FOR TONIGHT YOU ARE TRULY A ***MAN.***
THANK YOU, FATHER.
NOW, LET US ENJOY THIS FEAST WITH OUR BROTHERS... BEFORE ***DUTY*** CALLS AT ***MIDNIGHT!***

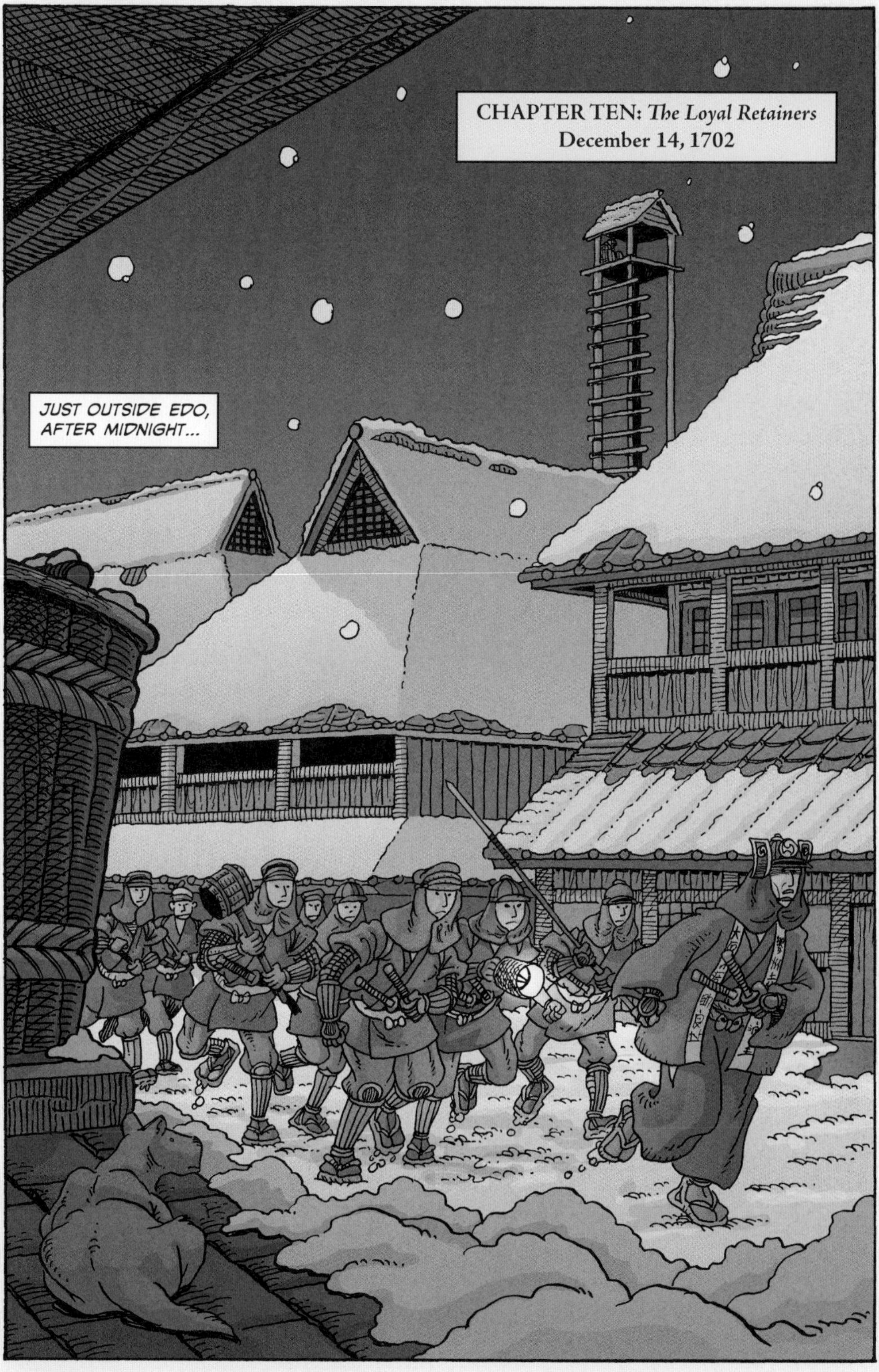
CHAPTER TEN: The Loyal Retainers
December 14, 1702
JUST OUTSIDE EDO, AFTER MIDNIGHT...

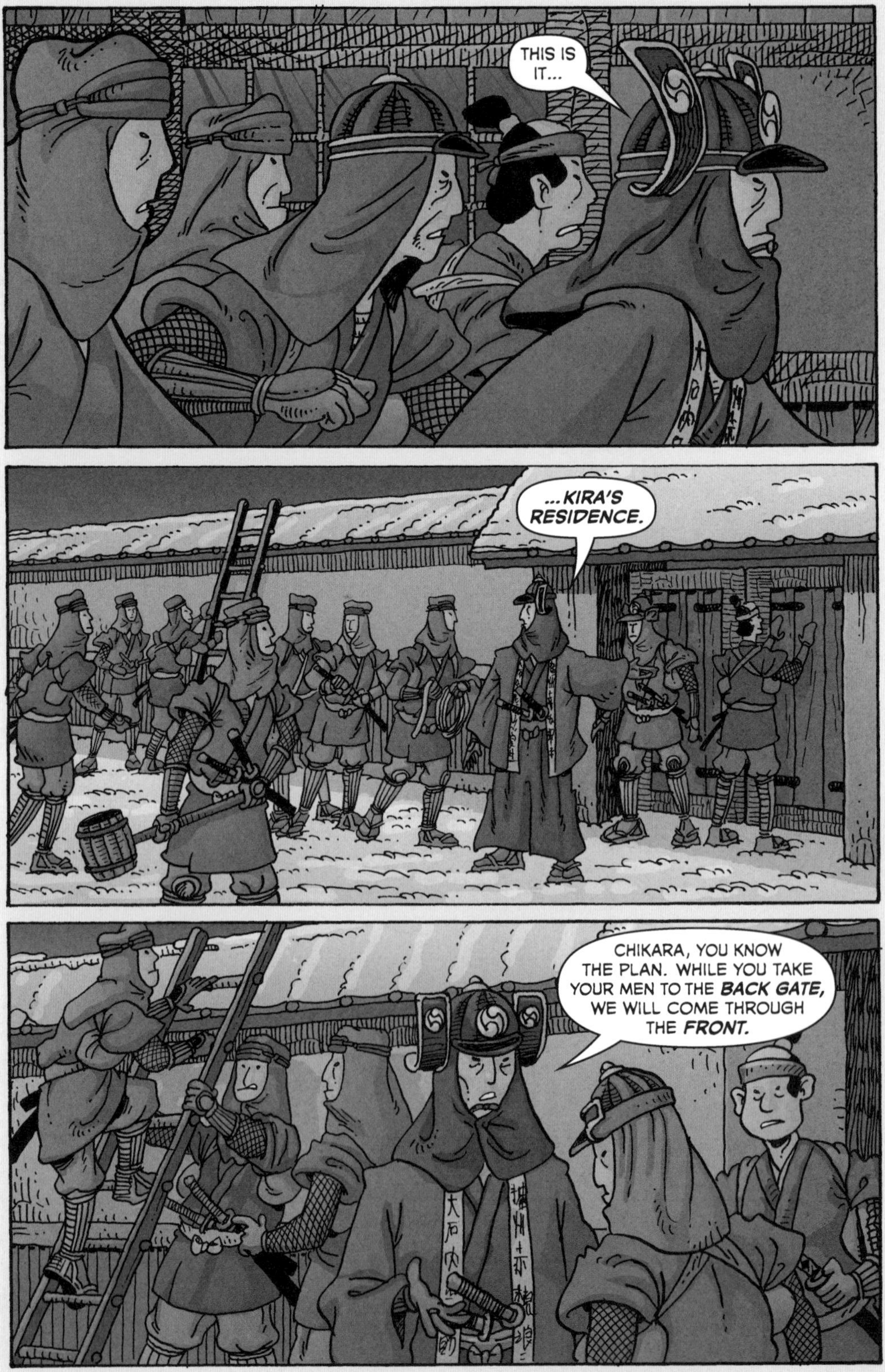
THIS IS IT...
...KIRA'S RESIDENCE.
CHIKARA, YOU KNOW THE PLAN. WHILE YOU TAKE YOUR MEN TO THE BACK GATE, WE WILL COME THROUGH THE FRONT.

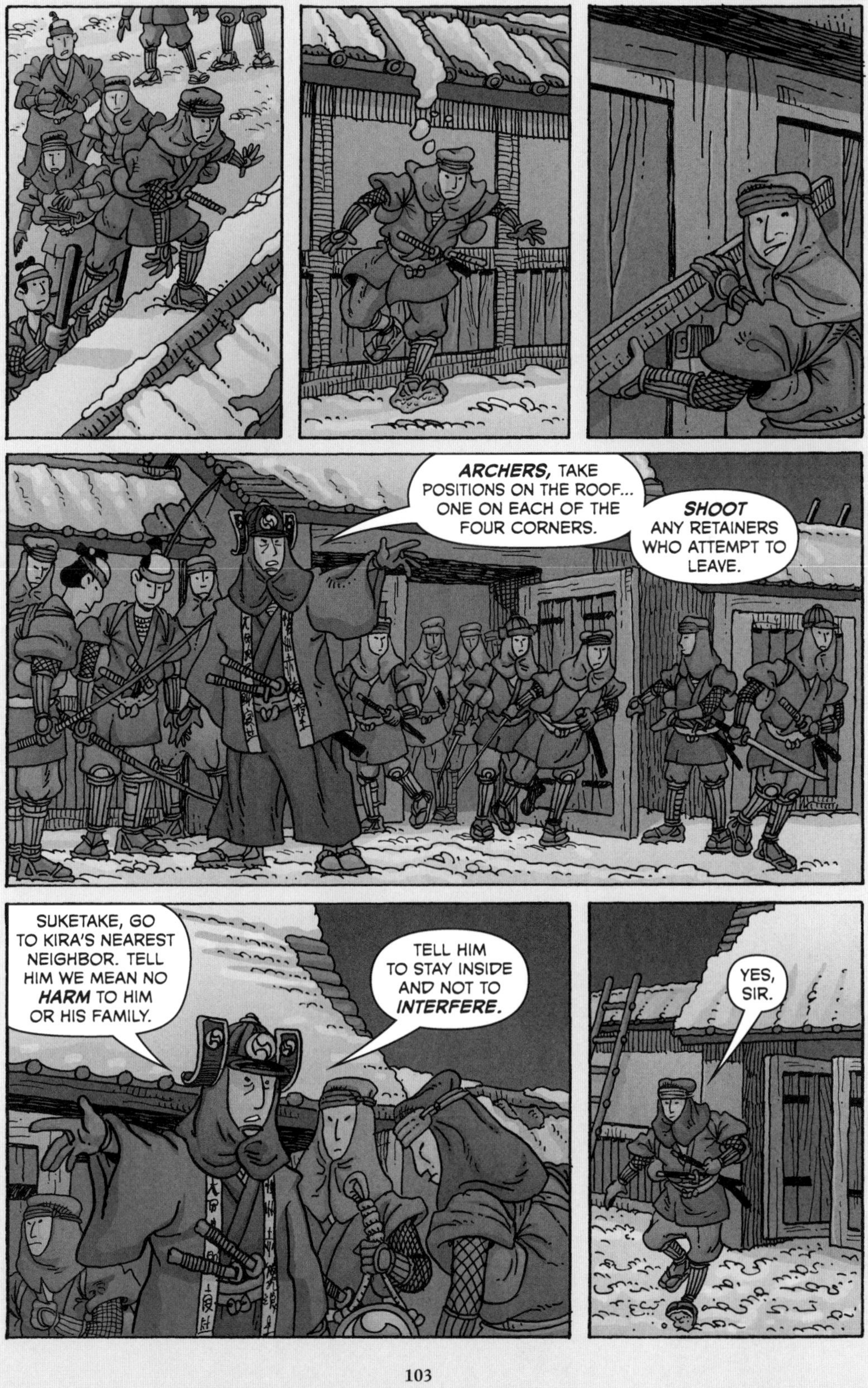
ARCHERS, TAKE POSITIONS ON THE ROOF... ONE ON EACH OF THE FOUR CORNERS.
SHOOT ANY RETAINERS WHO ATTEMPT TO LEAVE.
SUKETAKE, GO TO KIRA'S NEAREST NEIGHBOR. TELL HIM WE MEAN NO HARM TO HIM OR HIS FAMILY.
TELL HIM TO STAY INSIDE AND NOT TO INTERFERE.
YES, SIR.

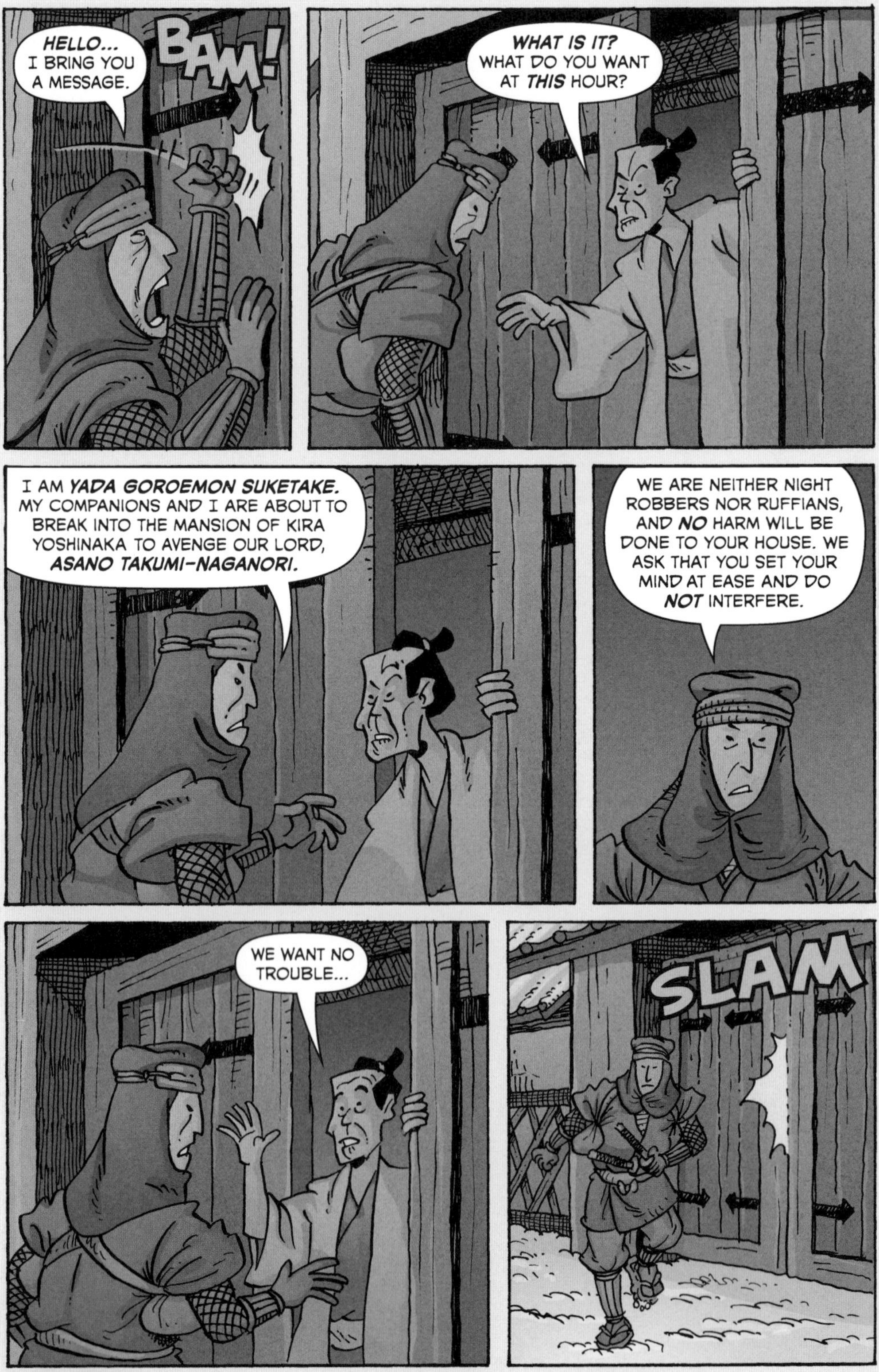
HELLO... I BRING YOU A MESSAGE.
BAM!
WHAT IS IT? WHAT DO YOU WANT AT THIS HOUR?
I AM YADA GOROEMON SUKETAKE. MY COMPANIONS AND I ARE ABOUT TO BREAK INTO THE MANSION OF KIRA YOSHINAKA TO AVENGE OUR LORD, ASANO TAKUMI-NAGANORI.
WE ARE NEITHER NIGHT ROBBERS NOR RUFFIANS, AND NO HARM WILL BE DONE TO YOUR HOUSE. WE ASK THAT YOU SET YOUR MIND AT EASE AND DO NOT INTERFERE.
WE WANT NO TROUBLE...
SLAM

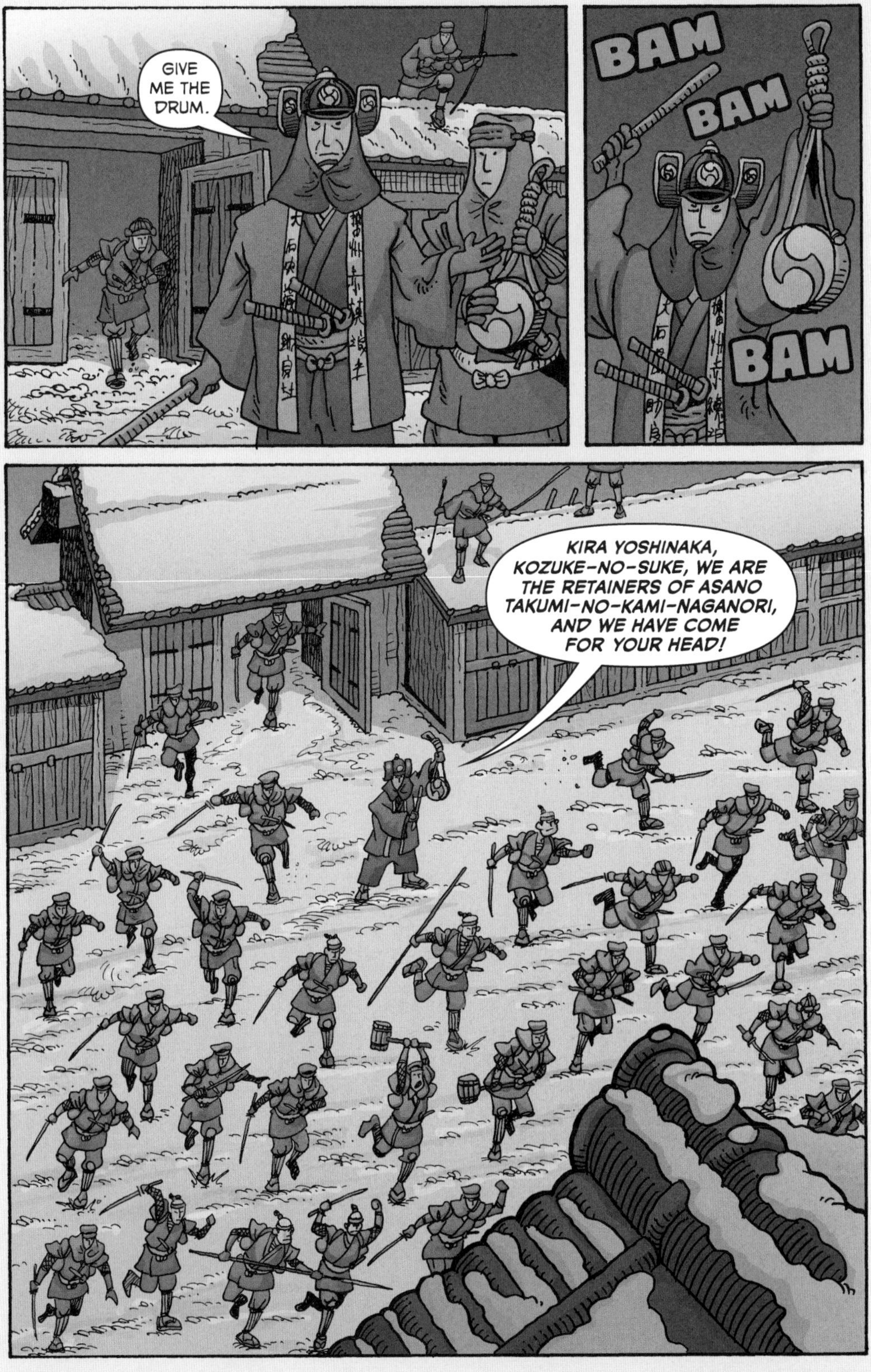
GIVE ME THE DRUM.
BAM
BAM
BAM
KIRA YOSHINAKA, KOZUKE-NO-SUKE, WE ARE THE RETAINERS OF ASANO TAKUMI-NO-KAMI-NAGANORI, AND WE HAVE COME FOR YOUR HEAD!

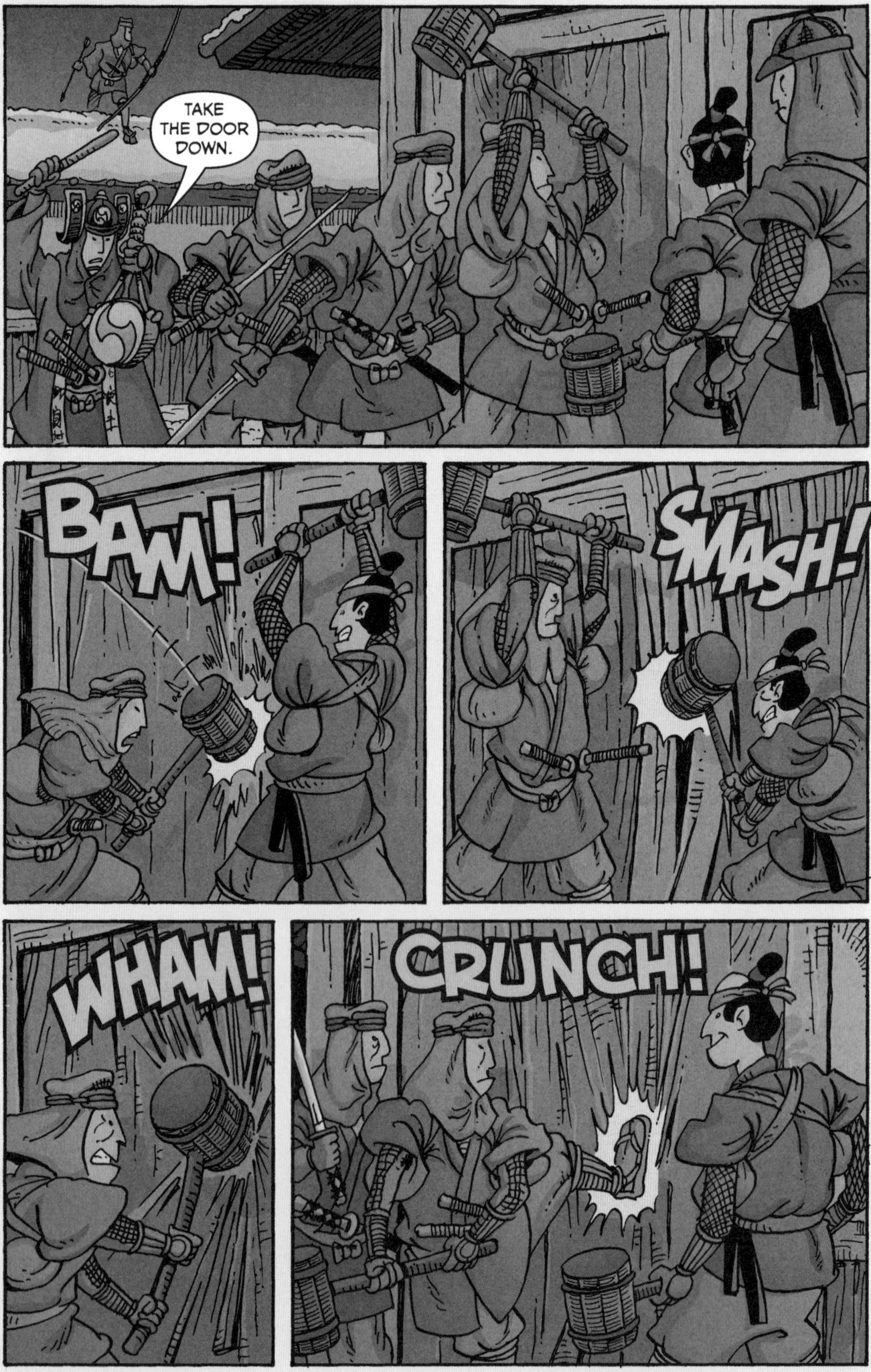
TAKE THE DOOR DOWN.
BAM!
SMASH!
WHAM!
CRUNCH!

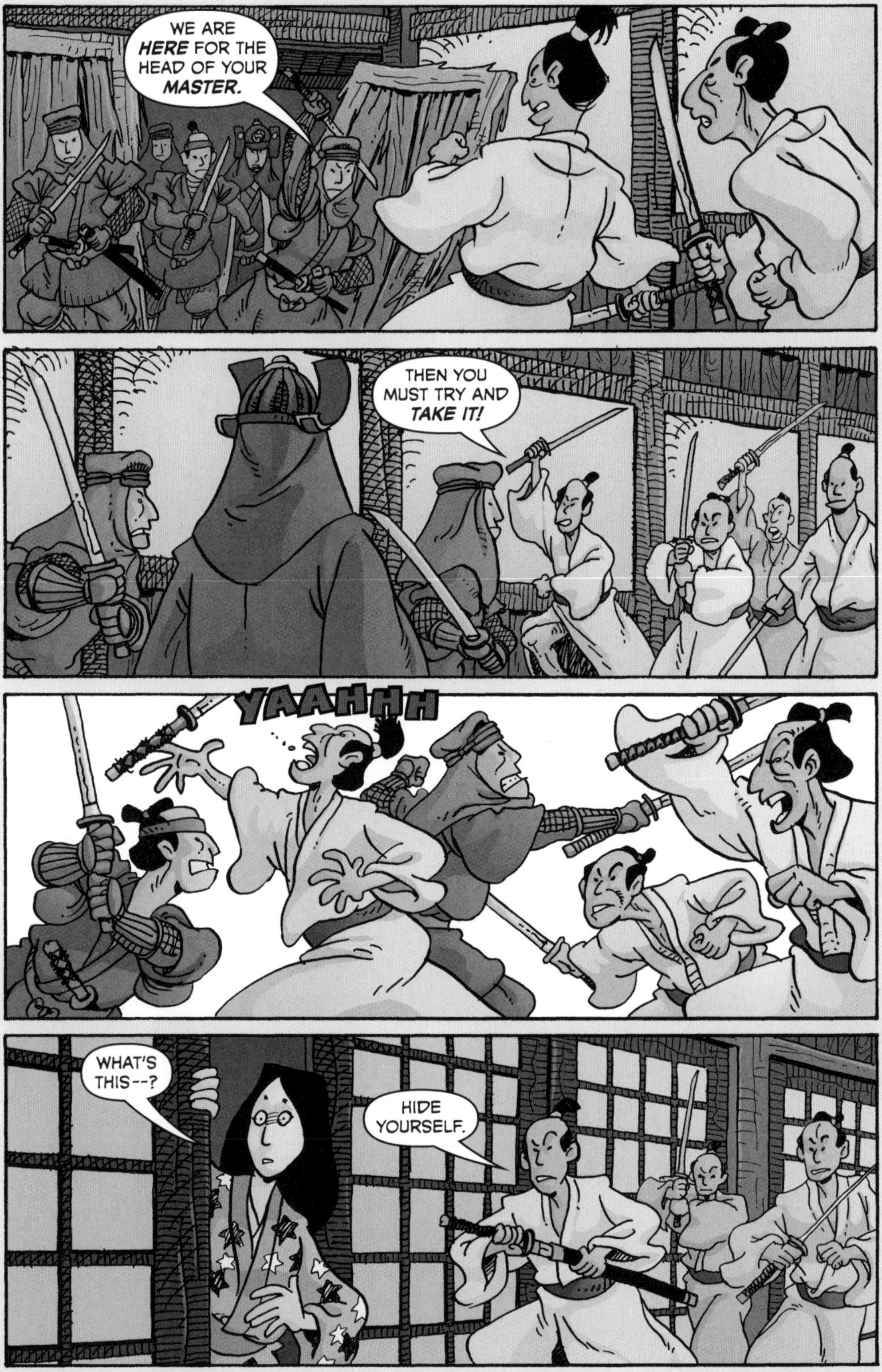
WE ARE HERE FOR THE HEAD OF YOUR MASTER.
THEN YOU MUST TRY AND TAKE IT!
YAAHHH
WHAT'S THIS--?
HIDE YOURSELF.

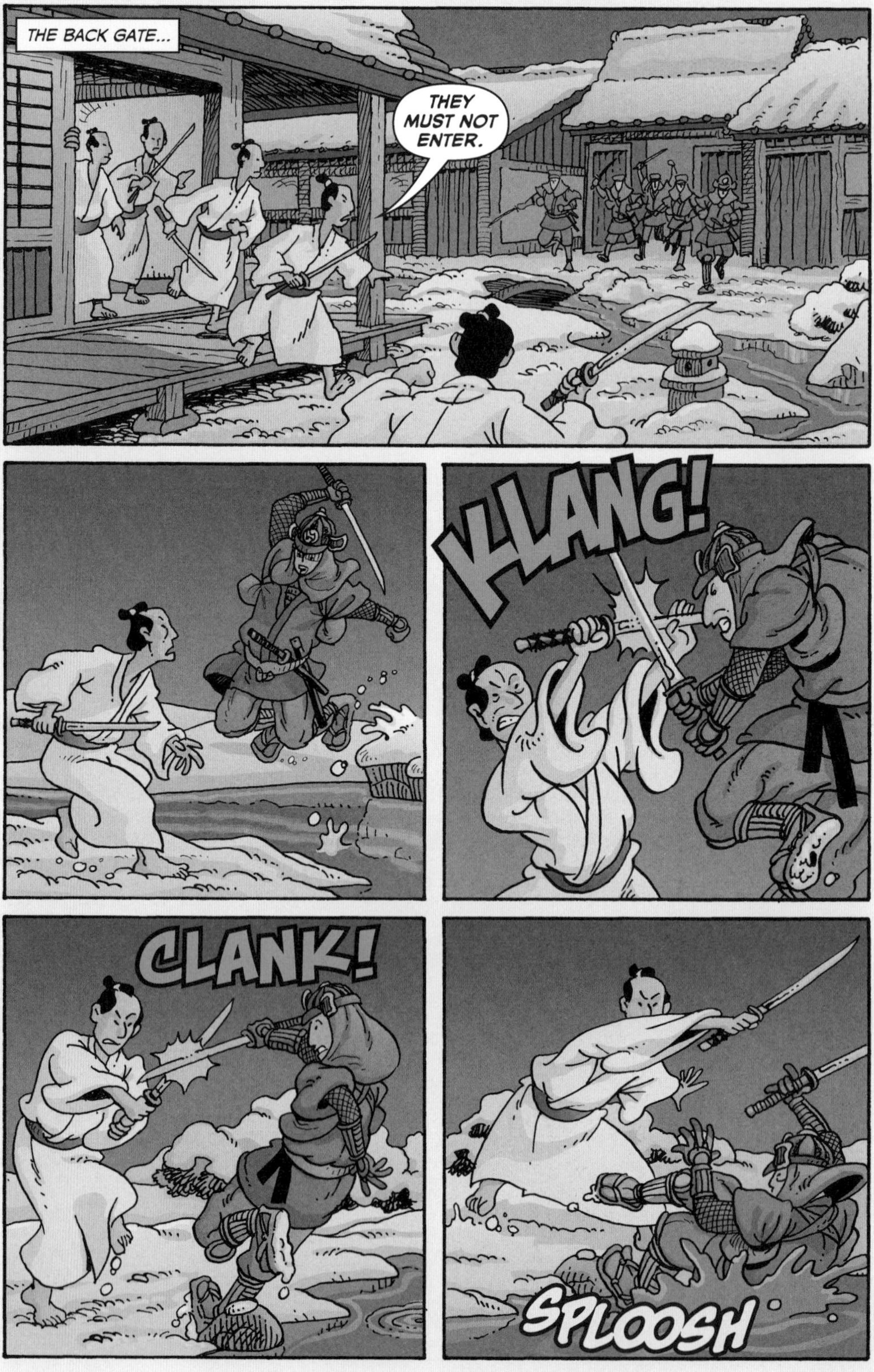
THE BACK GATE...
THEY MUST NOT ENTER.
KLANG!
CLANK!
SPLOOSH

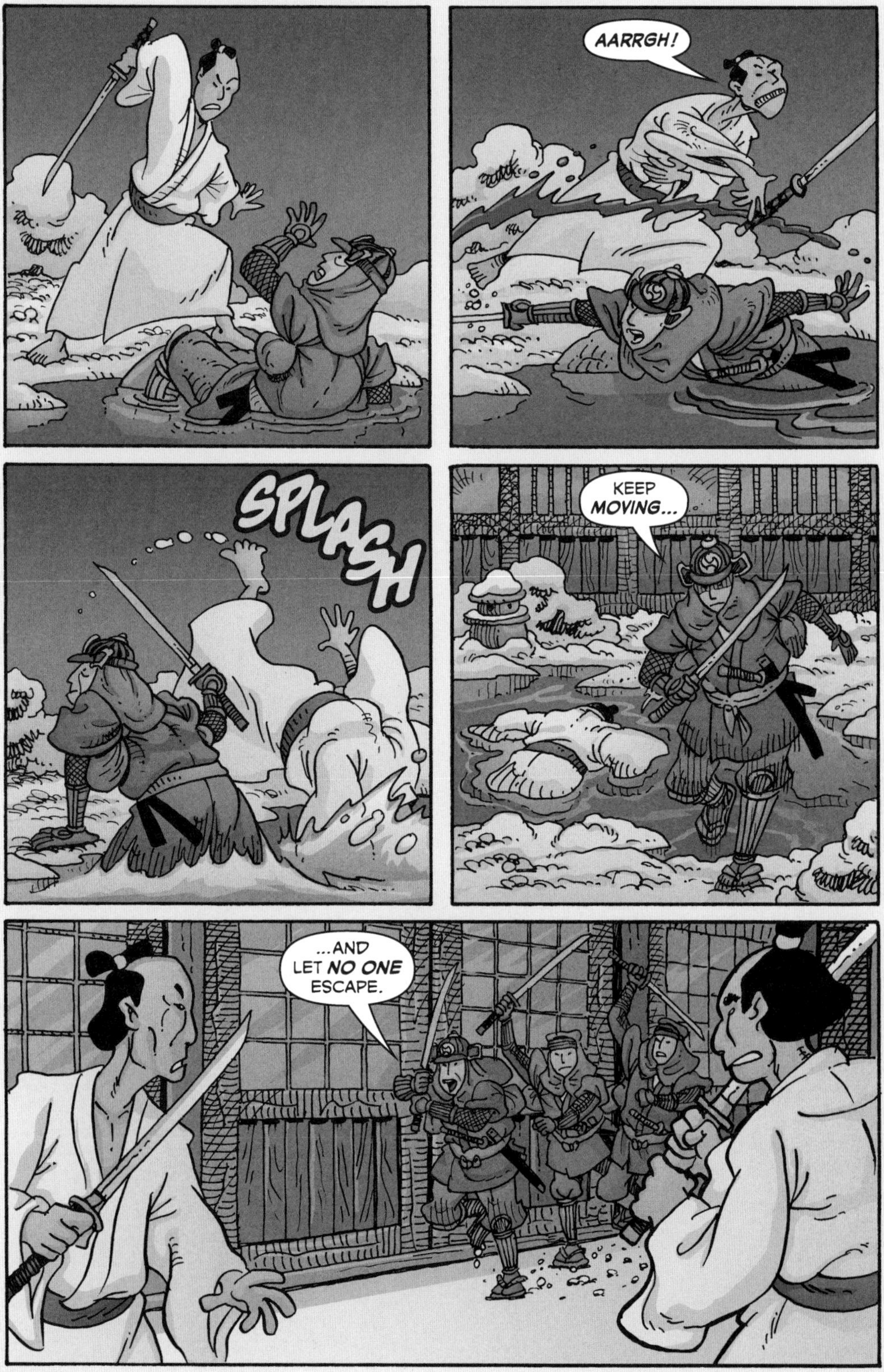
AARRGH!
SPLASH
KEEP MOVING...
...AND LET NO ONE ESCAPE.

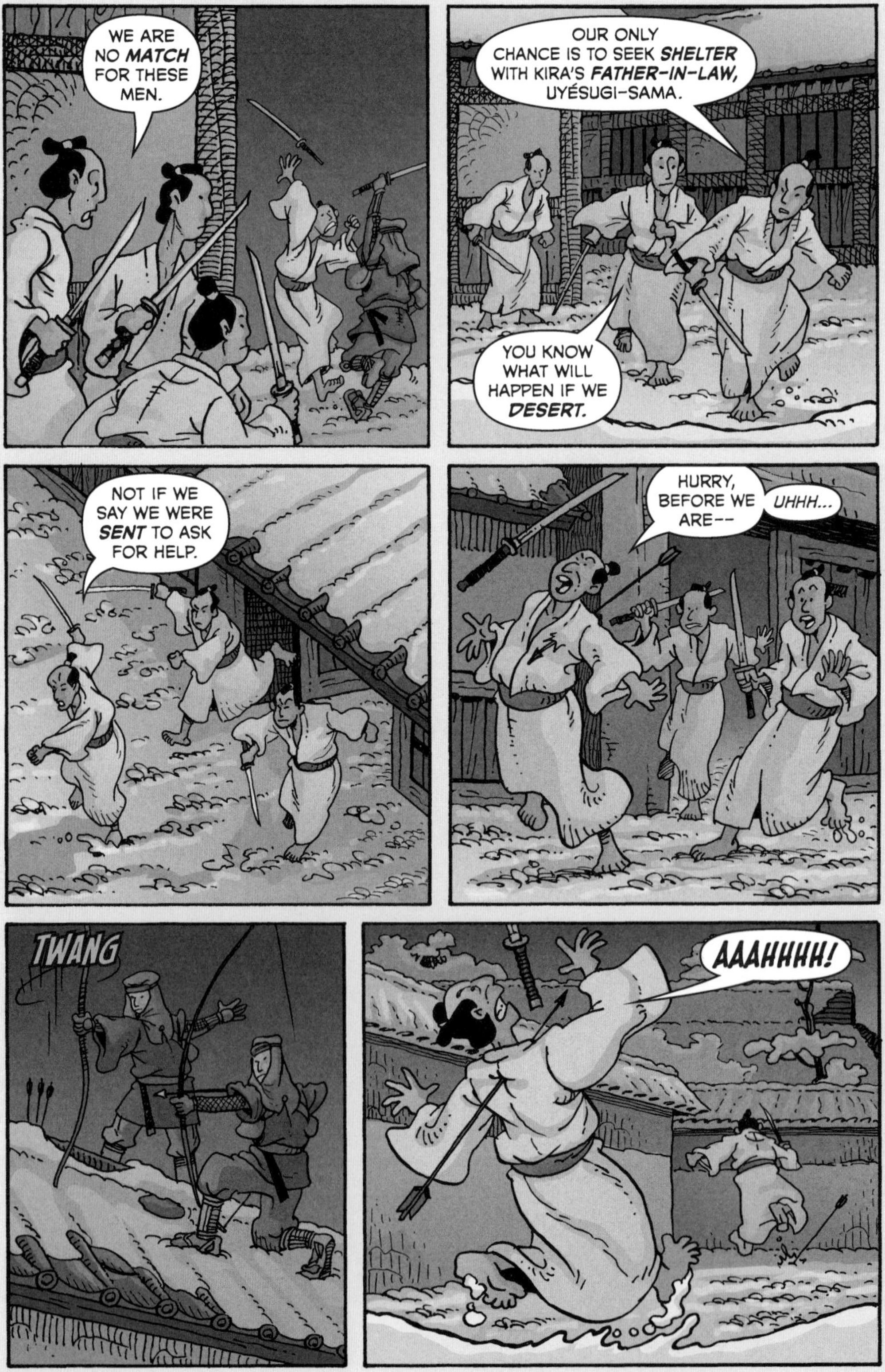

WE ARE NO MATCH FOR THESE MEN.
OUR ONLY CHANCE IS TO SEEK SHELTER WITH KIRA'S FATHER-IN-LAW, UYÉSUGI-SAMA.
YOU KNOW WHAT WILL HAPPEN IF WE DESERT.
NOT IF WE SAY WE WERE SENT TO ASK FOR HELP.
HURRY, BEFORE WE ARE--
UHHH...
TWANG
AAAHHHH!

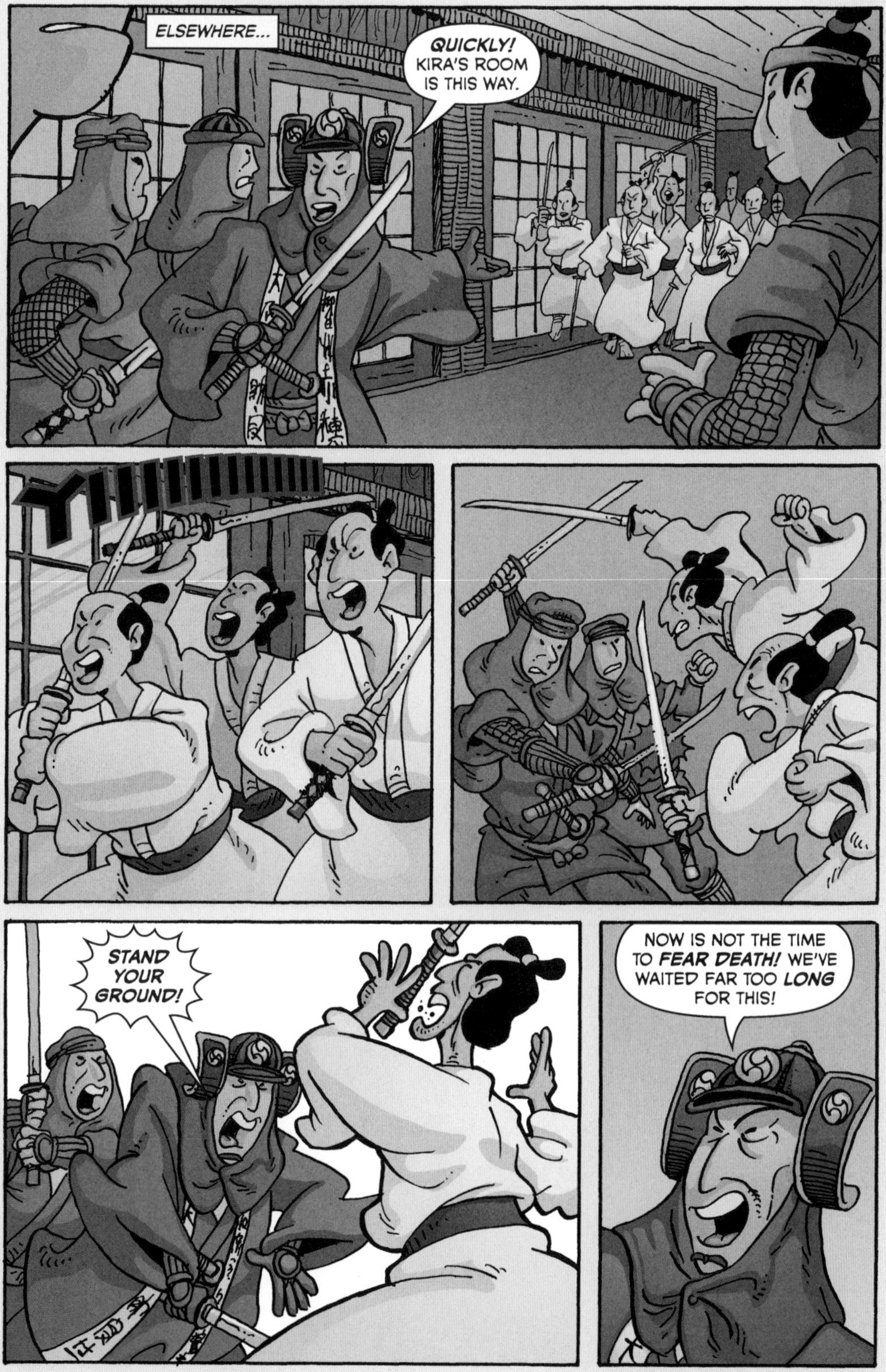
ELSEWHERE...
QUICKLY! KIRA'S ROOM IS THIS WAY.
STAND YOUR GROUND!
NOW IS NOT THE TIME TO FEAR DEATH! WE'VE WAITED FAR TOO LONG FOR THIS!

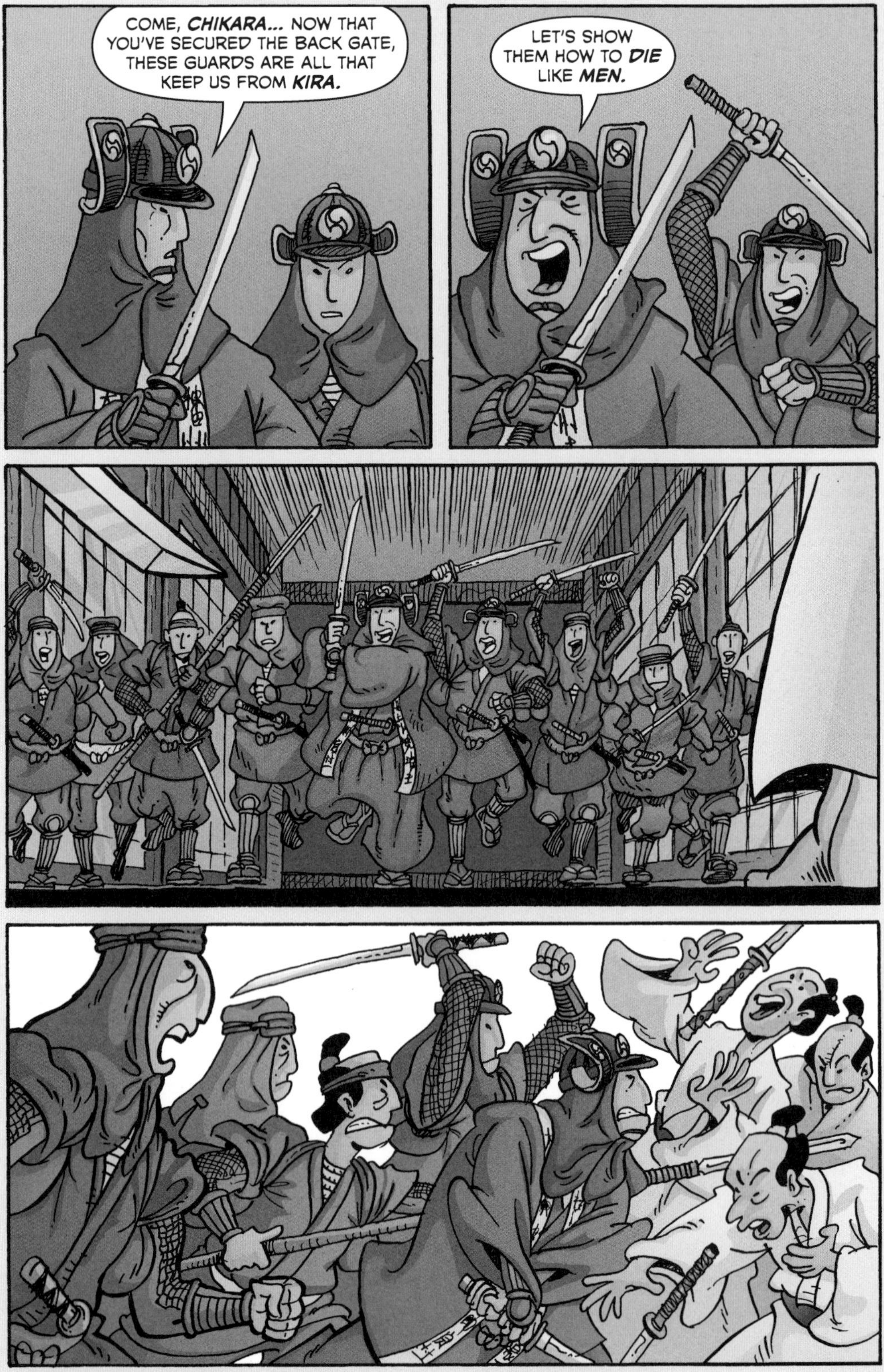
COME, CHIKARA... NOW THAT YOU'VE SECURED THE BACK GATE, THESE GUARDS ARE ALL THAT KEEP US FROM KIRA.
LET'S SHOW THEM HOW TO DIE LIKE MEN.

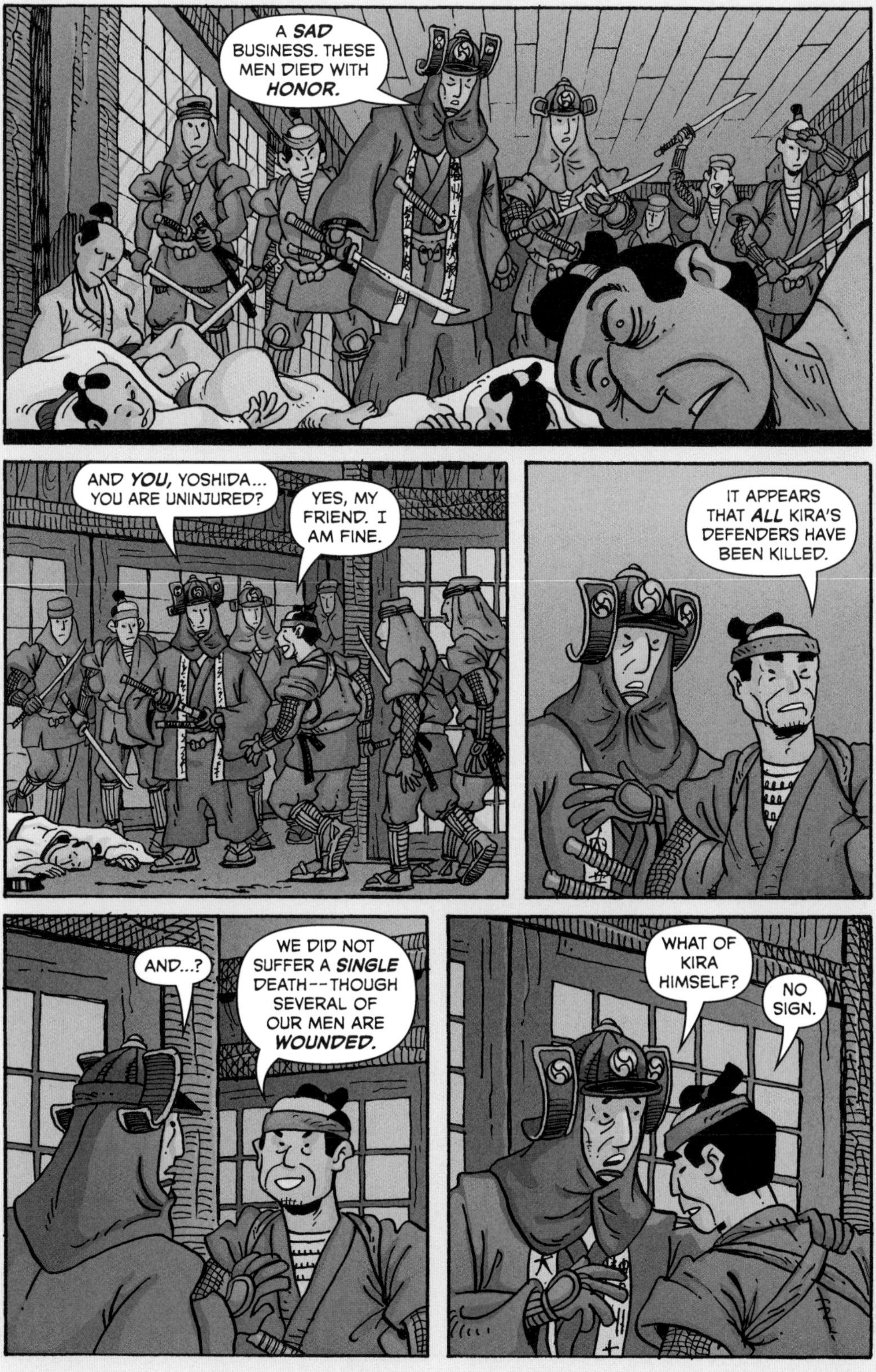
A SAD BUSINESS. THESE MEN DIED WITH HONOR.
AND YOU, YOSHIDA... YOU ARE UNINJURED?
YES, MY FRIEND. I AM FINE.
IT APPEARS THAT ALL KIRA'S DEFENDERS HAVE BEEN KILLED.
AND...?
WE DID NOT SUFFER A SINGLE DEATH--THOUGH SEVERAL OF OUR MEN ARE WOUNDED.
WHAT OF KIRA HIMSELF?
NO SIGN.

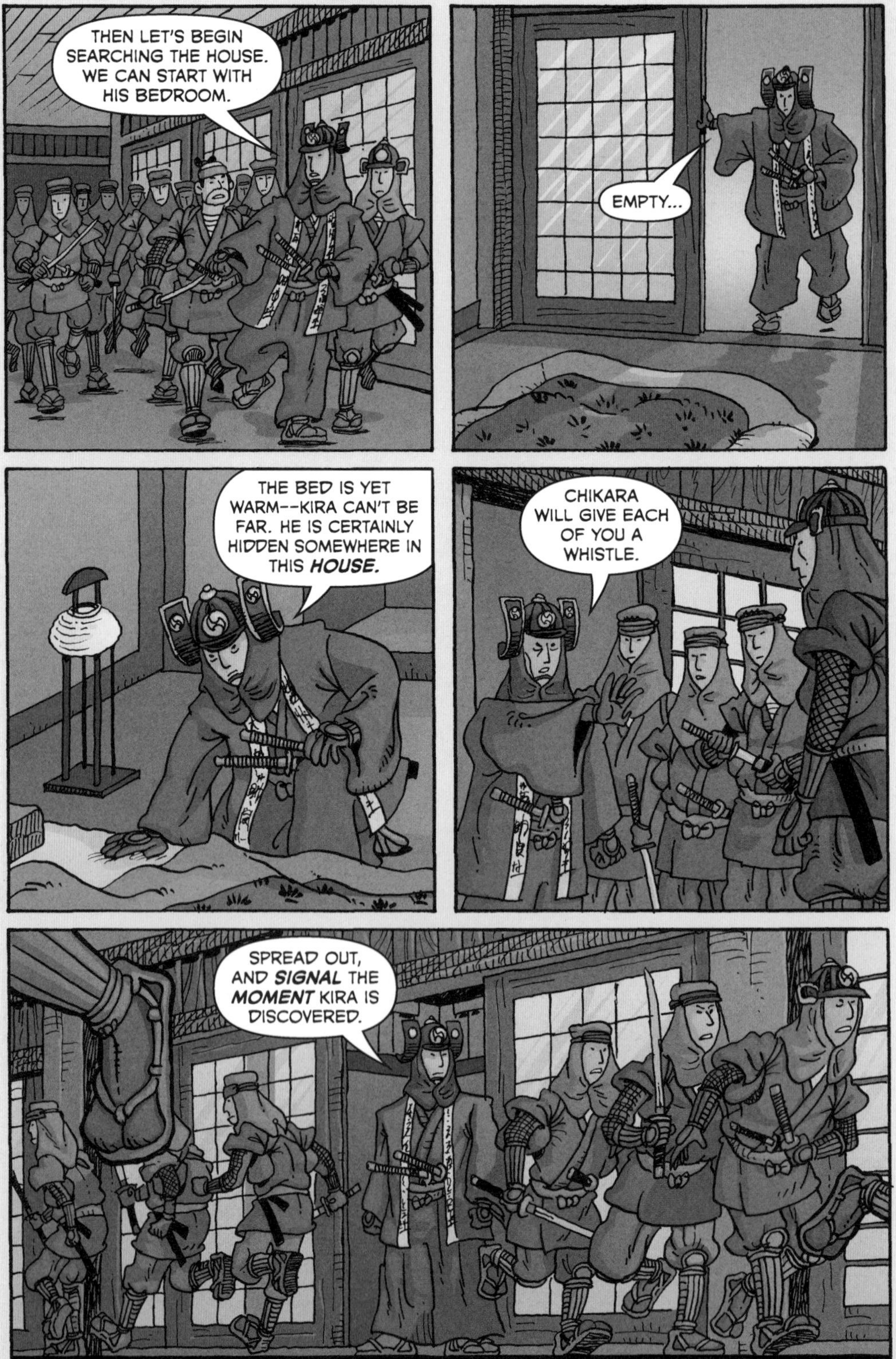
THEN LET'S BEGIN SEARCHING THE HOUSE. WE CAN START WITH HIS BEDROOM.
EMPTY...
THE BED IS YET WARM--KIRA CAN'T BE FAR. HE IS CERTAINLY HIDDEN SOMEWHERE IN THIS HOUSE.
CHIKARA WILL GIVE EACH OF YOU A WHISTLE.
SPREAD OUT, AND SIGNAL THE MOMENT KIRA IS DISCOVERED.

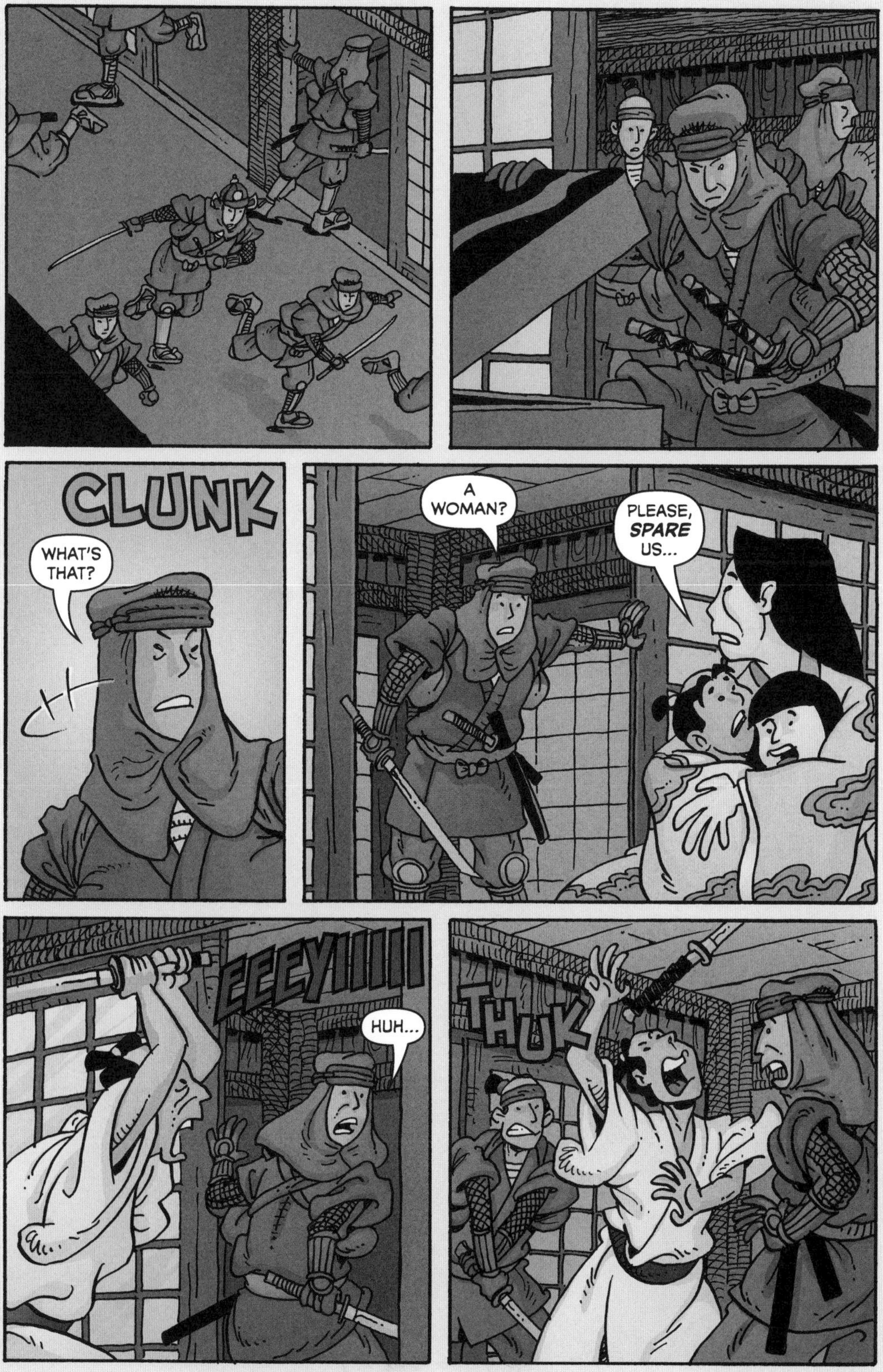
CLUNK
WHAT'S THAT?
A WOMAN?
PLEASE, SPARE US...
EEEYIIIII
HUH...
THUK

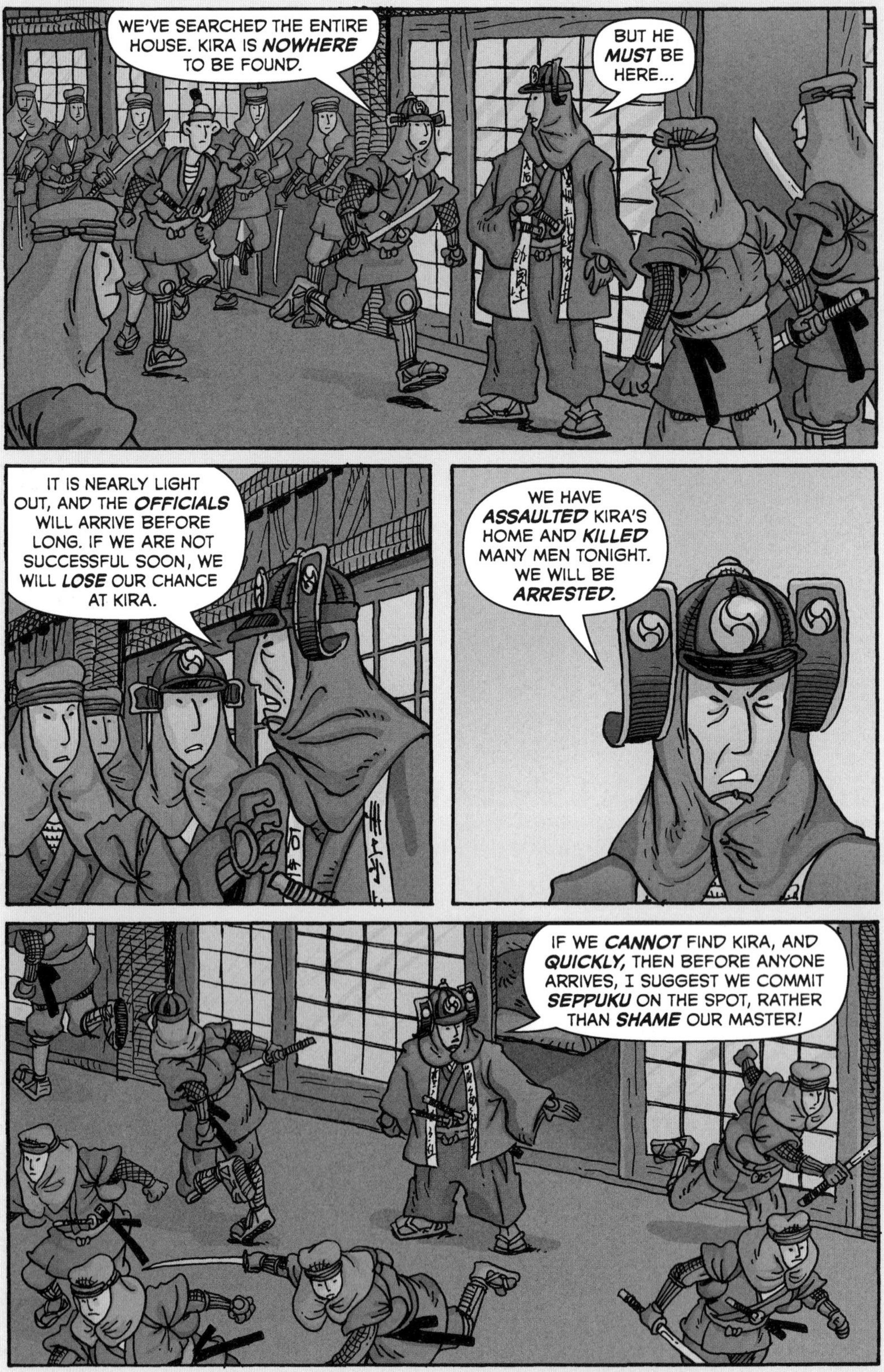
WE'VE SEARCHED THE ENTIRE HOUSE. KIRA IS NOWHERE TO BE FOUND.
BUT HE MUST BE HERE...
IT IS NEARLY LIGHT OUT, AND THE OFFICIALS WILL ARRIVE BEFORE LONG. IF WE ARE NOT SUCCESSFUL SOON, WE WILL LOSE OUR CHANCE AT KIRA.
WE HAVE ASSAULTED KIRA'S HOME AND KILLED MANY MEN TONIGHT. WE WILL BE ARRESTED.
IF WE CANNOT FIND KIRA, AND QUICKLY, THEN BEFORE ANYONE ARRIVES, I SUGGEST WE COMMIT SEPPUKU ON THE SPOT, RATHER THAN SHAME OUR MASTER!

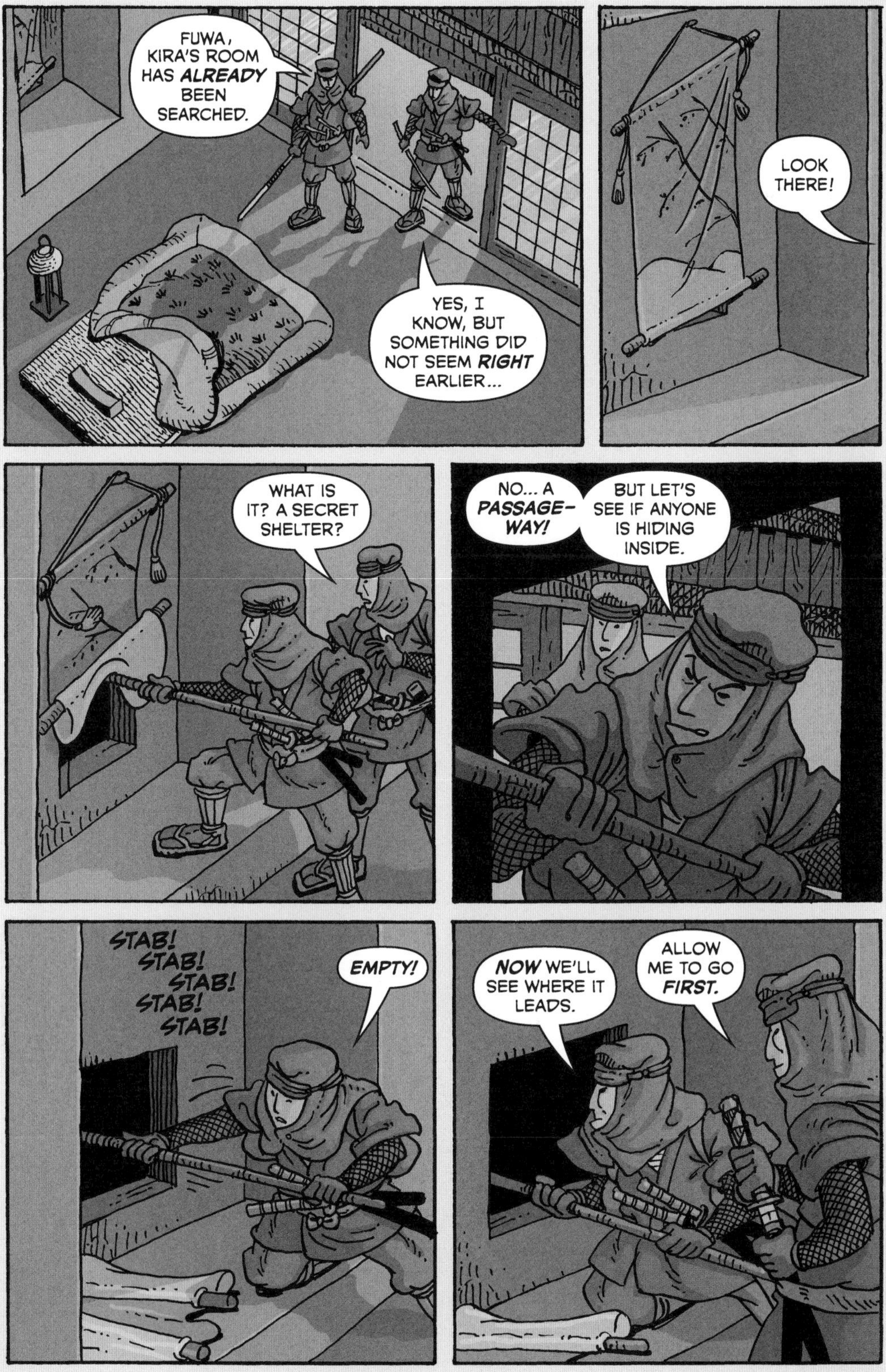
FUWA, KIRA'S ROOM HAS ALREADY BEEN SEARCHED.
YES, I KNOW, BUT SOMETHING DID NOT SEEM RIGHT EARLIER...
LOOK THERE!
WHAT IS IT? A SECRET SHELTER?
NO... A PASSAGE-WAY!
BUT LET'S SEE IF ANYONE IS HIDING INSIDE.
STAB! STAB! STAB! STAB! STAB!
EMPTY!
NOW WE'LL SEE WHERE IT LEADS.
ALLOW ME TO GO FIRST.

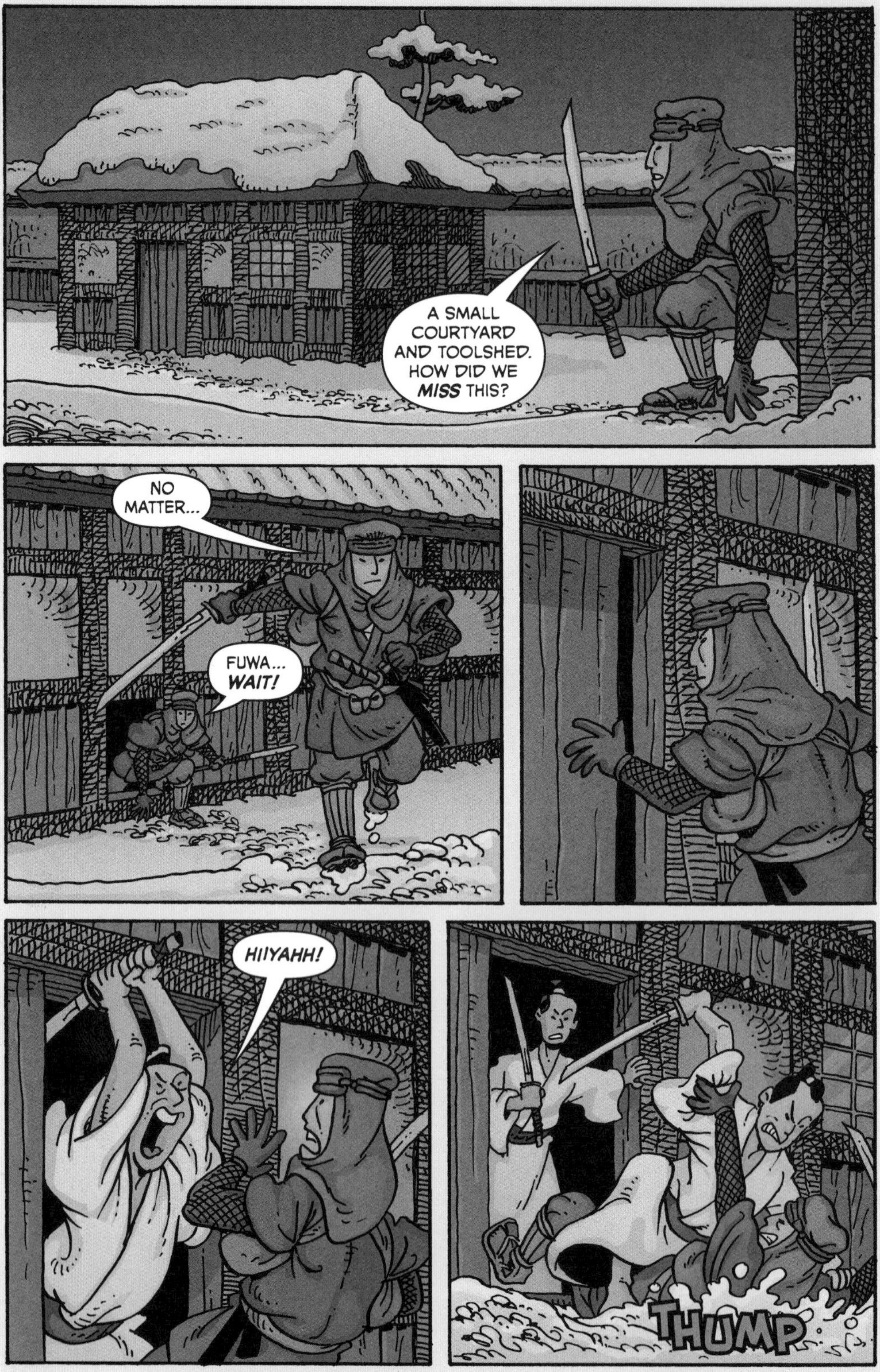
A SMALL COURTYARD AND TOOLSHED. HOW DID WE *MISS* THIS?
NO MATTER...
FUWA... *WAIT!*
HIIYAHH!
THUMP

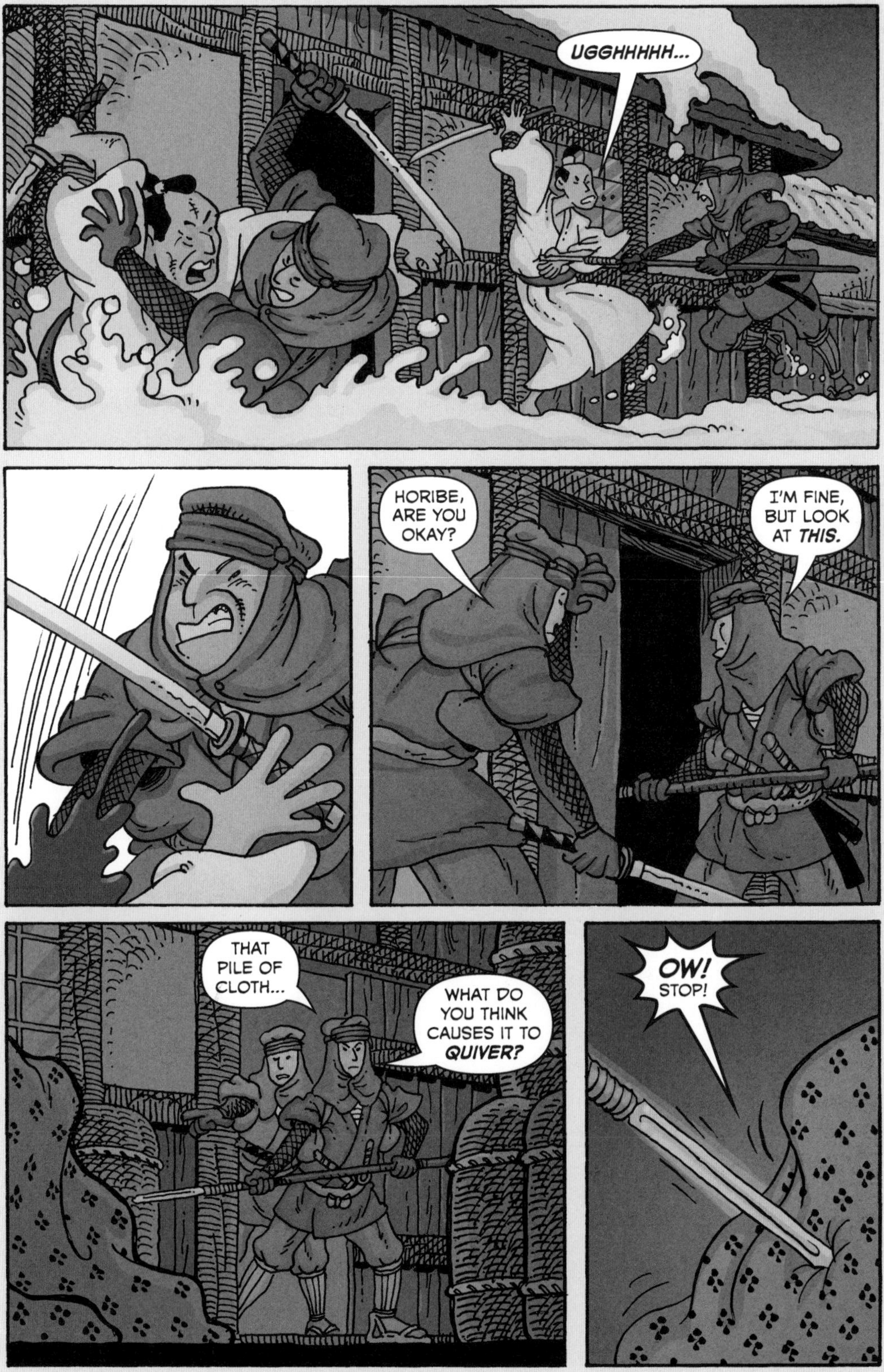
UGGHHHHH...
HORIBE, ARE YOU OKAY?
I'M FINE, BUT LOOK AT THIS.
THAT PILE OF CLOTH...
WHAT DO YOU THINK CAUSES IT TO QUIVER?
OW! STOP!

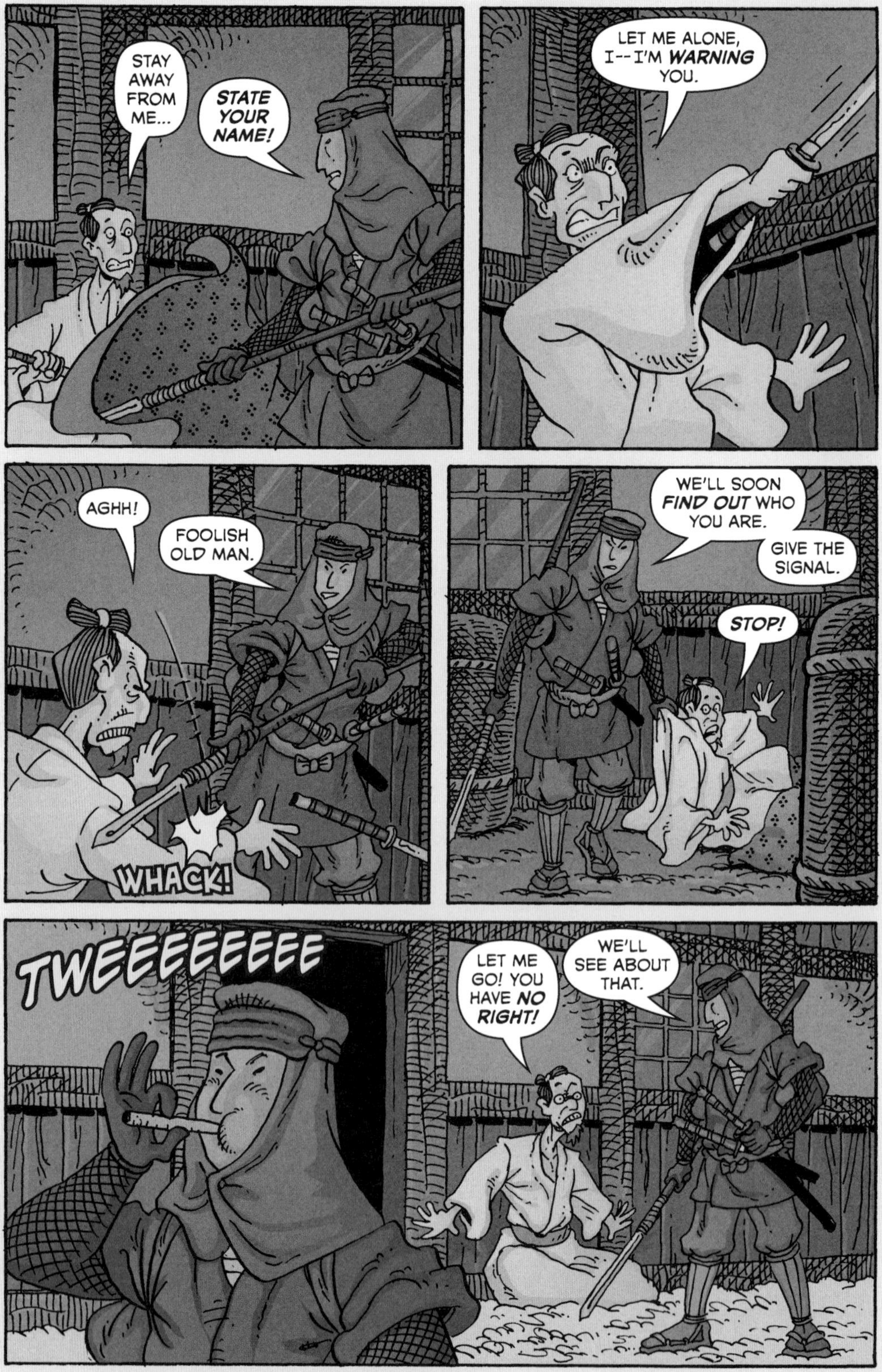
STAY AWAY FROM ME...
STATE YOUR NAME!
LET ME ALONE, I--I'M WARNING YOU.
AGHH!
FOOLISH OLD MAN.
WHACK!
WE'LL SOON FIND OUT WHO YOU ARE.
GIVE THE SIGNAL.
STOP!
TWEEEEEEEE
LET ME GO! YOU HAVE NO RIGHT!
WE'LL SEE ABOUT THAT.

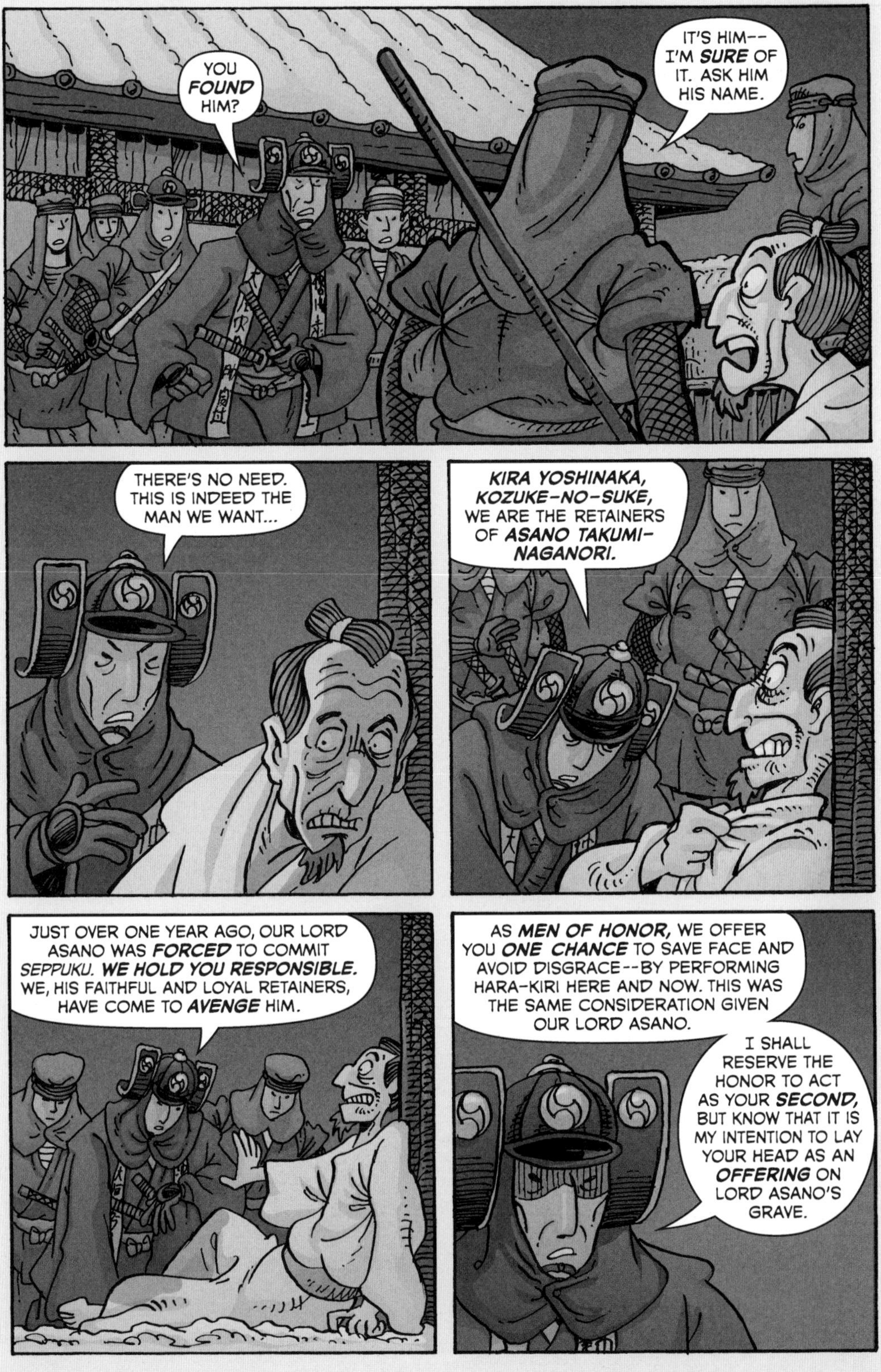
YOU FOUND HIM?
IT'S HIM-- I'M SURE OF IT. ASK HIM HIS NAME.
THERE'S NO NEED. THIS IS INDEED THE MAN WE WANT...
KIRA YOSHINAKA, KOZUKE-NO-SUKE, WE ARE THE RETAINERS OF ASANO TAKUMI-NAGANORI.
JUST OVER ONE YEAR AGO, OUR LORD ASANO WAS FORCED TO COMMIT SEPPUKU. WE HOLD YOU RESPONSIBLE. WE, HIS FAITHFUL AND LOYAL RETAINERS, HAVE COME TO AVENGE HIM.
AS MEN OF HONOR, WE OFFER YOU ONE CHANCE TO SAVE FACE AND AVOID DISGRACE--BY PERFORMING HARA-KIRI HERE AND NOW. THIS WAS THE SAME CONSIDERATION GIVEN OUR LORD ASANO.
I SHALL RESERVE THE HONOR TO ACT AS YOUR SECOND, BUT KNOW THAT IT IS MY INTENTION TO LAY YOUR HEAD AS AN OFFERING ON LORD ASANO'S GRAVE.

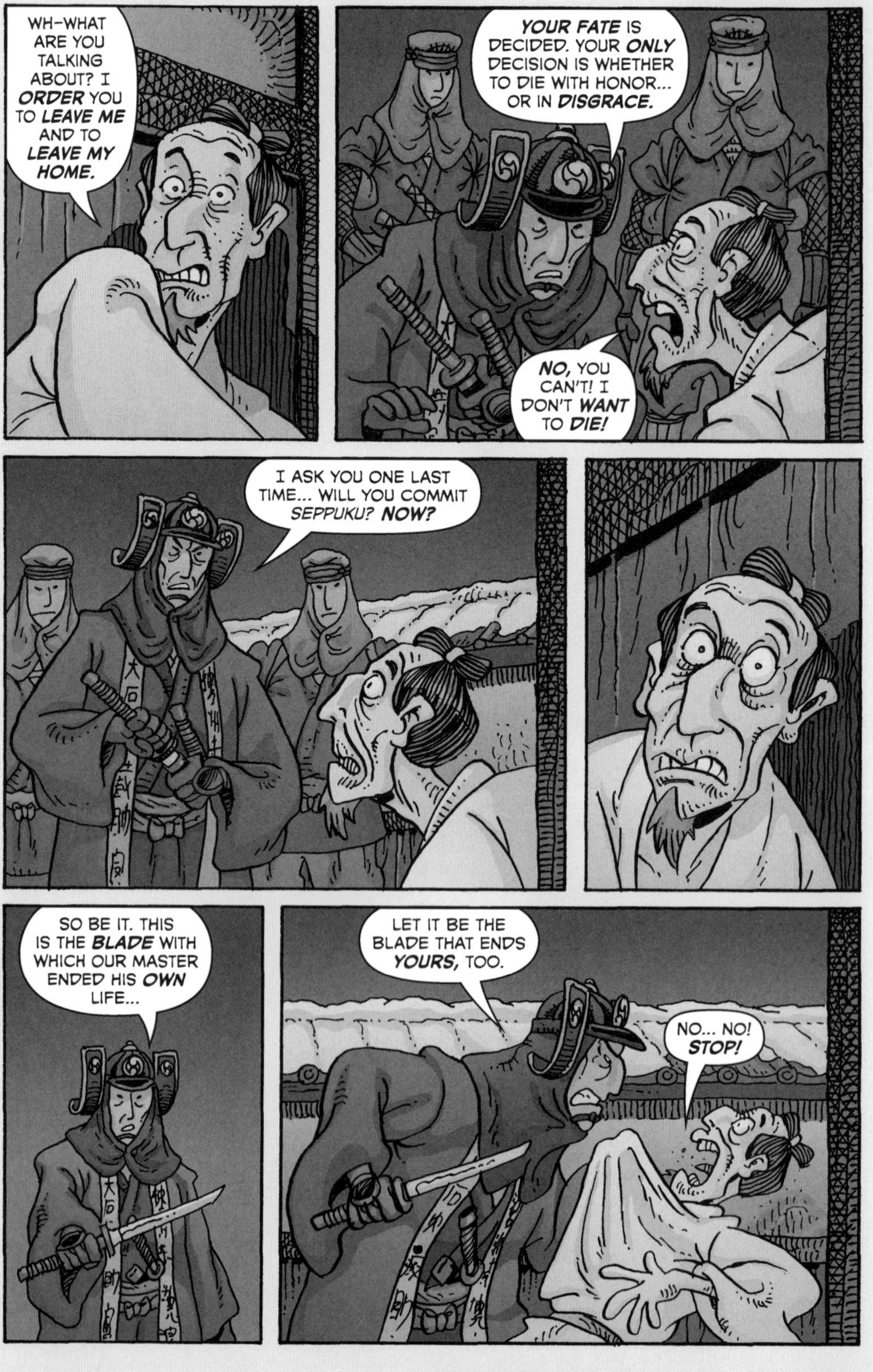
WH-WHAT ARE YOU TALKING ABOUT? I ORDER YOU TO LEAVE ME AND TO LEAVE MY HOME.
YOUR FATE IS DECIDED. YOUR ONLY DECISION IS WHETHER TO DIE WITH HONOR... OR IN DISGRACE.
NO, YOU CAN'T! I DON'T WANT TO DIE!
I ASK YOU ONE LAST TIME... WILL YOU COMMIT SEPPUKU? NOW?
SO BE IT. THIS IS THE BLADE WITH WHICH OUR MASTER ENDED HIS OWN LIFE...
LET IT BE THE BLADE THAT ENDS YOURS, TOO.
NO... NO! STOP!

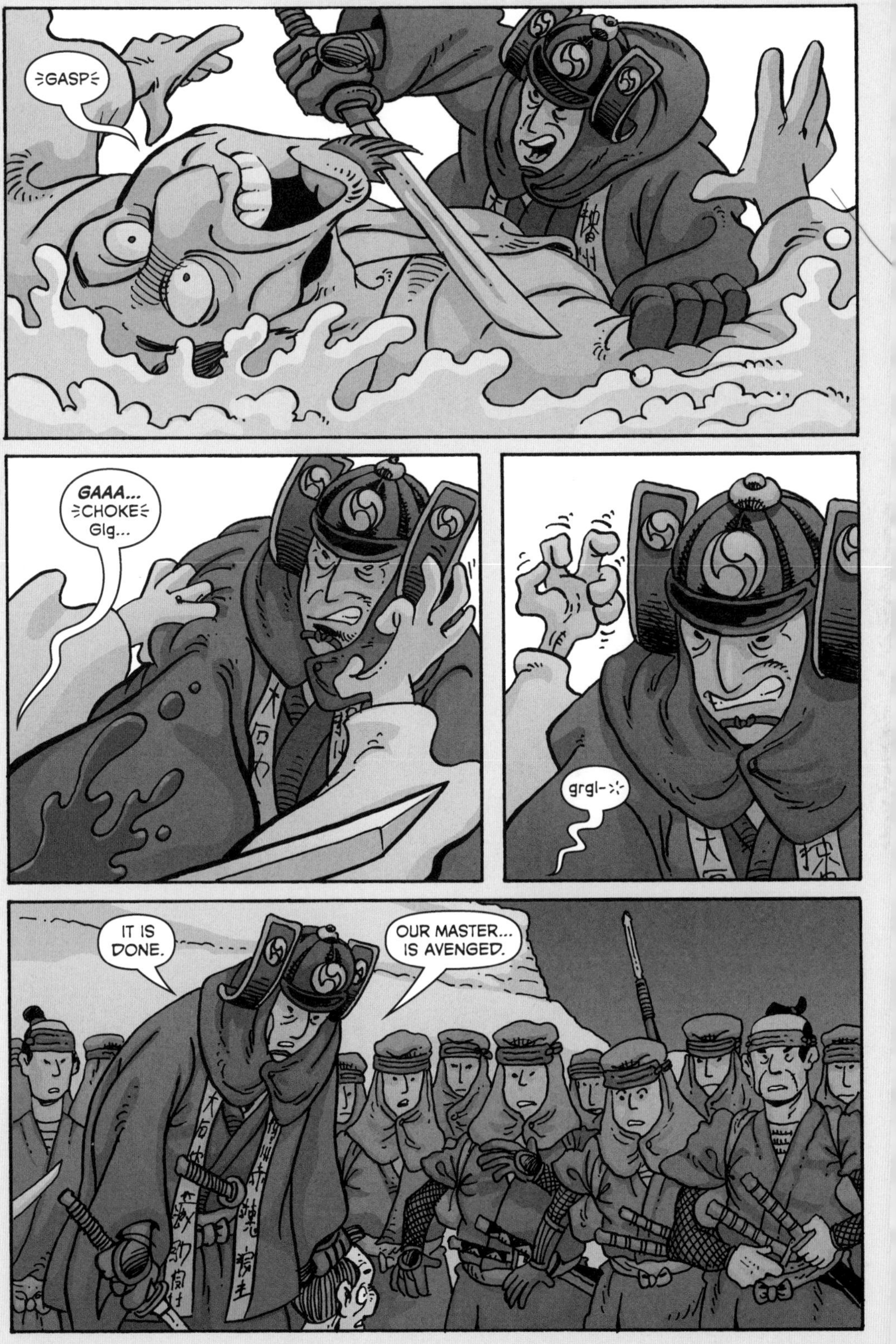

GASP
GAAA... CHOKE Glg...
grgl-
IT IS DONE.
OUR MASTER... IS AVENGED.

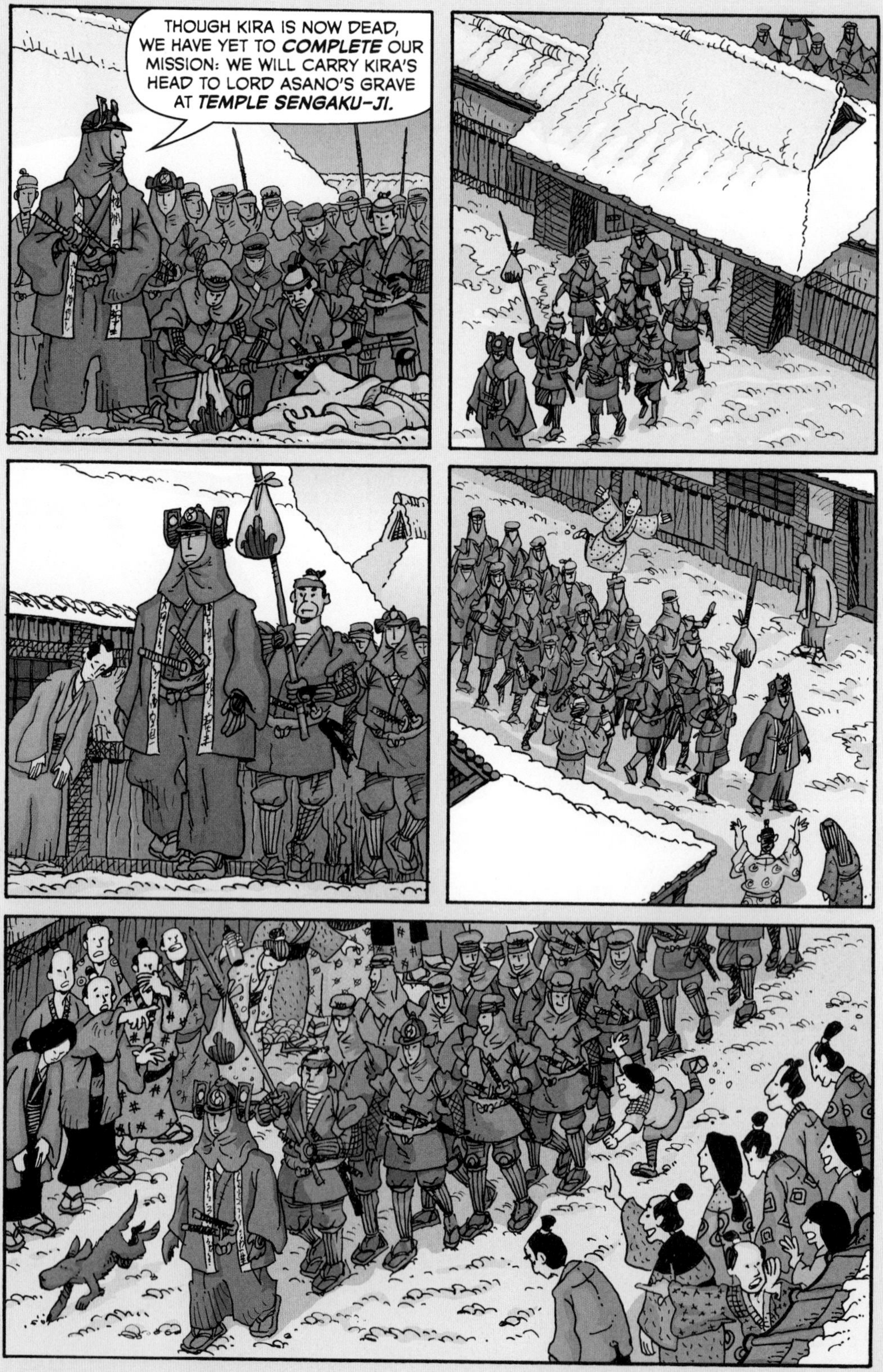
THOUGH KIRA IS NOW DEAD, WE HAVE YET TO COMPLETE OUR MISSION: WE WILL CARRY KIRA'S HEAD TO LORD ASANO'S GRAVE AT TEMPLE SENGAKU-JI.

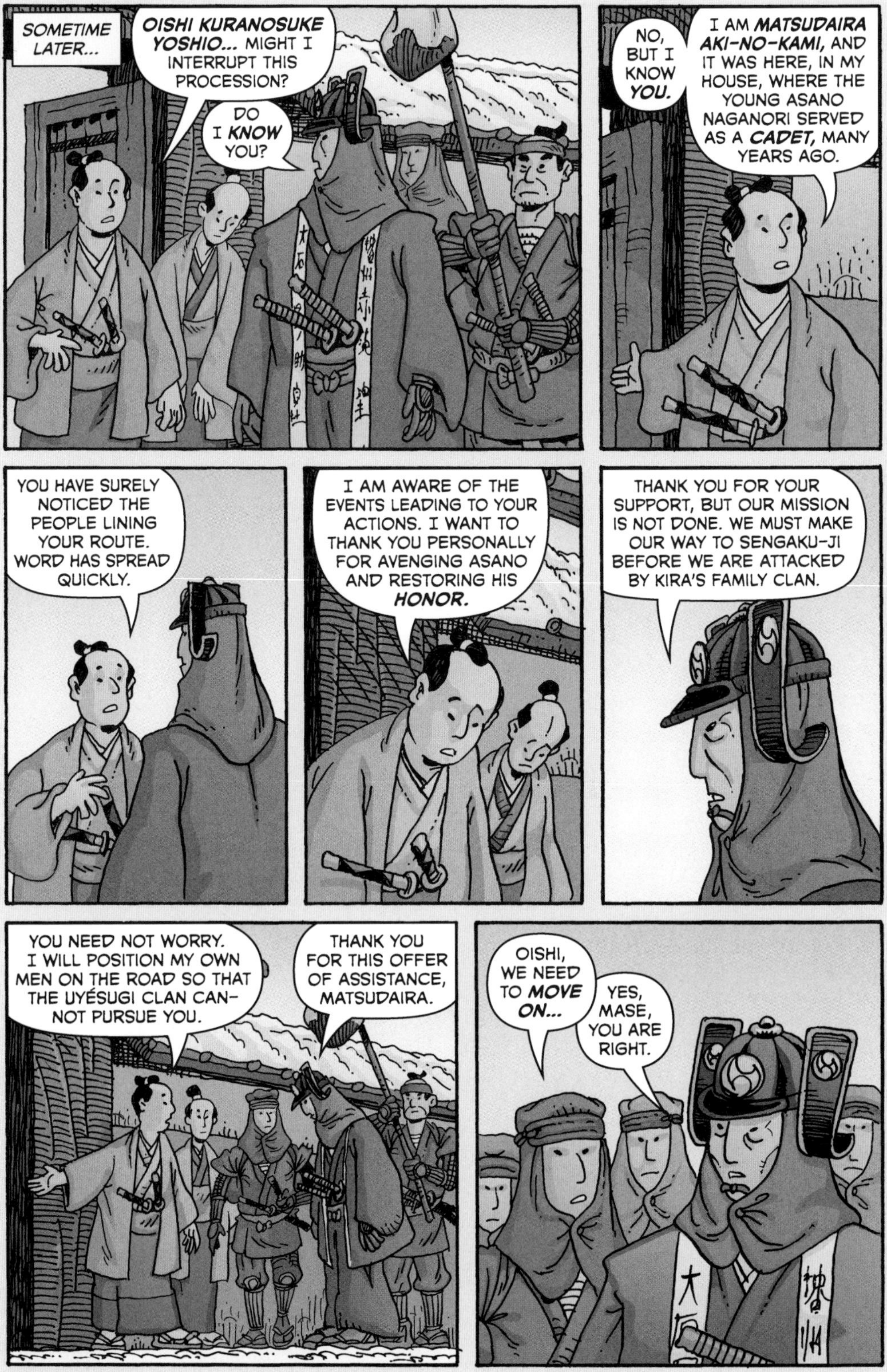
SOMETIME LATER...
OISHI KURANOSUKE YOSHIO... MIGHT I INTERRUPT THIS PROCESSION?
DO I KNOW YOU?
NO, BUT I KNOW YOU.
I AM MATSUDAIRA AKI-NO-KAMI, AND IT WAS HERE, IN MY HOUSE, WHERE THE YOUNG ASANO NAGANORI SERVED AS A CADET, MANY YEARS AGO.
YOU HAVE SURELY NOTICED THE PEOPLE LINING YOUR ROUTE. WORD HAS SPREAD QUICKLY.
I AM AWARE OF THE EVENTS LEADING TO YOUR ACTIONS. I WANT TO THANK YOU PERSONALLY FOR AVENGING ASANO AND RESTORING HIS HONOR.
THANK YOU FOR YOUR SUPPORT, BUT OUR MISSION IS NOT DONE. WE MUST MAKE OUR WAY TO SENGAKU-JI BEFORE WE ARE ATTACKED BY KIRA'S FAMILY CLAN.
YOU NEED NOT WORRY. I WILL POSITION MY OWN MEN ON THE ROAD SO THAT THE UYÉSUGI CLAN CAN-NOT PURSUE YOU.
THANK YOU FOR THIS OFFER OF ASSISTANCE, MATSUDAIRA.
OISHI, WE NEED TO MOVE ON...
YES, MASE, YOU ARE RIGHT.

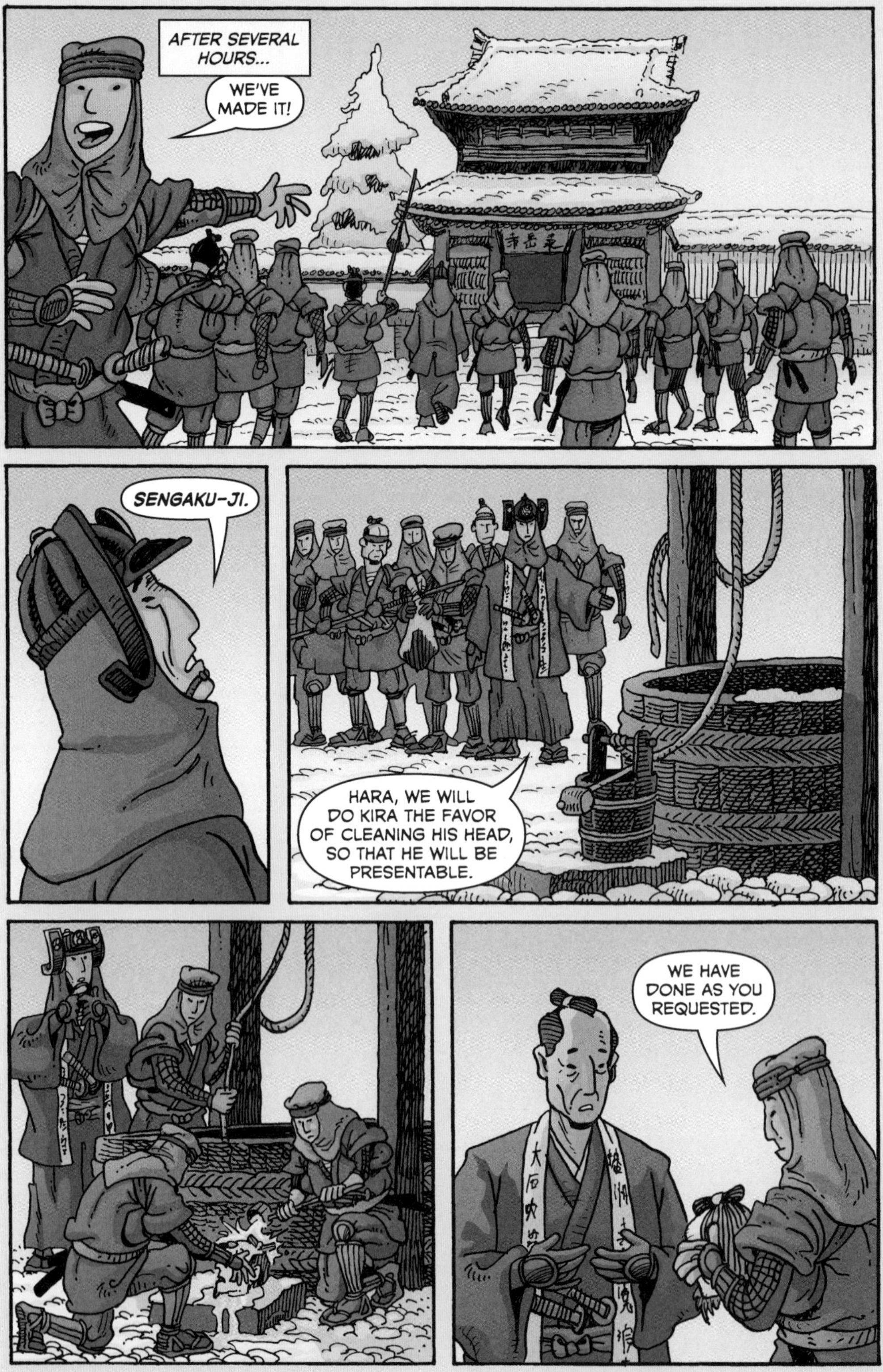
AFTER SEVERAL HOURS...
WE'VE MADE IT!
SENGAKU-JI.
HARA, WE WILL DO KIRA THE FAVOR OF CLEANING HIS HEAD, SO THAT HE WILL BE PRESENTABLE.
WE HAVE DONE AS YOU REQUESTED.

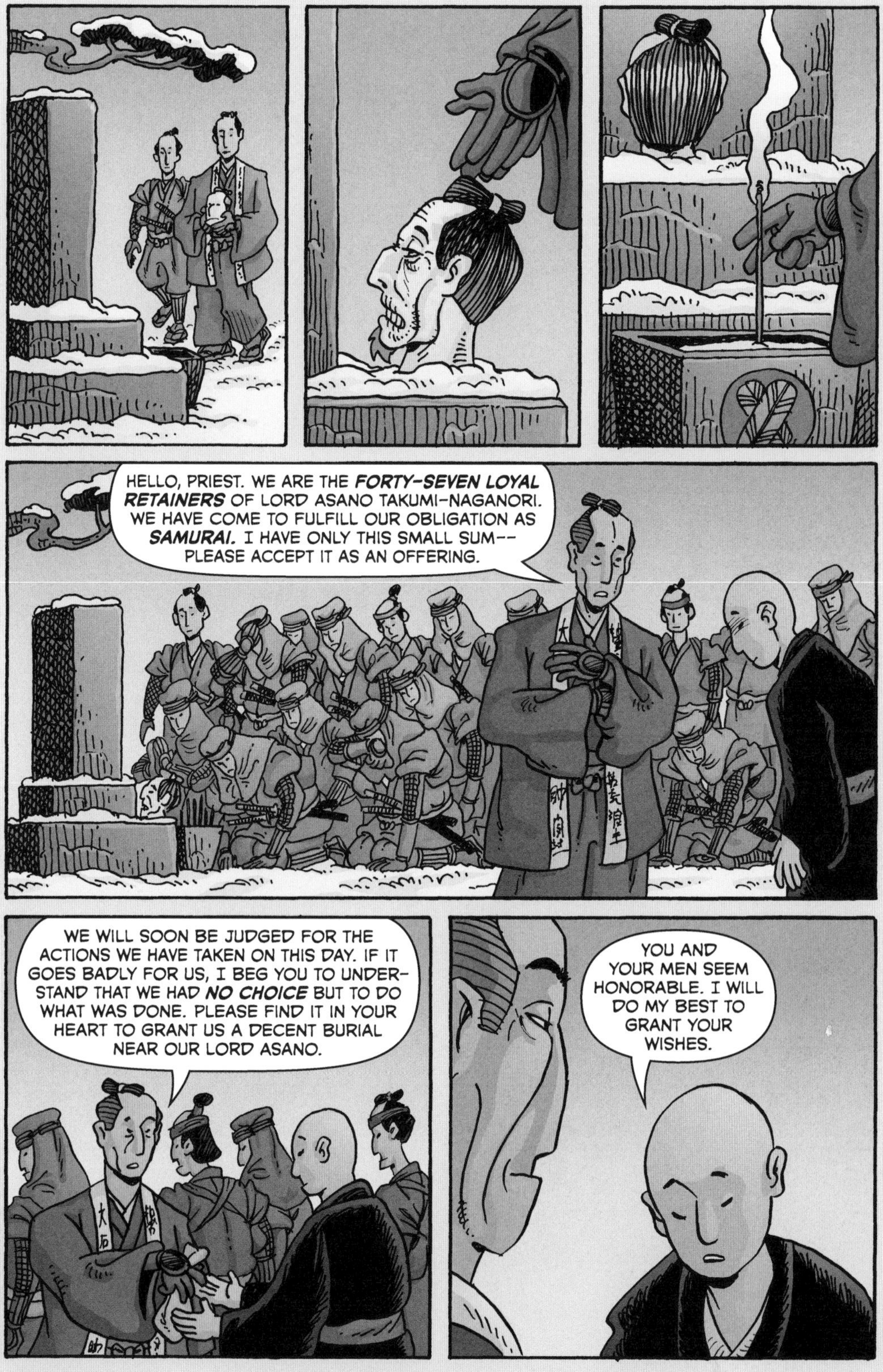
HELLO, PRIEST. WE ARE THE ***FORTY-SEVEN LOYAL RETAINERS*** OF LORD ASANO TAKUMI-NAGANORI. WE HAVE COME TO FULFILL OUR OBLIGATION AS ***SAMURAI.*** I HAVE ONLY THIS SMALL SUM-- PLEASE ACCEPT IT AS AN OFFERING.
WE WILL SOON BE JUDGED FOR THE ACTIONS WE HAVE TAKEN ON THIS DAY. IF IT GOES BADLY FOR US, I BEG YOU TO UNDERSTAND THAT WE HAD ***NO CHOICE*** BUT TO DO WHAT WAS DONE. PLEASE FIND IT IN YOUR HEART TO GRANT US A DECENT BURIAL NEAR OUR LORD ASANO.
YOU AND YOUR MEN SEEM HONORABLE. I WILL DO MY BEST TO GRANT YOUR WISHES.

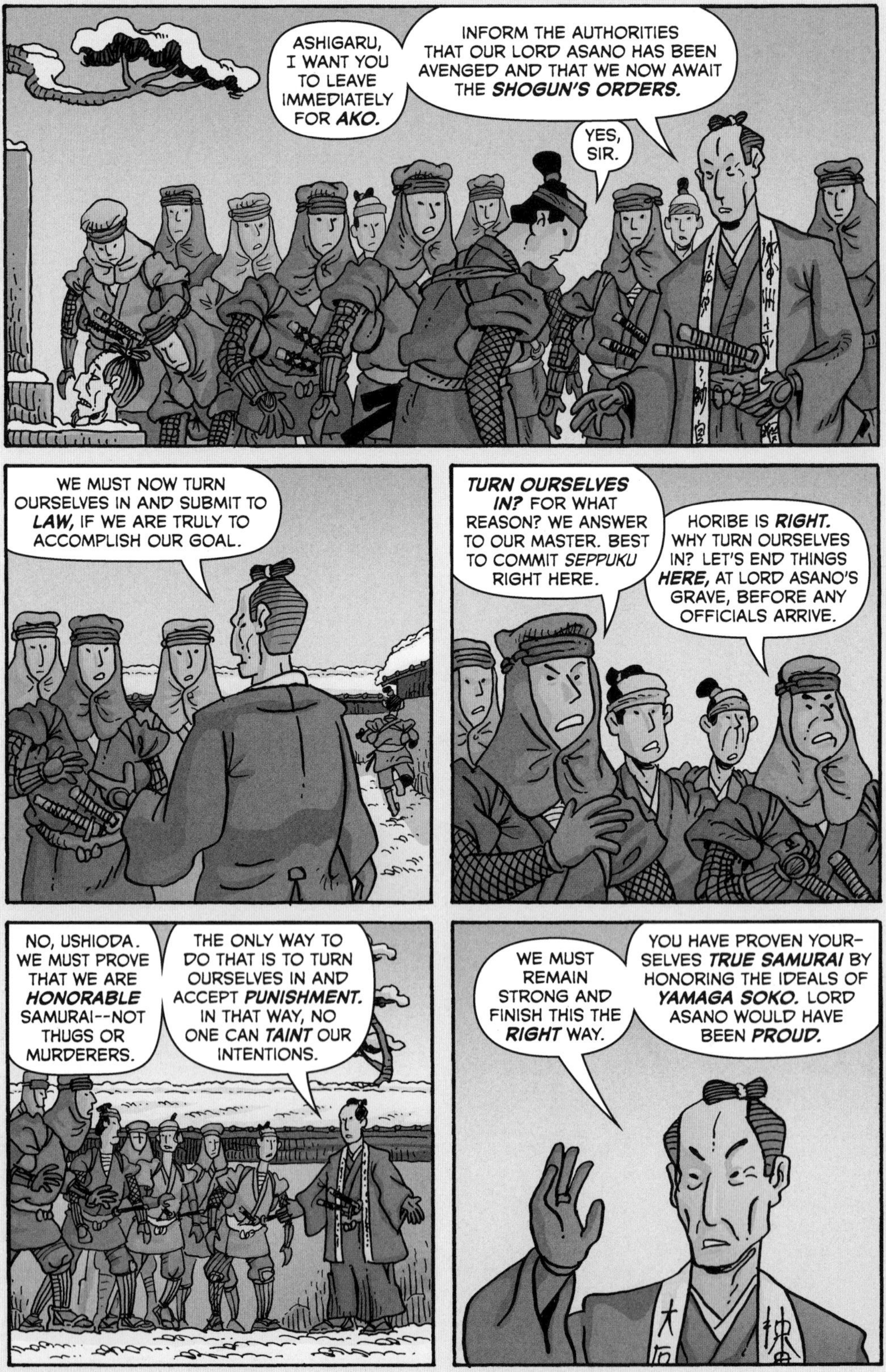
ASHIGARU, I WANT YOU TO LEAVE IMMEDIATELY FOR AKO.
INFORM THE AUTHORITIES THAT OUR LORD ASANO HAS BEEN AVENGED AND THAT WE NOW AWAIT THE SHOGUN'S ORDERS.
YES, SIR.
WE MUST NOW TURN OURSELVES IN AND SUBMIT TO LAW, IF WE ARE TRULY TO ACCOMPLISH OUR GOAL.
TURN OURSELVES IN? FOR WHAT REASON? WE ANSWER TO OUR MASTER. BEST TO COMMIT SEPPUKU RIGHT HERE.
HORIBE IS RIGHT. WHY TURN OURSELVES IN? LET'S END THINGS HERE, AT LORD ASANO'S GRAVE, BEFORE ANY OFFICIALS ARRIVE.
NO, USHIODA. WE MUST PROVE THAT WE ARE HONORABLE SAMURAI--NOT THUGS OR MURDERERS.
THE ONLY WAY TO DO THAT IS TO TURN OURSELVES IN AND ACCEPT PUNISHMENT. IN THAT WAY, NO ONE CAN TAINT OUR INTENTIONS.
WE MUST REMAIN STRONG AND FINISH THIS THE RIGHT WAY.
YOU HAVE PROVEN YOURSELVES TRUE SAMURAI BY HONORING THE IDEALS OF YAMAGA SOKO. LORD ASANO WOULD HAVE BEEN PROUD.

THE SHOGUN'S PALACE IN EDO...

THEY **MUST** BE BROUGHT TO JUSTICE! THEY HAVE **BROKEN THE LAW**...

YES, BUT THEY HAVE **ADMIRERS.** I MUST ADMIT, I INCLUDE MYSELF IN THAT NUMBER. AND MUCH OF THE PUBLIC IS IN FAVOR OF THEIR **RELEASE.**

BUT THEY HAVE DEFIED **YOUR ORDERS!**

FOR THE **HONOR** OF THEIR **MASTER.**

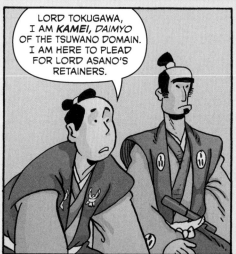

LORD TOKUGAWA, I AM **KAMEI,** DAIMYO OF THE TSUWANO DOMAIN. I AM HERE TO PLEAD FOR LORD ASANO'S RETAINERS.

I WOULD BEG YOU TO **SPARE** THE FORTY-SEVEN, IN RECOGNITION OF BOTH THEIR GREAT DISPLAY OF **BUSHIDO** AND THEIR **DEFENSE** OF THEIR LORD ASANO'S HONOR.

AS YOU KNOW, I WAS PRESENT AT THE ORIGINAL INCIDENT, AND ASANO WAS CEASELESSLY **GOADED** AND **INSULTED.** KIRA WAS AS MUCH TO **BLAME** AS--

YES, YES... WE'VE HEARD ALL THAT. DESPITE YOUR CLAIM, THEY SHOULD STILL BE **PUNISHED** ACCORDING TO LAW. IF THEIR CRIME IS OVER-LOOKED FOR SENTIMENTAL REASONS, THE RULE OF LAW IS BELITTLED AND THE SHOGUNATE **WEAKENED.**

THIS PLACES ME IN A DIFFICULT POSITION.

129

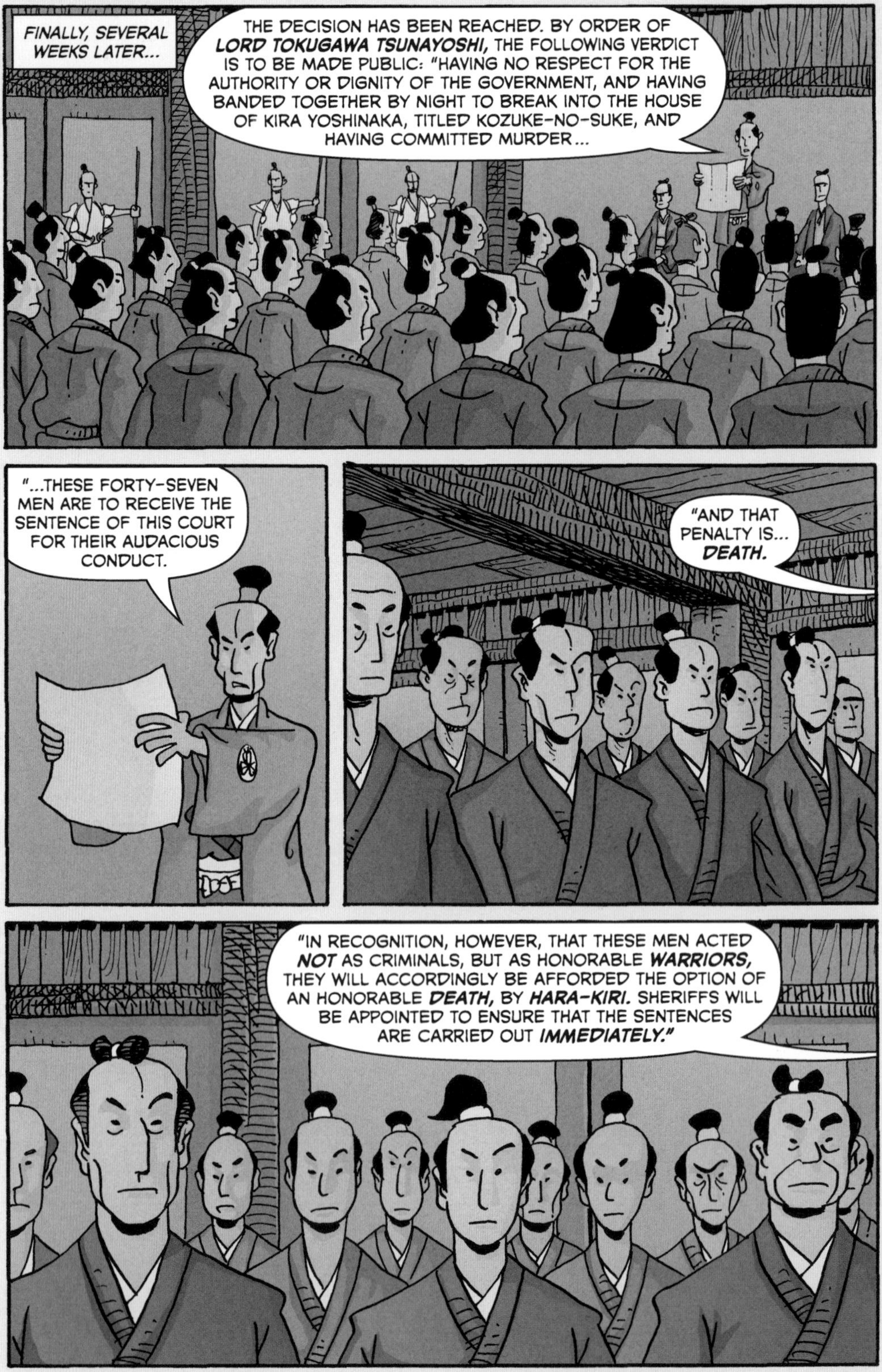
FINALLY, SEVERAL WEEKS LATER...
THE DECISION HAS BEEN REACHED. BY ORDER OF LORD TOKUGAWA TSUNAYOSHI, THE FOLLOWING VERDICT IS TO BE MADE PUBLIC: "HAVING NO RESPECT FOR THE AUTHORITY OR DIGNITY OF THE GOVERNMENT, AND HAVING BANDED TOGETHER BY NIGHT TO BREAK INTO THE HOUSE OF KIRA YOSHINAKA, TITLED KOZUKE-NO-SUKE, AND HAVING COMMITTED MURDER...
"...THESE FORTY-SEVEN MEN ARE TO RECEIVE THE SENTENCE OF THIS COURT FOR THEIR AUDACIOUS CONDUCT.
"AND THAT PENALTY IS... DEATH.
"IN RECOGNITION, HOWEVER, THAT THESE MEN ACTED NOT AS CRIMINALS, BUT AS HONORABLE WARRIORS, THEY WILL ACCORDINGLY BE AFFORDED THE OPTION OF AN HONORABLE DEATH, BY HARA-KIRI. SHERIFFS WILL BE APPOINTED TO ENSURE THAT THE SENTENCES ARE CARRIED OUT IMMEDIATELY."

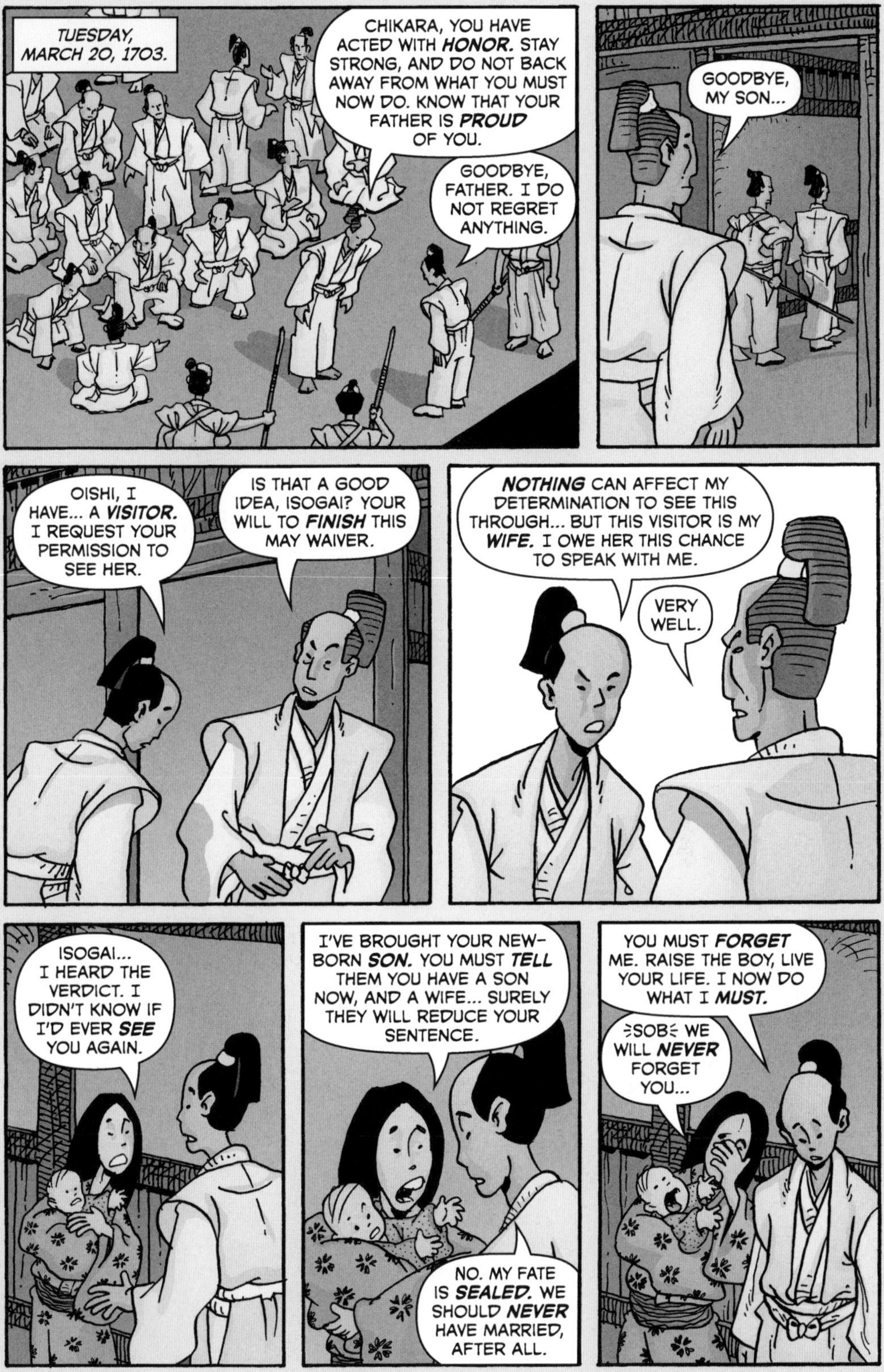
TUESDAY, MARCH 20, 1703.
CHIKARA, YOU HAVE ACTED WITH HONOR. STAY STRONG, AND DO NOT BACK AWAY FROM WHAT YOU MUST NOW DO. KNOW THAT YOUR FATHER IS PROUD OF YOU.
GOODBYE, FATHER. I DO NOT REGRET ANYTHING.
GOODBYE, MY SON...
OISHI, I HAVE... A VISITOR. I REQUEST YOUR PERMISSION TO SEE HER.
IS THAT A GOOD IDEA, ISOGAI? YOUR WILL TO FINISH THIS MAY WAIVER.
NOTHING CAN AFFECT MY DETERMINATION TO SEE THIS THROUGH... BUT THIS VISITOR IS MY WIFE. I OWE HER THIS CHANCE TO SPEAK WITH ME.
VERY WELL.
ISOGAI... I HEARD THE VERDICT. I DIDN'T KNOW IF I'D EVER SEE YOU AGAIN.
I'VE BROUGHT YOUR NEW-BORN SON. YOU MUST TELL THEM YOU HAVE A SON NOW, AND A WIFE... SURELY THEY WILL REDUCE YOUR SENTENCE.
NO. MY FATE IS SEALED. WE SHOULD NEVER HAVE MARRIED, AFTER ALL.
YOU MUST FORGET ME. RAISE THE BOY, LIVE YOUR LIFE. I NOW DO WHAT I MUST.
SOB WE WILL NEVER FORGET YOU...

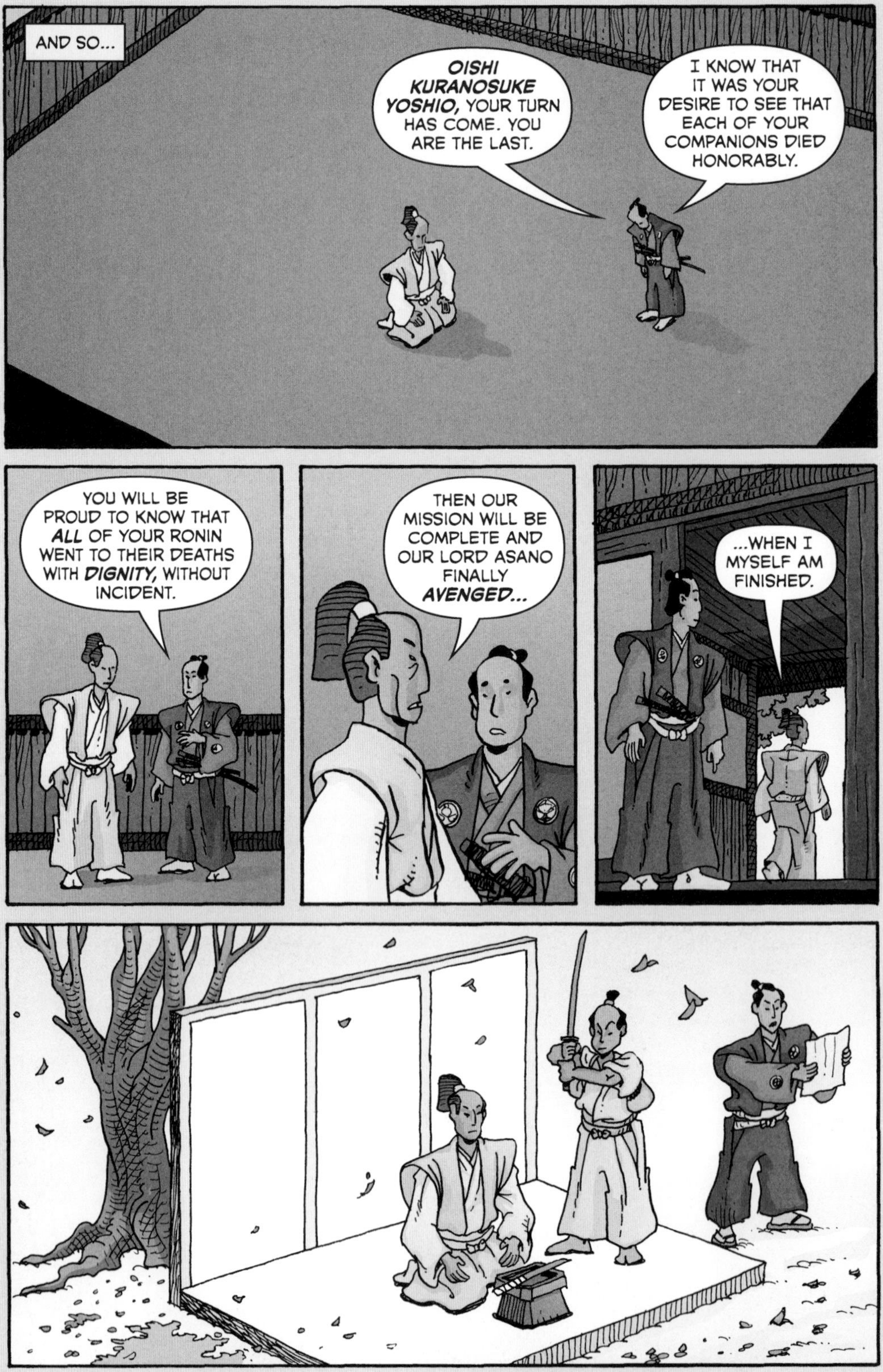
AND SO...
OISHI KURANOSUKE YOSHIO, YOUR TURN HAS COME. YOU ARE THE LAST.
I KNOW THAT IT WAS YOUR DESIRE TO SEE THAT EACH OF YOUR COMPANIONS DIED HONORABLY.
YOU WILL BE PROUD TO KNOW THAT ALL OF YOUR RONIN WENT TO THEIR DEATHS WITH DIGNITY, WITHOUT INCIDENT.
THEN OUR MISSION WILL BE COMPLETE AND OUR LORD ASANO FINALLY AVENGED...
...WHEN I MYSELF AM FINISHED.

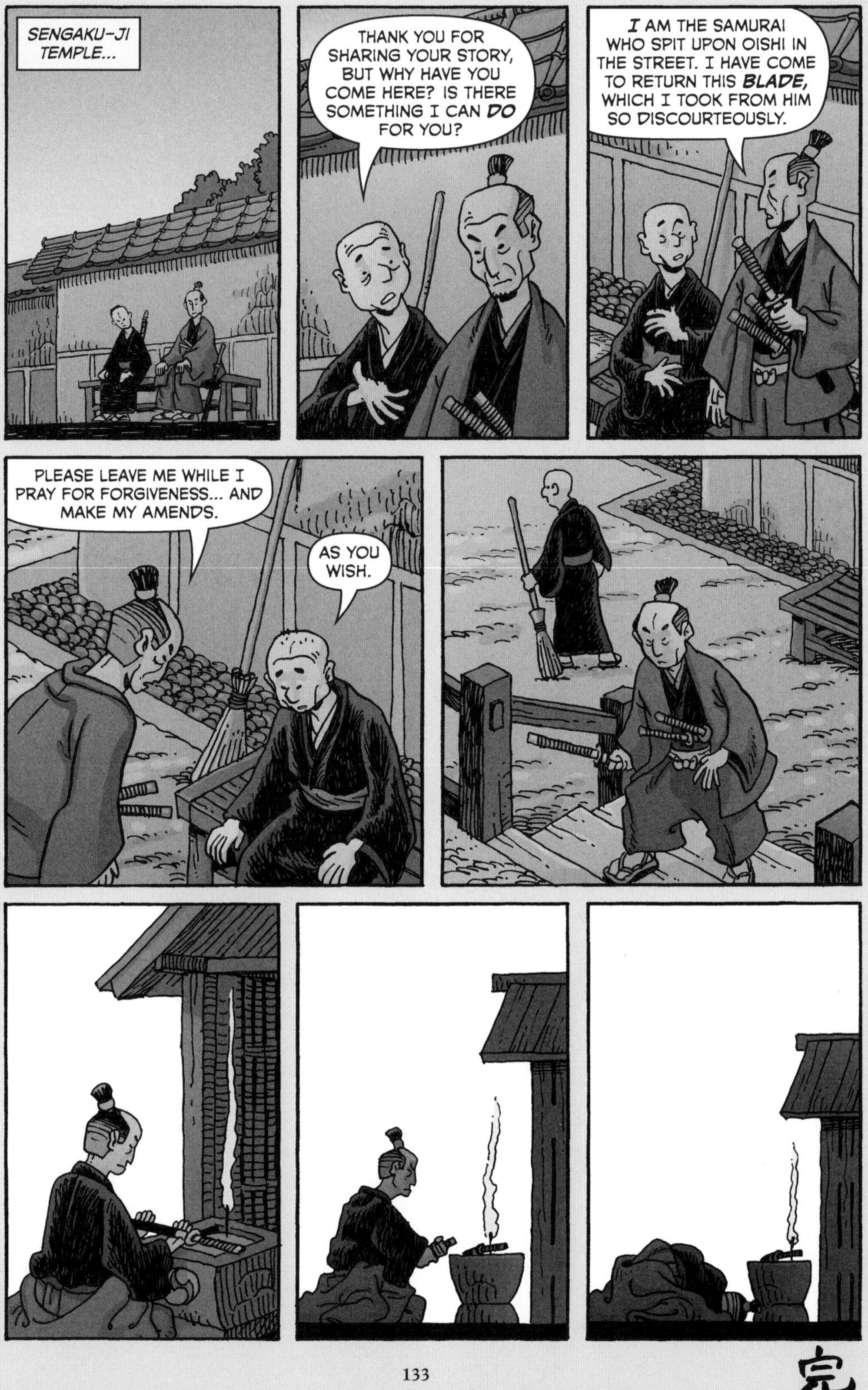
SENGAKU-JI TEMPLE...
THANK YOU FOR SHARING YOUR STORY, BUT WHY HAVE YOU COME HERE? IS THERE SOMETHING I CAN DO FOR YOU?
I AM THE SAMURAI WHO SPIT UPON OISHI IN THE STREET. I HAVE COME TO RETURN THIS BLADE, WHICH I TOOK FROM HIM SO DISCOURTEOUSLY.
PLEASE LEAVE ME WHILE I PRAY FOR FORGIVENESS... AND MAKE MY AMENDS.
AS YOU WISH.

完

四十七浪人
THE 47 RONIN

Oishi Kuranosuke Yoshio

Yoshida Chuzaemon Kanetora — Okano Kineimon Kanehide

Hara Soemon Mototoki — Kaiga Yazaemon Tomonobu

Kataoka Goemon Takafusa — Otaka Gengo Tadao

Mase Kyuidaefu Masaaki — Okajima Yasoemon Tsunetatsu

Onodera Junai Hidekazu — Yoshida Sawaemon Kanesada

Hazama Kihei Mitsunobu — Takebayashi Tadshicki Takashige

Isogai Jurozaemon Masahisa — Kurahashi Densuke Takeyuki

Horibe Yahei Kanamaru — Hazama Shinroku Mitsukaze

Chikamatsu Kanroku Yukishige — Muramatsu Kihei Hidenao

Tomi Morisuke Emon Masao — Sugino Toseiji Tsugufusa

Ushioda Matanojo Takaatsu — Katsuta Shizaemon Takeaki

Hayamizu Tozaemon Misutora — Maebara Isuke Munefusa

Akaue Genzoshigetaka — Onodera Koemon Hidetomi

Okuda Magodaiu Shigemori — Hazama Jujiro Mitsuoki

Yada Goroemon Suketake — Okuda Sadaemon Yukitaka

Oishi Sezaemon Nobukiyo — Yatouemon Shiki Norikane

Oishi Chikara Yoshikane — Muramatsu Sandaifu Takanao

Horibe Yasube Takeyasu — Mase Magokuro Masatatsu

Nakamura Kansuke Masatatsu — Kayano Wasuke Tsunenari

Sugaya Hanojo Masatoshi — Yokokawa Kanbei Munetoshi

Fuwa Kazuemon Masatane — Mimura Jirozaemon Kanetsune

Kimura Okaemon Sadayuki — Kanzaki Yogoro Noriyasu

Semba Saburoe Misutada — Ashigaru Terasaki Kichiemon

*Different sources use slightly different spellings of some of the names,
a result of the various interpretations of the sounds represented by
Japanese characters when translated into English.*

BEHIND THE SCENES OF 47 RONIN

136
COVER GALLERY

142
THE ROAD TO THE 47 RONIN

144
INTERVIEW WITH THE RONIN

147
ABOUT KAZUO KOIKE

149
OGATA GEKKO: THE PRINTS

152
AUTHOR BIOS

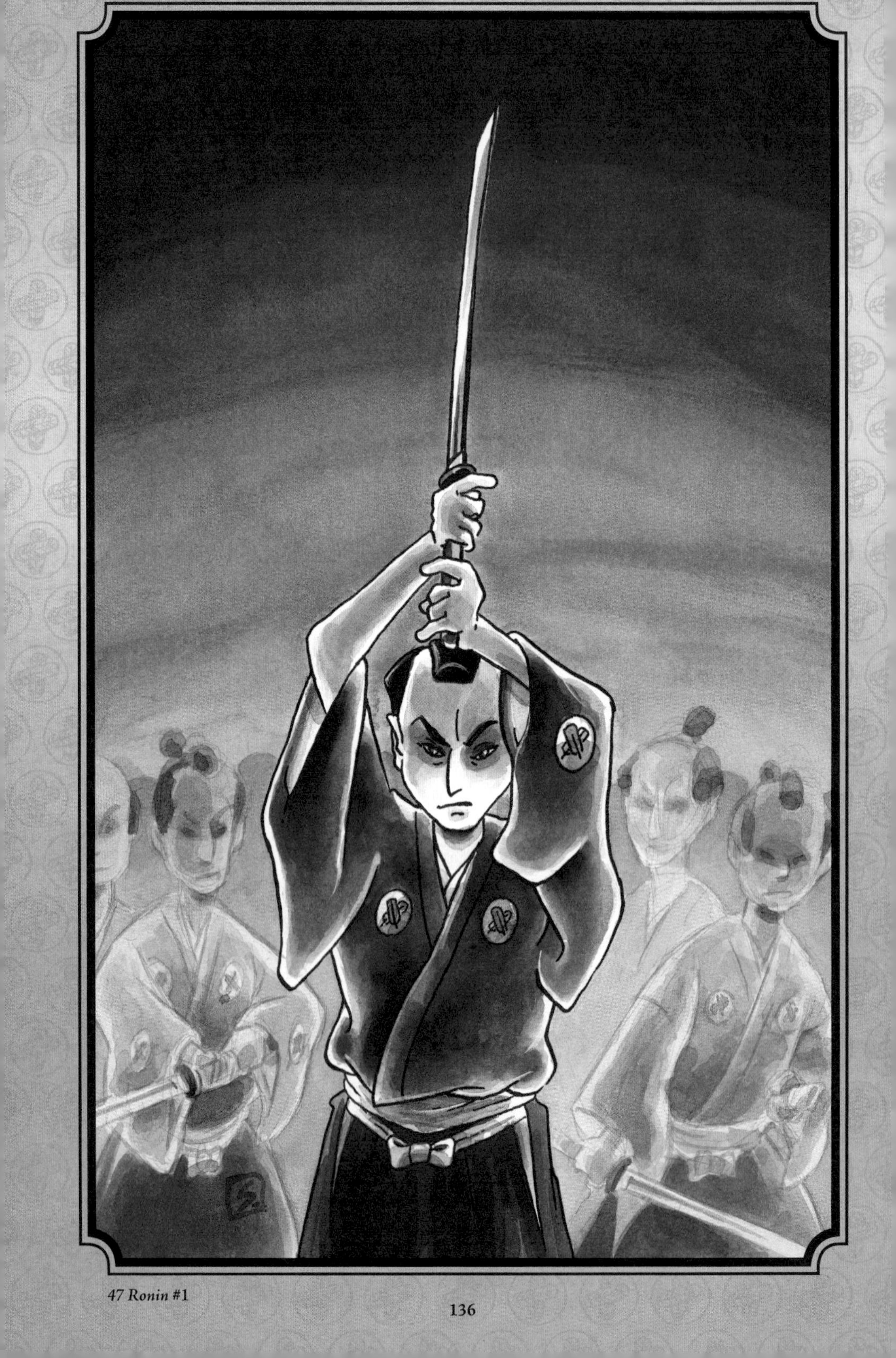

47 Ronin #1

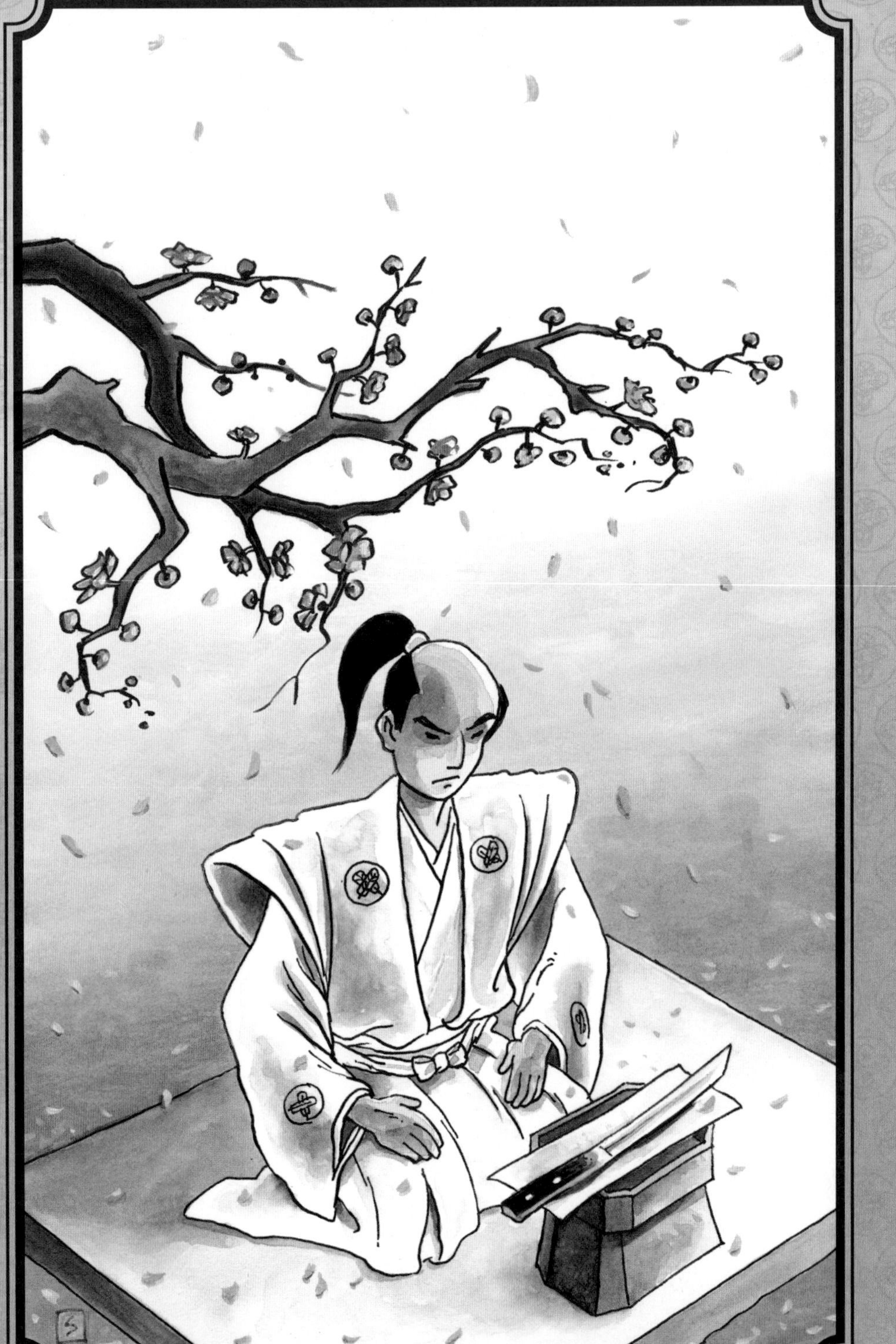

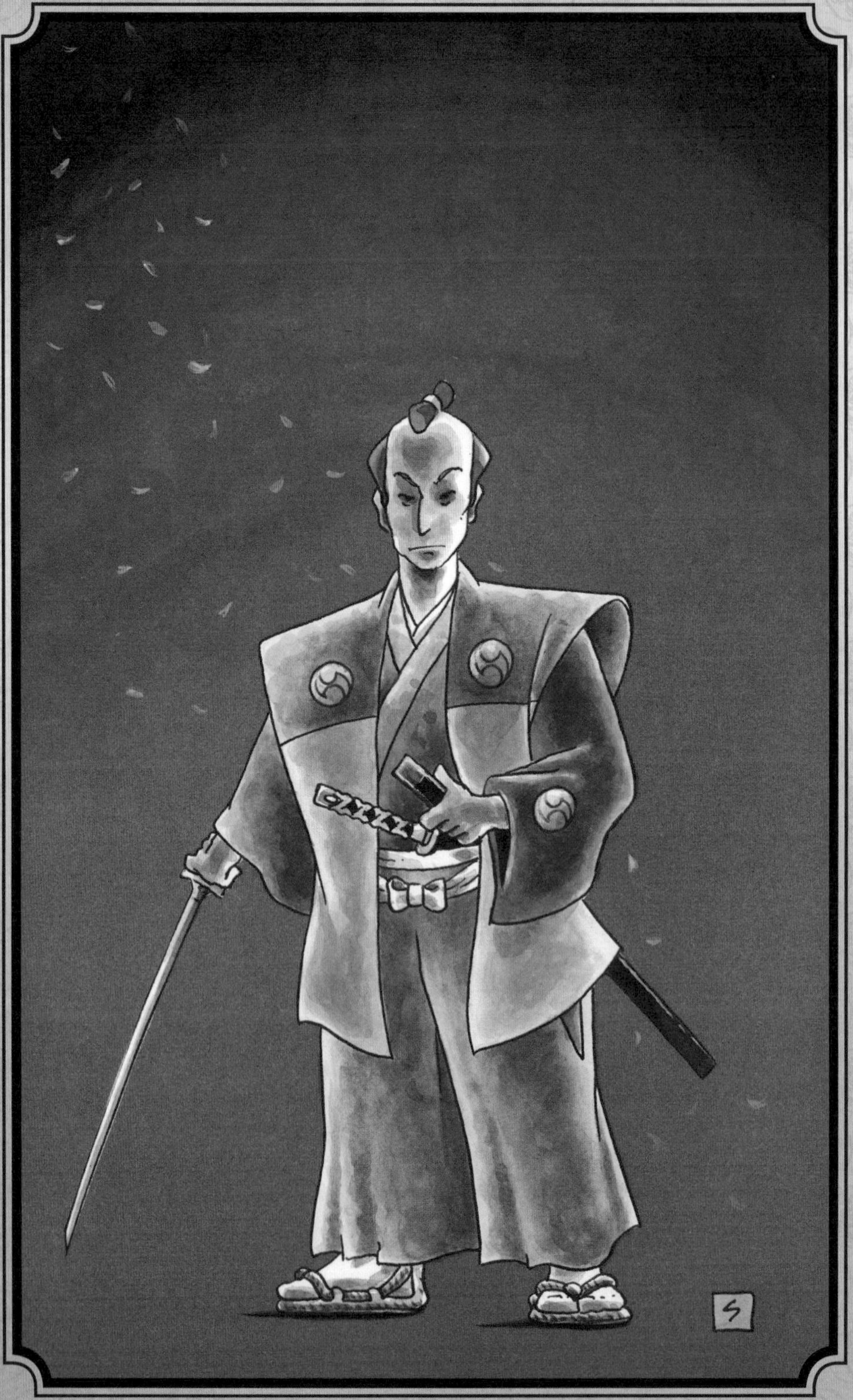
S

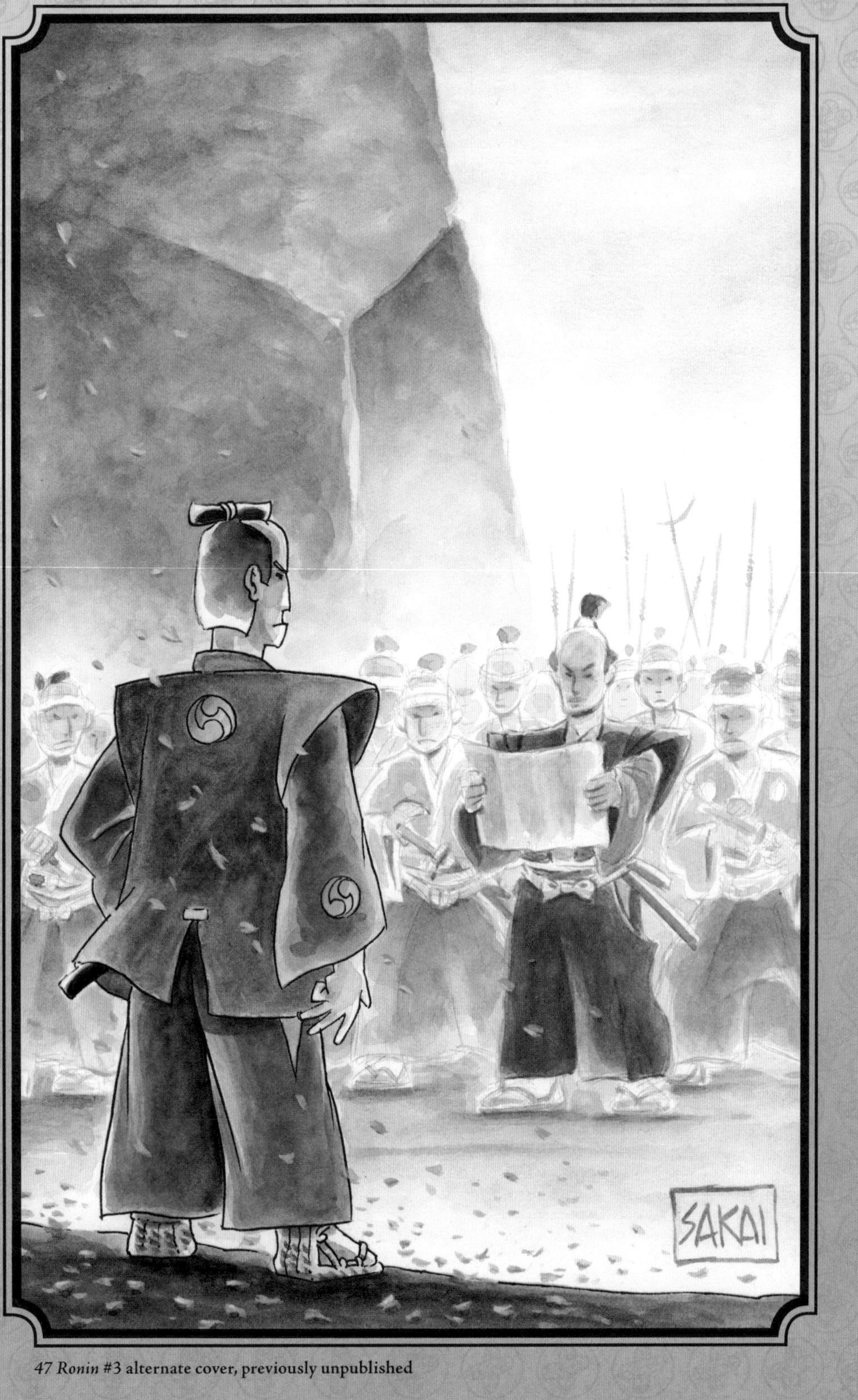
SAKAI

47 Ronin #3 alternate cover, previously unpublished

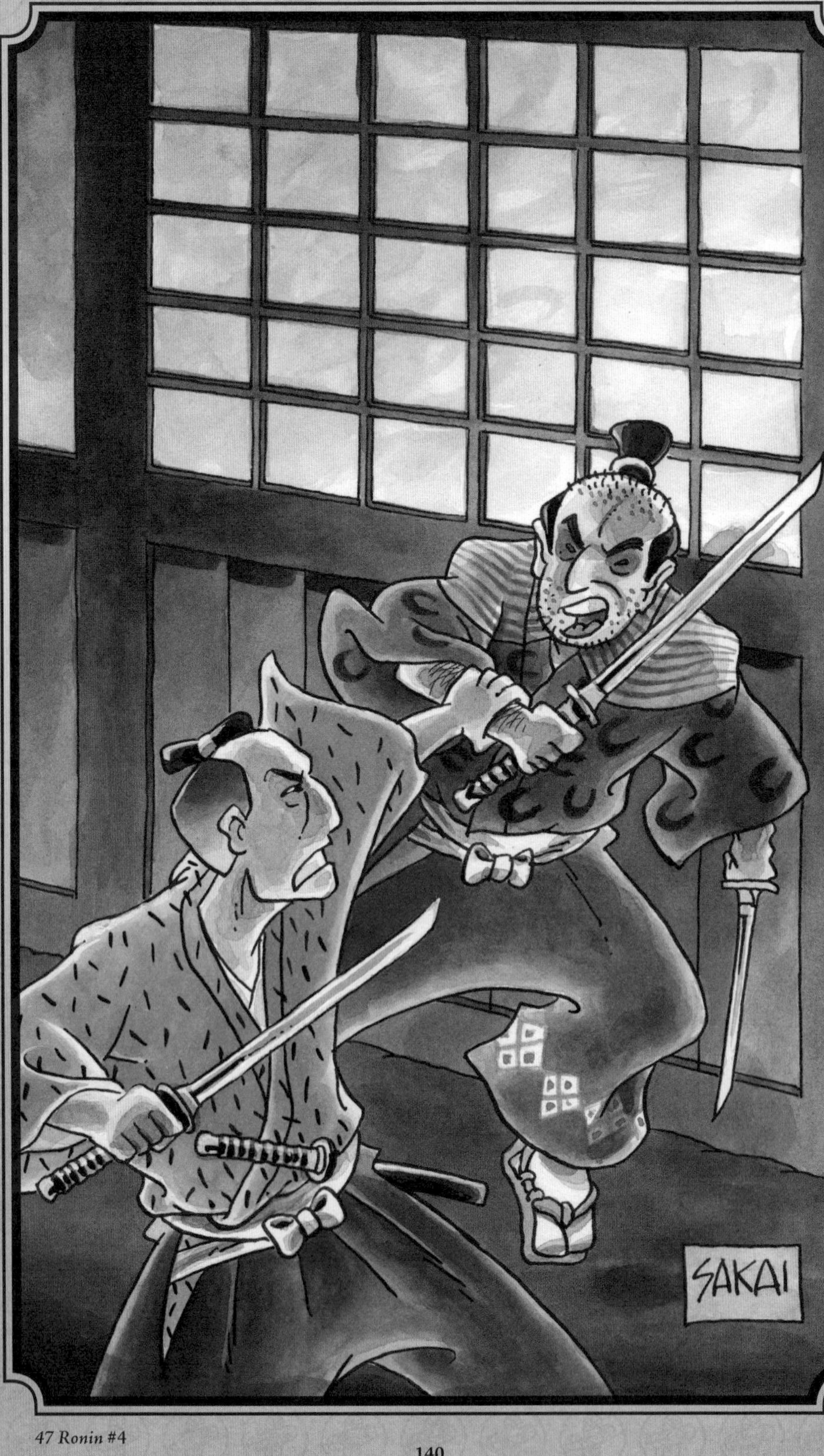
SAKAI

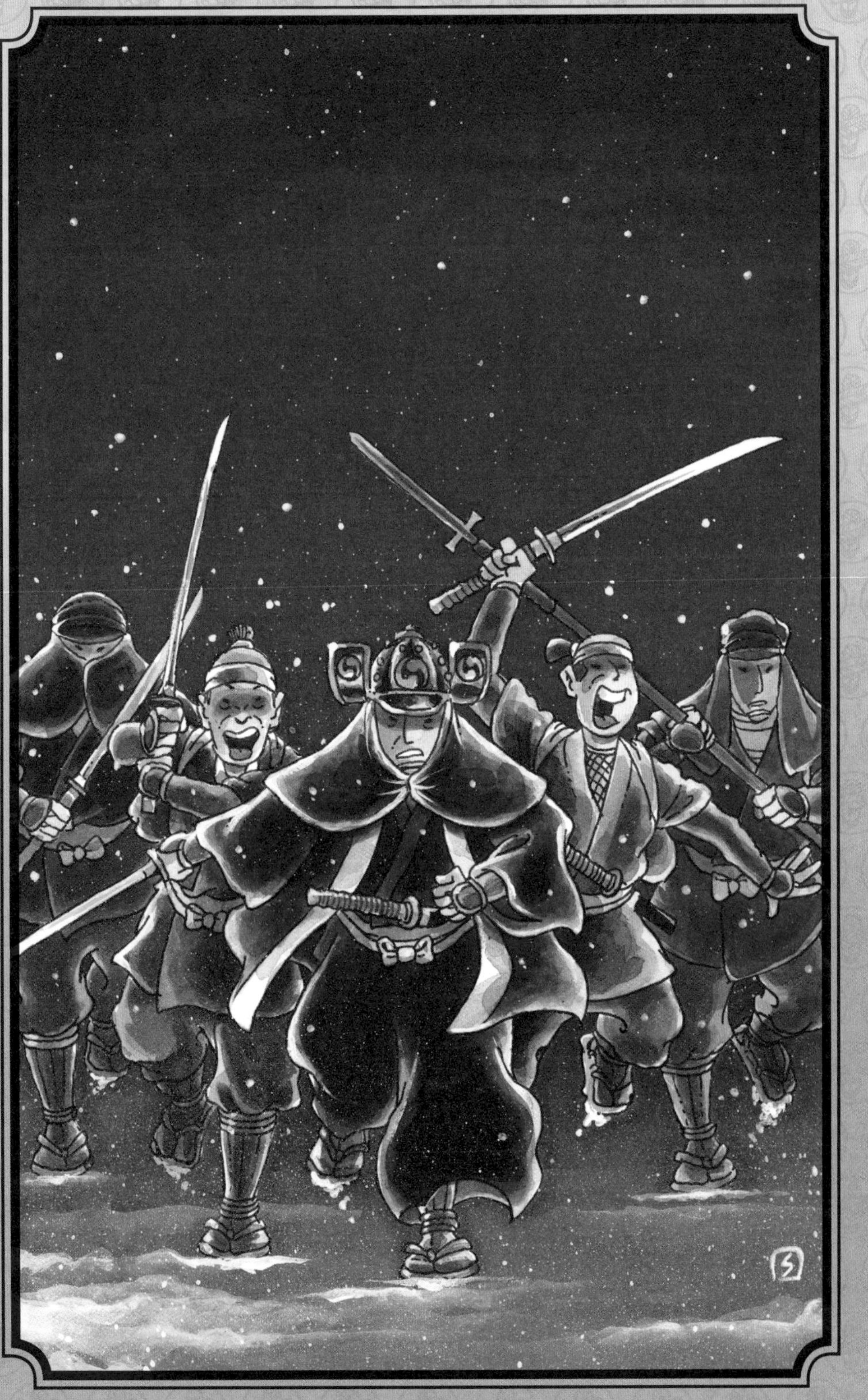

THE ROAD TO THE 47 RONIN
by Mike Richardson

THE LEGEND OF THE 47 RONIN is based on real events that took place in the earliest part of eighteenth-century Japan. From the very beginning, a fictionalized version of the actual incident, titled *Chūshingura* (with names and dates changed to avoid censorship), caught the imagination of the Japanese people and was retold through *bunraku* (puppet plays) and *kabuki* (Japanese theater). Centuries later, an old saying, "*To know the 47 Ronin is to know Japan,*" still rings true.

I first heard the tale of the Loyal Retainers sometime around 1986, from Randy Stradley. We had just launched Dark Horse, and both of us had a fascination with Japanese films, comics, and animation. At the time, I was chasing down the rights to Kazuo Koike's *Lone Wolf and Cub* (illustrated by Goseki Kojima) for our fledgling company, while watching every samurai film I could get my hands on. During one of our discussions about director Akira Kurosawa (*Seven Samurai, Hidden Fortress, Yojimbo, Throne of Blood,* etc.), Randy asked if I knew the story of the 47 Ronin. I didn't. He briefly told me of Oishi's quest to avenge his master while finding honor for himself and his companions. I was entranced.

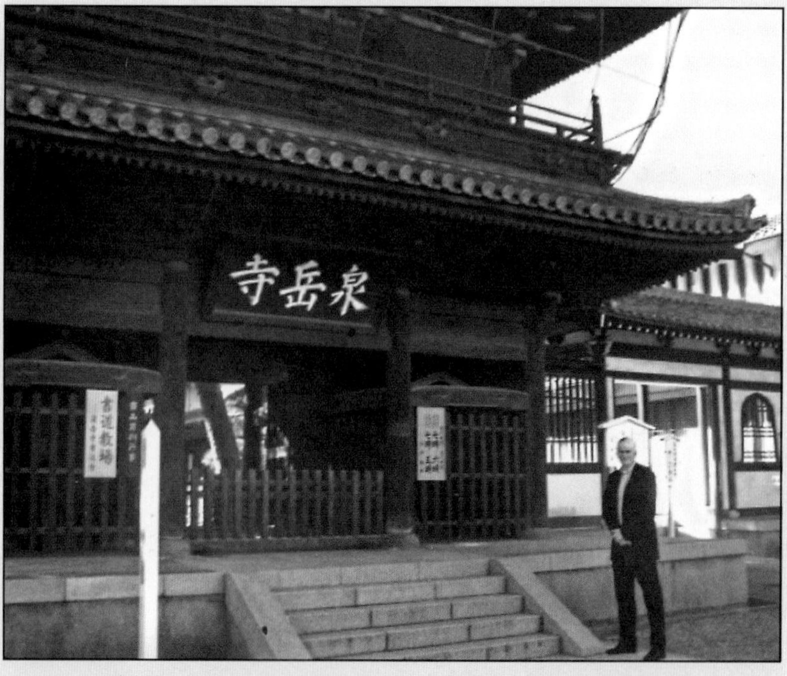
泉岳寺

Mike Richardson at Sengaku-ji Temple, where the 47 Ronin are buried.

What's more, I learned that the story was true. A short time later, Randy brought in a book about the incident, titled, appropriately enough, *The 47 Ronin*. After reading it, I was obsessed with the story and determined to see Dark Horse tell it in comics form.

Time has a way of slipping by, and though the project was never far from my mind, years went by without any real attempt to move it forward. A variety of creators professed interest, but for one reason or another none ever signed on. During those years, I continued my research, with visits to Sengaku-ji Temple, where I burned incense at the grave of each of the forty-seven, and to Kira's home (or what's left of it). I read everything I could get my hands on and, of course, watched most of the many movies on the subject—most notably Kenji Mizoguchi's two-part masterpiece filmed circa WWII. Over the course of a couple decades, I gathered photos, saved related clippings and articles, and built a file containing anything that might be helpful. Finally, I began speaking about the project with my friend Kazuo Koike during my trips to Japan. Koike offered his suggestions and insights on the story, encouraging me to move forward with the project. I finally wrote the first outline in 2008 and sent it to him for review. Numerous revisions followed. There were many versions of the incident, and I had to narrow them down to a tale that would fit a four-issue comics series. Eventually the four issues became five, and the planned twenty-two pages per issue expanded, as I found it impossible to tell the story in the original eighty-eight pages I had allotted myself.

I need to take a step backwards. Once I'd decided to write the story myself, I had to find just the right person to draw it. I considered artists from both Japan and America, and one from Europe. It was crucial to the project to find someone who was familiar with the customs, clothing, and politics of the period. I particularly wanted to find someone who could evoke, but not copy, the woodblock prints of Ogata Gekko. After much head-scratching and some anxiety, I suddenly realized that the perfect artist was right in front of me: Stan Sakai, whose award-winning series *Usagi Yojimbo* had been at Dark Horse for over fifteen years. Having himself created stories of samurai for most of his career, Stan was exactly the artist for this tale! While his long-running series features anthropomorphic characters, their actions, emotions, and desires are decidedly human, and it is evident from his work that he knows the period. A phone call to a surprised Stan ultimately led to his enthusiastic decision to join the project, and a twenty-five-year-old dream was finally on the road to completion.

INTERVIEW WITH THE RONIN

by Brendan Wright with Stan Sakai

STAN SAKAI has been a part of the Dark Horse stable for nearly twenty years, but for most of that time he has kept busy writing, drawing, and lettering Usagi Yojimbo, *his samurai epic of a wandering rabbit ronin.* 47 Ronin *marks Stan's first extended collaboration, and non-Usagi project, at Dark Horse. Shortly after the release of issue #1, Stan answered a few questions posed by associate editor Brendan Wright about the series.*

Is *47 Ronin* the longest project you've ever illustrated that you didn't also write?

Yes, it is. The only stories authored by someone else that I've drawn were short stories, and even those can be counted on one hand.

Mike Richardson has already talked about how long he's wanted to tell this story. As it's such a well-known tale, do you have a history with it as well?

I first heard this story when I was in about the third grade. Almost anyone of Japanese descent who knows anything about his or her culture must have heard of it.

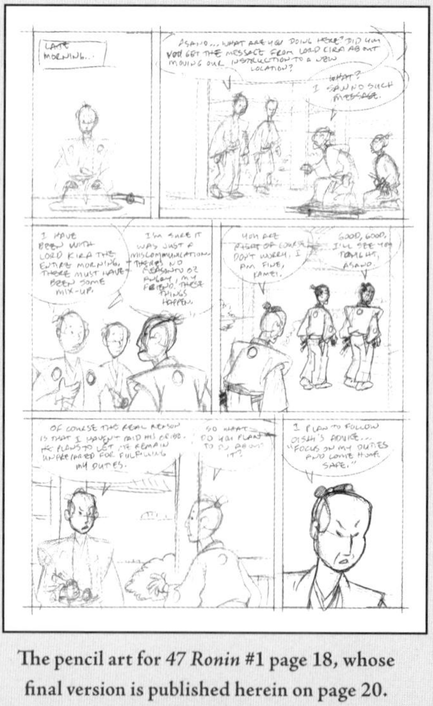
LATE MORNING...
WHAT? I SAW NO SUCH MESSAGE.
I HAVE BEEN WITH LORD KIRA THE ENTIRE MORNING. THERE MUST HAVE BEEN SOME MIX-UP.
GOOD, GOOD. I'LL SEE YOU TONIGHT, ASANO.
I PLAN TO FOLLOW OISHI'S ADVICE... "FOCUS ON MY DUTIES AND COME HOME SAFE."

The pencil art for *47 Ronin* #1 page 18, whose final version is published herein on page 20.

What has the back-and-forth between you and Mike been like?

Mike has written full scripts, but he is very open to my own input and thoughts, however minor they may be. I send in pencils for approval and for Mike to write the final script. I'm not used to sending in pencil art, as my pencils tend to be very loose. I've had to tighten up my pencils, and, even then, they're pretty vague. I do most of the art in the inking stage, but the pencils give a good idea of the storytelling.

I can't think of another project of yours that you haven't lettered yourself. How has leaving space for balloons, rather than drawing them in yourself, changed your approach to composing a panel?

Actually, I *do* include the dialogue in the penciling stage. That way, I can be sure that there's enough space for the lettering. Also, it makes it much easier for Mike and editor Diana to follow the story when I turn in the pencils. Tom Orzechowski came on board to letter the books. He is a seasoned professional and has a great design sense, so the lettering never interferes with the art.

One of the prints from which Richardson and Sakai drew inspiration, by Ogata Gekko.

Color is so important to this story, in the use of seasons and particularly the cherry blossoms, and in the many different clan color schemes. What's been your collaboration process with Lovern Kindzierski?

Lovern sent in a few pages of the first issue, and I saw that his palette complemented the art perfectly. From there, he has been working pretty much on his own.

How much research did Mike present to you when you came onto the project? What additional reference did you look at while preparing?

I was impressed with the amount of research Mike had done for the project. Soon after I agreed to do this, he sent dozens of emails with attachments showing locations, woodcuts, costumes, and other details. Of course, I already had a lot of reference of my own. I have eight versions of the movie *Chūshingura* (Mike told me he has a dozen), as well as novels, reference books, and even the opera on CD.

You've made reference to drawing inspiration from traditional Japanese prints. Was this an idea you had right away or one you hit on after trying a few other approaches. What specifically did you take from that style?

I had that idea right away for drawing faces. The rest of the anatomy is pretty much my own. I like the stylized look of people in those old prints.

What were some of the challenges of drawing *actual* settings and clan clothing rather than the settings and clothing for *fictionalized* clans in *Usagi*?

Locations were difficult. Many of the structures no longer exist. Edo Castle has suffered through two fires since that time, however I was able to build on existing structures. Edo Castle is not as imposing as others in Japan, so I took a lot of artistic license and, when given the choice, I went with more interesting and dramatic images, rather than sticking to reality. It was the same with clan crests. The major crests were easy enough, but many were difficult to research. When in doubt, I allied characters with the major clans.

The big question: how much of an adjustment was it to draw so many human samurai instead of the anthropomorphized characters you usually draw?

There's not that much difference to drawing humans. My characters are still very stylized. It's mostly a matter of getting the proportions correct. I should point out that my character designs look nothing like the real people did. I've made Oishi much nobler-looking, Asano is younger and more innocent, and Kira really looks the part of the villain.

Was anything more difficult than you expected? Less difficult?

I terribly underestimated the time this project would take. I can generally finish a Usagi story in about five weeks—that's from writing to finished art. *47 Ronin*, however, takes about a full month to pencil one issue and another month to ink it. I also took a couple months at the beginning to prepare for the series. I am putting a lot more detail into the backgrounds than I usually do, to give the feel of eighteenth-century Japan. Since Mike writes in full-script style, it's very easy to work from. I do rough page breakdowns on the backs of the original art. With *Usagi*, I have to break down the entire story before starting any penciling, to determine pacing and composition, and I often have to go back once or twice to revise the breakdowns. Mike has already taken care of the pacing for me.

Has drawing *47 Ronin* led you to learn things about the story that you didn't know, or did you pretty much already know it inside and out?

The big revelation is that the legend of the 47 Ronin is far from the truth. Much of what I took for gospel turns out to be speculation or outright fabrication. Kira may not have been the villain he is portrayed as, Asano not quite the innocent, and Oishi not as noble. We don't even know why exactly Lord Asano attacked Kira. We just know he had "a grudge." The story of the 47 Ronin is regarded as Japan's national legend, and, in a line from *The Man Who Shot Liberty Valance*, "When the legend becomes fact, print the legend." The myth of the *ronin* is intertwined with fact so tightly that I don't think there can really be an objective telling of the tale. That's why there are so many versions of the story. This is one of them.

ABOUT KAZUO KOIKE
by Mike Richardson

KAZUO KOIKE is the Japanese author of such manga titles as *Lone Wolf and Cub*, *Crying Freeman*, *Samurai Executioner*, and *Lady Snowblood*. Koike also teaches a college course, *Gekika Sonjuku*, to aspiring manga artists. He is an avid golfer—and, I should mention, has beaten me on two continents! In addition to writing golf manga, Koike also owns Japan's premier golf magazine, *Alba*, which stands for *albatross*. And until 2006, Koike's own clubs were made under his personal supervision in his office building.

I once asked Koike if there was any similarity between swinging a samurai sword and a golf club, and he told me that there is, in fact, a particular stroke used by samurai swordsmen that closely resembles the golf swing. In feudal times, he said, samurai had their blades made to certain specifications, and only specific sword-makers were patronized by samurai. Not too slow on the uptake, I asked Koike if his practice of

having his clubs made under his personal specifications by master club-makers was an attempt to emulate the blade-makers of the past. He looked at me as though he had been caught, then smiled, but would not answer.

———————————

I first met Kazuo Koike under rather uncomfortable circumstances. I had been chasing his "baby-cart" series for over a decade and had entered into a deal with a company claiming to represent Koike's interests in the matter. After drafting a basic plot outline, I pitched an updated version of the character to these "representatives," who responded positively. Writer Mike Kennedy and artist Francisco Ruiz Velasco were hired to work on the series, and *Lone Wolf 2100* was born. Unfortunately, it turned out, much to my dismay, that Koike had *not* been consulted about the project!

Sometime around 1998, I was able, finally, to arrange a meeting in Japan with the legendary writer. It was then that I learned the truth about our own project and that Koike's previous dealings with American companies had not been so great. From that unfortunate beginning, our relationship only improved. Dark Horse would eventually publish the entire run of *Lone Wolf and Cub*, as well as other titles Koike had authored. Over the years, our business relationship has developed into a friendship, one that I sincerely value.

In 2005, during one of my visits to Japan, I spoke to Koike of my interest in writing a graphic novel based on the legend of the 47 Ronin. The story is very much a part of Japanese culture, and I wanted to hear his thoughts regarding an "outsider" actually adapting the tale. Koike greeted the idea with great enthusiasm and urged me to go forward with the project, offering to oversee the scripting. Years and numerous revisions later, *47 Ronin* is a reality. I couldn't let this opportunity pass without mentioning that much of the credit for its existence is owed to my friend, Kazuo Koike.

OGATA GEKKO: THE PRINTS
by Mike Richardson

AS MENTIONED elsewhere herein, the idea of creating a graphic novel based on the legend of the 47 Ronin has been with me for decades. Thankfully, I was able to finally complete the project with two comics giants. Stan Sakai, who has built legions of fans for his career-long masterwork, *Usagi Yojimbo*, was an ideal collaborator and artist. His exquisite drawings breathed life into the story we told. Of course, Kazuo Koike was our inspiration and spiritual guide, keeping us on the right path and preventing us from straying too far from the proper perspective. There is one other artist who deserves mention: Ogata Gekko.

Kayano Sanbei Shigetsugu

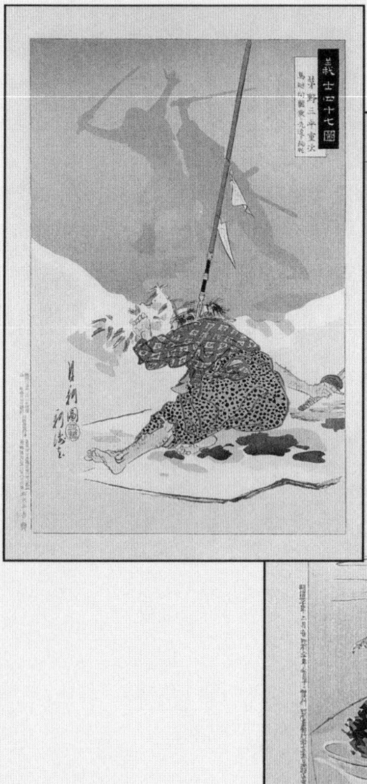

Kanzaki Yogoro Noriyasu

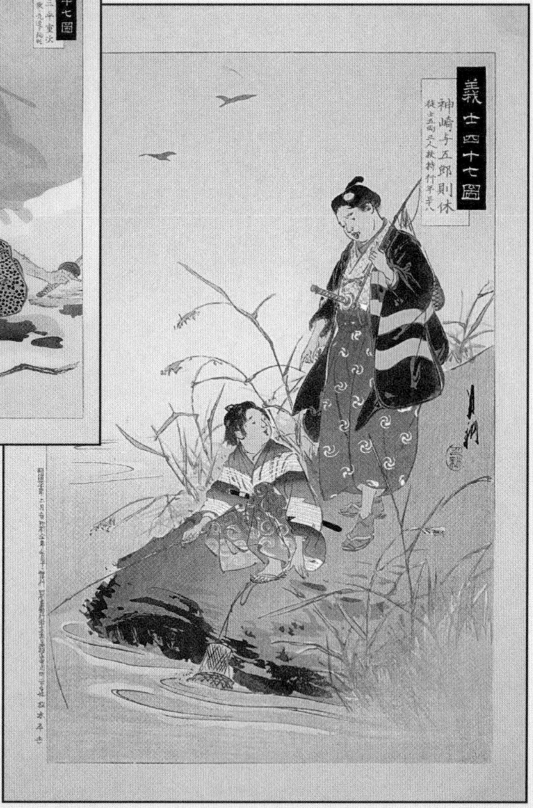
義士四十七圖
神崎与五郎則休

Maebara Isuke Munefusa

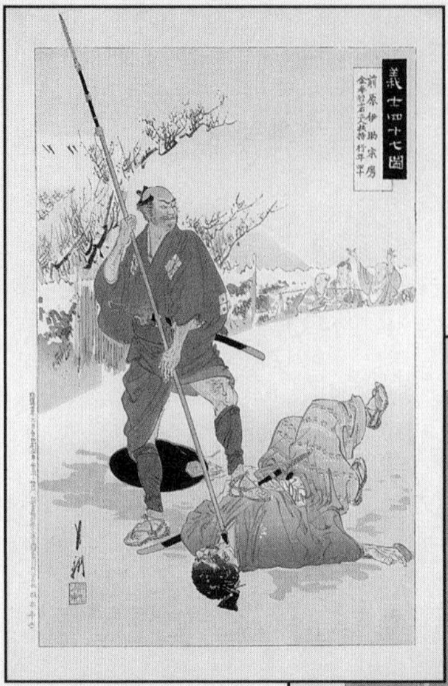
義士四十七図

Ogata Gekko (1859–1920) was an important Japanese artist of the Meiji Period who created an amazing set of woodblock prints based on the legend of the 47 Ronin.

Yoshida Sawaemon Kanesada

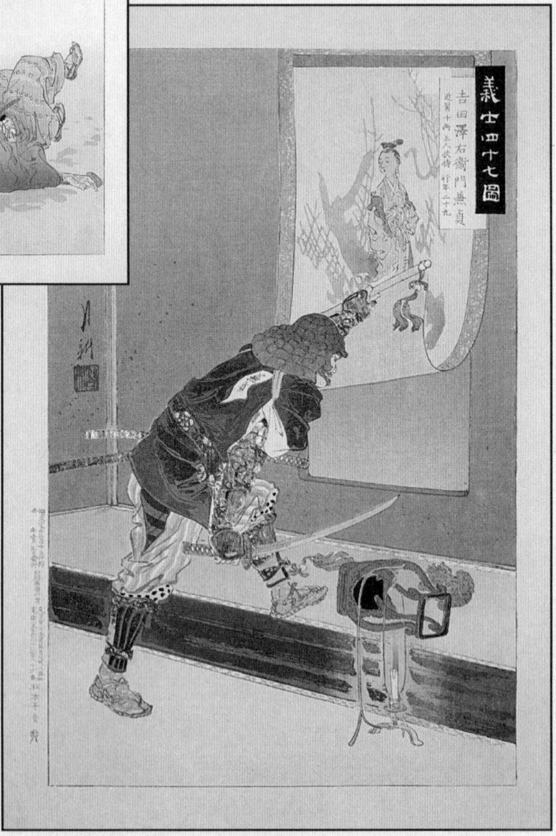
義士四十七図
吉田澤右衛門兼貞

Gekko was born Nagami Masanosuke in the Kobayashi district in Oke-cho. He became an orphan at the age of sixteen, but was soon adopted and took on the family name of Ogata. He gave himself the tag of Gekko, which means *moonlight*. He made his living by creating illustrations for books, magazines, and newspapers, and by designing lacquer-ware. He is especially renowned for his Sino-Japanese War prints, informing the Japanese public about the events of that conflict. Though most likely self-taught, Gekko himself went on to teach art students for nearly three decades.

Muramatsu Kihei Hidenao

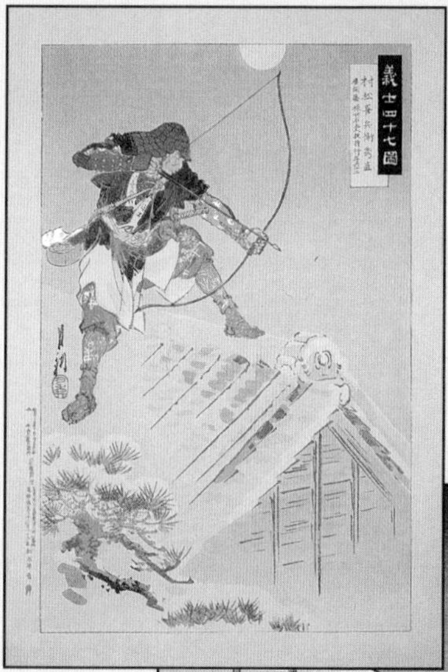
義士四十七圖

I discovered Ogata Gekko's work while researching *47 Ronin* and eventually shared his stunning prints of the ronin with Stan. We both agreed that our tale should be presented in a visual style heavily influenced by Gekko's masterful work. It is our hope that by mentioning his influence on our own book, we can inspire others also to learn about this great artist.

Night Attack

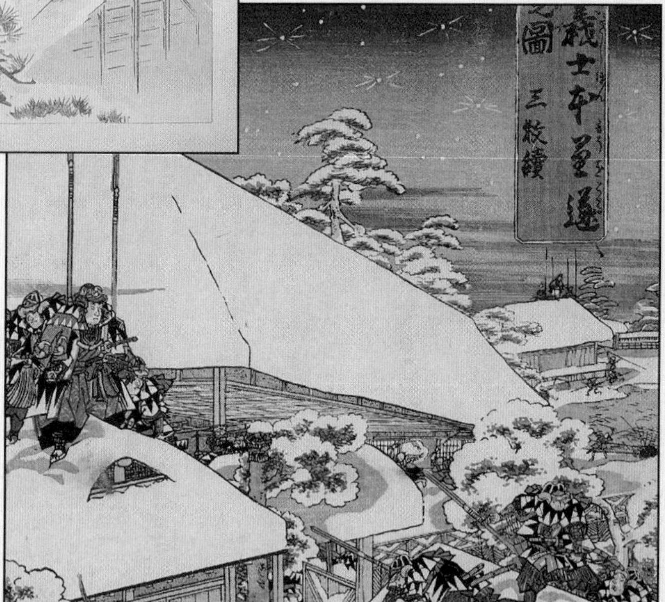
義士本望遂之圖
三枚續

AUTHOR BIOS

MIKE RICHARDSON founded Dark Horse Comics in 1986, as an offshoot of his Oregon comic-book retail chain, Things From Another World. He pursued the idea of establishing an ideal atmosphere for creative professionals, and twenty-seven years later, the company has grown to become the third-largest comics publisher in the United States.

Richardson has also written many comic book series and original graphic novels in addition to *47 Ronin*, including *Star Wars: Crimson Empire*, *The Occultist*, *Living with the Dead*, *Cut*, *The Secret*, and *Cravan*.

Born in Kyoto, Japan, **STAN SAKAI** grew up in Hawaii and now lives in California with his wife, Sharon. They have two children, Hannah and Matthew. Stan received a Fine Arts degree from the University of Hawaii and furthered his studies at the Art Center College of Design in Pasadena, California.

Stan's most beloved creation, Usagi Yojimbo, first appeared in comics in 1984. Since then, Stan has been the recipient of many prestigious comics industry honors, including several Eisner Awards for his storytelling talent as well as for his hand-lettering on Sergio Aragonés's *Groo*, the *Spider-Man* Sunday newspaper strips, and *Usagi Yojimbo*.

Though widely respected as a powerful writer of graphic fiction, **KAZUO KOIKE** has spent a lifetime reaching beyond the bounds of the comics medium. Aside from co-creating and writing the successful *Lone Wolf and Cub* and *Crying Freeman* manga, Koike has hosted television programs; founded a golf magazine; produced movies; written popular fiction, poetry, and screenplays; and mentored some of Japan's top manga talent.

Koike's commitment to character is clear: "Comics are carried by the characters. If a character is well created, the comic becomes a hit." Kazuo Koike's continued success in comics and literature has proven the philosophy true.